Advance P
Atonement in the Apocalypse: A

While many colorful threads exist in the tapestry of the Apocalypse, the thread of the atonement is not often teased out. Robert Canoy, with an adept and perceptive reading of the biblical text, traces this thread and illustrates it as a major focus both for the original audience and contemporary. This book will challenge readers to see the redemptive work of Christ through the apocalyptic lens of the author of the Apocalypse.

—*David M. May*
Professor of New Testament
Central Baptist Theological Seminary

In this careful, detailed analysis, Robert Canoy offers an insightful examination of the idea of atonement in the book of Revelation. Canoy demonstrates why Revelation's redemption language needs to be understood in light of the book's own historical and theological concerns rather than made to fit the views of other biblical writers or later theories of atonement. This is an excellent study of an often overlooked, though crucial, topic in the Apocalypse. Canoy's work is the result of informed exegesis, critical dialogue with other scholars, and theological reflection on the significance of John's understanding of the redemptive work of God (for ancient as well as contemporary readers).

—*Mitchell G. Reddish*
Professor and Chair of Religious Studies
Stetson University

Atonement in the Apocalypse: An Exposé of the Defeat of Evil, is a fresh and insightful work that features the often neglected theme of atonement in John's apocalypse. Canoy's contribution offers a unique and refreshing perspective on foundational theological themes so prominently (and intricately) woven through John's work. The work is solidly biblical, written with clarity for both scholars and laypersons in mind, and it challenges the reader to revisit important themes and images in Revelation that are either ignored or misappropriated in fanciful eschatological systems. Canoy's work is a serious and helpful attempt to add yet one more voice to the conversation.

—*Danny West*
Professor of Preaching and Pastoral Studies, School of Divinity,
Gardner-Webb University

Smyth & Helwys Publishing, Inc.
6316 Peake Road
Macon, Georgia 31210-3960
1-800-747-3016
©2017 by Robert W. Canoy

Library of Congress Cataloging-in-Publication Data

Names: Canoy, Robert W., author.
Title: Atonement in the Apocalypse : an exposé of the defeat of evil / by
Robert W. Canoy.
Description: Macon : Smyth & Helwys, 2017. | Includes bibliographical
references.
Identifiers: LCCN 2017005334 | ISBN 9781573129466 (pbk. : alk. paper)
Subjects: LCSH: Atonement--Biblical teaching. | Bible. Revelation--Criticism,
interpretation, etc.
Classification: LCC BS2825.6.A8 C36 2017 | DDC 228/.06--dc23
LC record available at https://lccn.loc.gov/2017005334

ATONEMENT

IN THE

APOCALYPSE

An Exposé
of the
Defeat of Evil

ROBERT W. CANOY

ALSO BY ROBERT W. CANOY

Israel and Rome:
A Study-Tour Guidebook and Devotional Resource

Turkey and Greece:
A Study-Tour Guidebook and Devotional Resource

Israel and Egypt:
A Study-Tour Guidebook and Devotional Resource

This book is dedicated to my teachers
who saw something in me
that I seek to see in my own students

ACKNOWLEDGMENTS

Like most books, this one has been written over a lifetime. Truth is, each time that I was privileged to teach Revelation, those who attended the studies (either in an academic setting or in churches) consistently asked about a book where they could find these thoughts in writing. I customarily pointed them to a list of very fine commentaries or monographs to discover the answers to most of their questions. Admittedly, there were no books written specifically about atonement in Revelation to which I might direct them. Consequently, these inquirers' responses to me were nearly always the same: "Why don't you write such a book?"

My reply to their friendly suggestion was usually along the lines that there were already far too many books written about Revelation, so we hardly need another one. That response rarely satisfied the more persistent students. Accordingly, after seventeen years of teaching and serving administratively at the M. Christopher White School of Divinity at Gardner-Webb University, I requested and was granted a sabbatical leave in which to complete this project. As life (rather, death) would have it, during the preparatory phase for the sabbatical my father lost his battle with dementia and Alzheimer's, my wife's chronic health problems further deteriorated, and students and friends of mine faced an inordinate number of personal crises, not to mention the many local churches and their pastors that I knew that were having tremendous struggles. As these destructive and decreative forces took their toll on family, friends, and so many churches, I found myself asking what, if anything, Revelation's message of atonement, redemption, victory, and hope might have to say to these situations? One way I attempted to manage some of these personal stressors was to spend time in "the study" trying to be productive, namely, to address the subject of atonement as Revelation articulates it.

Those eager students (both academic and confessional ones) urged me not to "dial back" the details (including the Greek words and the biblical, theological, and mythological images with which they sometimes were and sometimes were not familiar) and not to neglect pointing out the theological implications at which Revelation is aiming. For these reasons various chapters in this book will be of greater or lesser interest to certain readers. Not coincidentally, what I have heard through the years from both academic students and confessional readers of the Revelation is that many of them typically proceed with theological convictions already established, or they read the text with an eye toward only certain academic details but with little interest in theological conclusions. I hope to have wedded these two perspectives appropriately in this work.

These same students expressed interest in a book about Revelation that is both textually sound and theologically oriented but not trapped in familiar debates about the when and where of the return of Christ or speculation about the millennial reign. They wanted a book that would direct them to the many valuable resources that I have found essential for arriving at John's theological conclusions, particularly about the implications of "the Lamb slain from the foundation of the world" / τοῦ ἀρνίου τοῦ ἐσφαγμένου ἀπὸ καταβολῆς κόσῃου (Rev 13:8). My attempt has been to provide such a book. Any failure to that end is my own, while any success is attributable to their persistence.

Smyth & Helwys Publishing has been first rate in every way, easy to work with, gracious, and yet necessarily firm with deadlines. Editor Leslie Andres' contribution has been outstanding as she moved the project along with precision, care, and wisdom. I also offer special thanks to student research assistant Mariah Q. Richardson who voluntarily tracked down sources and encouraged the work to completion. Clearly, this book is the work of many hands.

Above all, my hope is that the One who sits on the "throne of God and the Lamb" / θρόνου τοῦ θεοῦ καὶ τοῦ ἀρνίου (Rev 22:1, 3), who has been extraordinarily gracious and redemptive to me throughout my life, will be pleased with this effort and that this book will offer redemptive hope to others.

—RWC

Contents

Introduction

Among the things for which the book of Revelation (the Apocalypse) is well known, atonement is not a subject that gets a great deal of attention. While many books have been written on or about both Revelation and atonement, and from varieties of different perspectives, emphasis on atonement in the Apocalypse remains somewhat underdeveloped.[1] Certainly, the New Testament's final book does not use traditional biblical language, let alone familiar theological concepts associated with the classical views of the atonement[2] (*Christus Victor* / "Christ the Victor" perhaps being an exception[3]). For that reason, and likely others, the redemptive work of Jesus Christ has not been highlighted from the Apocalypse's perspective to the degree that it could be. The goal of this project is to reflect on the meaning and significance of Jesus' death as conveyed through the various images and metaphors the Apocalypse uses, particularly how the multimedia of Revelation 12 contribute to the subject.

To be sure, the importance of atonement has been well documented in most cultures. The English word "atonement" (or its colloquial equivalent "at-one-ment") implies that things can and often do go wrong in relationships: human relationships and the relationship that people have with God. Moreover, the human sense or desire to be right, or to have things that have gone wrong be made or declared right, is at the heart of atonement and its related expressions. This human (and divine) quest is specifically the case as atonement theories have been identified in Judaeo-Christian Scripture and as they have been further developed in Christian history. While the word "atonement" / ἱλαστήριον (*hilasterion*) is never specifically mentioned in Revelation and is a complex theological term, there is no debate that the Apocalypse maintains that God has done something redemptive through the death of Jesus Christ, the Lamb of God. The focus of this investigation, therefore, is to examine how Revelation contributes to an understanding of the meaning of atonement as the redemptive work accomplished by Jesus' death. In particular, what exactly does John declare God to have done when he pictured the "Lamb standing as having been slain" (Rev 5:6—ἀρνίον ἑστηκὸς ὡς ἐσφαγμένον) and "the Lamb having been slain from the foundation of the world" (13:8—τοῦ ἀρνίου τοῦ ἐσφαγμένου ἀπὸ καταβολῆς κόσμου)? Does the slain Lamb provide something propitiatory (to appease the wrath of God) or expiatory (to cover or remove the offense), as some interpreters have suggested is the meaning of atonement, or does Revelation communicate something else?

Closely related to atonement are the familiar biblical and theological terms *sacrifice* (as expiation, propitiation, or purification), *redemption, justification, reconciliation, regeneration, adoption, repentance, forgiveness, faith, cleansing, sanctification, glorification, sin,* and *salvation,* any and all of which are identified in one way or another by those seeking to understand what it means to be right with God and to be right with others. While there are certainly both major and minor differences in meaning and emphasis among the words *atonement, sacrifice,* and *redemption,* they will be used more or less interchangeably hereafter, yet, where appropriate, will be qualified as Revelation uses them in terms of their relationship to the more nuanced concepts mentioned above. By way of disclaimer, the following pages will not be a new commentary or an assessment of the classic atonement theories[4] found outside of Revelation (with sacrifice, expiation and propitiation, and redemption—as ransom—requiring a closer look). Revelation 12 will receive special attention as will all atonement-related concepts and images that John uses to inform readers of the significance of Jesus' and his followers' deaths. The chapters before the reader are principally an exploration of the signal contribution made by the book of Revelation as John develops the meaning of Jesus' atoning death. By using the exegetical contributions of representative contemporary scholarship—and pushing beyond them where appropriate—the Apocalypse's presentation of atonement will emerge.

Coming from the hand of St. John the Divine,[5] Revelation adds significantly to a Christian understanding of the meaning of redemption and to a Christian appropriation of its purpose in believers' lives. The Lamb of God of Revelation is pictured as slain, yet the Lamb is simultaneously victorious and redemptive. How John depicts this defeat-yet-victory as a single concept becomes clear when Revelation 12 is examined alongside other texts in the Apocalypse that either anticipate it or build upon it. Although the word *sacrifice* and other traditional terms associated with atonement are indirectly developed in Revelation, John has a variety of expressions to communicate the importance of atonement. At the heart of his revelation is Christ's redemptive accomplishment and the deliverance that Christ brings to his followers from pervasive evil powers.

For those who take seriously the reality of sin, offense, and wrong that are prevalent in the world, as well as sin's presence in their lives and the estrangement that results from it, the message of redemption found in the Apocalypse is inestimable. While no single perspective on atonement relates equally or fully well to all individuals' need of remedy for their separation from God, from other people, or dis-ease within themselves, John's viewpoint certainly serves as an important addition to other well-known views of atonement. Some may find the Apocalypse's perspective on the significance of the death of Jesus to be a welcome contribution to what they know already about the meaning of the cross in the Christian tradition. Others may find it to be an even more suitable expression that speaks truth to their need for personal reconciliation to God, their reconciliation to others, and their own spiritual and emotional well-being.

Because shifting worldviews have historically prompted theological and doctrinal thinking and rethinking of traditional theological concepts, such is the case for contemporary understanding of the meaning and significance of Jesus' death. Christian atonement theories, all of which have proceeded from both biblical texts and historical circumstances, continue to be analyzed and evaluated in most classical systematic, dogmatic, and Christian theologies.[6] Occasionally, however, new developments arise that challenge or supplement longstanding traditional views. For instance, in the last quarter of the twentieth century, Jürgen Moltmann's *The Crucified God: The Cross of Christ as the Foundation and Criticism of Christian Theology* propelled something of a reassessment of the meaning of atonement based on his articulation of Jesus' "God-forsaken" death on the cross.[7] Also at the close of the second and beginning of the third millennium, Black, Feminist, Womanist, and Post-modern theologies began to call into question the dominant atonement language used among evangelicals of exclusively satisfaction and substitution understandings of the cross (see ch. 1, "Propitiation and Expiation").[8] Their legitimate complaint was that such an abstract understanding of the cross often leaves things in culture and society pretty much the same; namely, if God were satisfied with Jesus' atoning death so much so that it addressed the sins of humanity, then why should people not merely continue to live their lives as they always have—particularly when it comes to how they relate to others, not to mention how they relate to the environment?[9]

More recently Alan Mann has taken up the matter from an even less-traditional perspective—that of postmodernity (if not post-Christianity)—in the second edition of his book *Atonement for a Sinless Society*.[10] Whether traditionalists agree with the thesis of his book, he admits that conventional satisfaction or substitution models of atonement do not touch the psyche of many people today. As he says, "Our responsibility is to discern the over-arching predicament of our time,"[11] which, drawing upon the research of Stephen Pattison, *Shame: Theory, Therapy, Theology*, he concludes is shame. As such, what do people do about shame in their lives, not guilt (as he traces this development in his second chapter)? Shame, he suggests, must be the focal point at which atonement aims today.[12]

Most recently Stephen Finlan, who through the years has written extensively on atonement, in his latest book *Sacrifice and Atonement: Psychological Motives and Biblical Patterns*, surveyed (as this title attests) psychological theories and how sacrifice and atonement seem to have provided an answer to injury, guilt, shame, and appeasement as well as concerns about purity through the "scapegoat" notions (advanced by René Girard) of certain religious contexts.[13] He even addresses how sacrifice and atonement speak to fear and traumatic childhood experiences.[14] What continues to prompt such theologians' rethinking is the simple but wisely asked question, "What does the death of the first-century man named Jesus have to do with a twenty-first-century person?" In answer to that question, traditional models of the atonement continue to be embraced, reevaluated, or occasionally (if unnecessarily) abandoned.

It is my intent that this book will add to the ongoing atonement conversation, but not by a lengthy retreading of the well-worn paths of the millennial views theorized about Revelation; those debates for the most part are unnecessary. This work, however, will touch occasionally on the various earlier perspectives on Revelation. What the reader will find mostly, however, is an examination of the biblical text of Revelation where atone-ment-related language is found en route to a theological reconstruction of John's sense of the redemptive work of Jesus Christ. Prior to taking up the main subject, I provide some preliminary groundwork relative to the Apocalypse. As such, these pages will include exegetical comments based on evaluative summaries of contemporary scholarship (not intended to be exhaustive) of more recent years by looking at classical commentaries of New Testament scholarship alongside both descriptive and prescriptive components developed across the six chapters of this work.

While this apocalypse / Ἀποκάλυψις (Rev 1:1), prophecy / τῆς προφ-ητείας (Rev 1:3), and epistle (see the letter format "to the seven churches in Asia, grace and peace to you" / ταῖς ἑπτὰ ἐκκλησίαις ταῖς ἐν τῇ Ἀσίᾳ· χάρις ὑμῖν καὶ εἰρήνη)[15] (1:4) speaks practically and pastorally to its first-century audience of seven churches of Asia Minor (Rev 2–3), it also provides "staurological" insights that are important for a proper theology of the cross both for the first listeners of the Apocalypse—"the ones who hear" / οἱ ἀκούοντες (Rev 1:3b)—and for readers who reflect theologically on Revelation today. Certainly the word "cross" (σταυρός—*stauros*) appears in Revelation only once, and that in verb form, in 11:8—"where also their Lord was crucified" / ὅπου κα κύριος αὐτῶν ἐσταυρώθη, but John mean-while uses a number of other related terms and images that speak to his understanding of the significance of Jesus' death.

In summary,

(1) chapter 1 is an introductory chapter that addresses general background, genre, and language of the Apocalypse as well as the meaning of atonement and sacrifice (including an examination of Revelation's meaning of the "wrath of the Lamb") as propitiation and expiation, and ransom, but it is not an exploration or evalua-tion of the classically known theories of atonement.

(2) Chapter 2 addresses one group of atonement-related concepts (Throne, Temple, and Altar) found in the Apocalypse outside of Revelation 12.

(3) Chapter 3 is a continuation of atonement language found else-where in Revelation.

(4) Chapter 4 povides an overview of the biblical character Satan (*ha satan*—הַשָּׂטָן), who figures prominently in Revelation 12, as well as the biblical character Michael, alongside John's use of "space and time," particularly how the timing of the death of Jesus, under the influence of Satan, relates to the timing of Satan's defeat and ouster from the heavenly courtroom described in Revelation 12.

(5) Chapter 5 is an investigation of Revelation 12 as it describes Satan's defeat via the cross including the theme of victory through suffering. Included in this discussion is the mythological story

from the "life" of Apollo—his birth and subsequent contest with Python in particular—from which John draws in part to illustrate something of his intended meaning in Revelation 12. Even so, this chapter explores how John's language relates to Satan and his defeat.

(6) Finally, chapter 6 concludes the work with a prescriptive theological emphasis that connects the aforementioned details in a constructive manner for application to the church and to Christian life.

Unless otherwise indicated, the translations of Greek words, phrases, and verses from Revelation found throughout are my own. While the textual and grammatical challenges found in the Apocalypse are not small, they will be engaged only at points where they have significant bearing on John's expression of atonement. The commentaries consulted throughout this work each take on the critical and technical issues with great care. To be sure, R. H. Charles's comment is not that much of an exaggeration: "No literary document of the Greek world exhibits such a vast multitude of solecisms. It would almost seem that the author of the Apocalypse deliberately set at defiance the grammarian and the ordinary rules of syntax."[16] Despite these (intended?) anomalies, John's message about the cross is nevertheless clearly articulated and understandable.

Notes

1. Note that in Allen, Paul, and Woodman's work on the Apocalypse there are no atonement-related themes: Garrick V. Allen, Ian Paul, and Simon P. Woodman, eds., *The Book of Revelation: Currents in British Research on the Apocalypse in Wissenschaftliche Untersuchungen zum Neuen Testament* (Tübingen: Mohr Siebeck, 2015). The subjects addressed in this work are Text, Structure, and Persuasion: Garrick V. Allen, "Reusing Scripture in the Book of Revelation: Techniques of Reuse and Habits of Reading"; Andrew Harker, "Prophetically Called Sodom and Egypt: The Affective Power of Revelation 11.1–13"; Ian Paul, "Source, Structure, and Composition in the Book of Revelation"; Context, Interpretation, and Genre: Richard Bauckham, "Judgment in the Book of Revelation"; Sarah Underwood Dixon, "'The Testimony of Jesus' in Light of Internal Self-References in the Books of Daniel and 1 Enoch"; Sean Michael Ryan, "'The Testimony of Jesus' and 'The Testimony of Enoch': An *emic* Approach to the Genre of the Apocalypse"; Michelle Fletcher, "Apocalypse Noir: How Revelation Defined and Defied a Genre"; Ronald Herms, "πνευματικῶς and Antagonists in Revelation 11 Reconsidered"; W. Gordon Campbell, "Facing Fire and Fury: One Reading of Revelation's Violence in the Context of Recent

Interpretation"; Simon P. Woodman, "*Fire* from Heaven: Divine Judgment in the Book of Revelation"; Paul Middleton, "Male Virgins, Male Martyrs, Male Brides: A Reconsideration of the 144,000 'who have not dirtied themselves with women' (Revelation 14.4)"; Shane J. Wood, "God's Triumphal Procession: Re-examining the Release of Satan in the Light of Roman Imperial Imagery"; Reception: Christopher Rowland, "British Interpretation of the Apocalypse: A Historical Perspective"; Ian Boxall, "The Mighty Angel and the Little Scroll: A Reception-Historical Study of Revelation 10"; Jonathan Downing, "The Women Clothed in the Sun: The Reception of Revelation 12 among Female British Prophets 1780–1814"; Afterword: Steve Moyise, "A Response to Currents in British Research on the Apocalypse."

2. N. T. Wright, *The Day the Revolution Began: Reconsidering the Meaning of Jesus's Crucifixion* (New York: HarperOne, 2016), for instance, is a recent treatment of the atonement that moves in a unique direction. In his book he makes no reference to Rev 12 (which figures prominently in this work below). Soon after its publication, Wright delivered a lecture, "Saving the World, Revealing the Glory: Atonement Then and Now" (St. Mellitus College, London, October 17, 2016), in which he summarized his conclusions about atonement. Essentially he avoids any traditional propitiatory or substitutionary connotations associated with Jesus' crucifixion emphasizing instead that atonement is God restoring the vocational covenant that was violated by Adam and Eve in the Genesis account. "The Covenant of Vocation" (ch. 4 particularly, 68–80) is his primary focus rather than the cross being a means of escape for believers from earthly sin in this fallen world to gain heaven in the life to come.

3. Martyn John Smith, *Divine Violence and the Christus Victor Atonement Model: God's Reluctant Use of Violence for Soteriological Ends* (Eugene OR: Pickwick, 2016), is a recent treatment of the *Christus Victor* subject with only minor emphasis, however, on the Apocalypse.

4. Smith, "Metaphor and Models," ch. 3 of *Divine Violence and the Christus Victor Atonement Model,* offers a summary analysis of the atonement theories as they relate to God's violence in the crucifixion.

5. George B. Caird, *The Revelation of St. John the Divine* (New York: Harper and Row, 1966). Because of the uncertainty about which "John" is the author Revelation, Caird's suggestion of "the Divine" seems an appropriate qualifier for the author. John most certainly is neither the author of the Gospel nor of the Epistles.

6. Millard J. Erickson, *Christian Theology*, 3rd ed. (Grand Rapids MI: Baker, 2013) 713–68, is but one example among many Christian theologies that examines atonement theories in detail. Any other book that bears a similar title does the same and often highlights a particular direction toward which the respective writer leans. Evangelical circles have highly favored substitutionary atonement, while in more mainline settings the exemplary or educational model has been embraced.

7. Jürgen Moltmann, *The Crucified God: The Cross of Christ as the Foundation and Criticism of Christian Theology* (New York: Harper and Row, 1974).

8. Examples include James H. Cone, *God of the Oppressed*, rev. ed. (Maryknoll NY: Orbis, 1997); Joan Carlson Brown and Rebecca Parker, "For God so Loved the World," *Christianity, Patriarchy, and Abuse: A Feminist Critique*, ed. Joan Carlson Brown and Carol R. Bohn (New York: Pilgrim Press, 1989); Rita Nakashima Brock, *Journeys by Heart: A Christology of Erotic Power* (New York: Crossroad, 1988); Delores Williams, *Sisters in the Wilderness: The Challenge of Womanist God-Talk* (Maryknoll NY: Orbis Books, 1993); Tina Pippin, *Death and Desire: The Rhetoric of Gender in the Apocalypse of John* (Louisville: Westminster/John Knox, 1992). See also Tina Pippin, "The Heroine and the Whore: Fantasy and the Female in the Apocalypse of John," *Semeia* 60 (1992): 67–82; Tina Pippin, "Eros and the End: Reading for Gender in the Apocalypse of John," *Semeia* 59 (1992): 193–217; Tina Pippin, "Jezebel Re-Vamped," *Semeia* 69/70: *Intertextuality and the Bible* (1995): 221–34; and Christopher A. Frilingos, *Spectacles of Empire: Monsters, Martyrs, and the Book of Revelation* (Philadelphia: University of Pennsylvania Press), 2004.

9. Michael S. Northcott, "Earth Left Behind? Ecological Readings of the Apocalypse of John in Contemporary America" in William John Lyons and Jorunn Økland, eds., The Way the World Ends? The Apocalypse of John in Culture and Ideology (Sheffield: Sheffield Phoenix, 2009) 230–31, says, "At the root of the anti-ecological rhetoric of dispensationalism lies the escapist doctrine of the 'rapture' which has become the lynchpin of the dispensationalist schema invented by Darby. Darby is said to have originated his account of an instant rapture after hearing about a vision which occurred to a small girl called Margaret Macdonald at a healing service in Glasgow in 1830. She received a vision of a two-stage return of Christ to earth. At the first return Christ comes secretly to rescue the raptured from the earth before the Great Tribulation and the battle of Megiddo or 'Armageddon'. At the second return Christ comes to reign over the earth in Jerusalem in the one-thousand year reign of peace which is said to be predicted in Revelation 21. The word rapture occurs nowhere in the Book of Revelation but it is a Latin translation of the Greek root *arpazo*, meaning 'catch up', and as used in 1 Thessalonians 4.17. The preaching of the rapture did not catch on in England but Darby made many evangelistic trips to the United States before, during, and after the American Civil War when the escapist theology of the rapture turned out to have widespread appeal. The doctrine of the rapture is what produces the peculiar division of world history into seven stages and it is the most significant innovation that Darby adds to his Joachimite forbears. And it is this teaching which singularly reshapes the modern millennialist reading of the Book of Revelation. . . .

"This escapist reading of the Apocalypse has found a particularly influential form in the best-selling *Left Behind* novelistic series of Timothy LaHaye and Jerry Jenkins. Since the terror attacks on America in 2001, an event that many dispensationalists interpreted as a 'sign of the end,' each new issue in this fictional series has made it to the top of the New York Times bestseller list. . . .

"For the dispensationalist, history is reaching an end point where the earth is given over to Satan and the rule of antichrist and only those who believe, and are soon to be raptured, may be saved from the destructive events that this rule will unleash. Consequently, many Christians of this theological persuasion when faced with intractable social or ecological problems such as global warming turn to the maxim of Darby, 'the Church must be entirely passive'. The created order is already on the way to perdition and there is nothing that Christians can do to save it."

See Thomas D. Ice, "Margaret MacDonald," in M. Couch, ed., *Dictionary of Premillennial Theology: A Practical Guide to the People, Viewpoints, and History of Prophetic Studies* (Grand Rapids MI: Kregel, 1996) 243. See also Ernest R. Sandeen, *The Roots of*

Fundamentalism: British and American Millenarianism 1800–1930 (Grand Rapids MI: Baker, 1970).

10. Alan Mann, *Atonement for a Sinless Society*, 2nd ed. (Eugene OR: Cascade, 2014).

11. Ibid., 4.

12. Stephen Pattison, *Shame: Theory, Therapy, Theology* (Cambridge: Cambridge University Press, 2000).

13. Stephen Finlan, *Sacrifice and Atonement: Psychological Motives and Biblical Patterns* (Minneapolis: Fortress, 2016).

14. Ibid., 59–74.

15. Here and hereafter the Greek text edited by M. W. Holmes, *The Greek New Testament: SBL Edition* (Lexham Press, Society of Biblical Literature, 2011–2013), will be used.

16. R. H. Charles, *Studies in the Apocalypse* (Edinburgh: T & T Clark, 1913) 81.

Outline of *Atonement in the Apocalypse*

CHAPTER 1

Genre, Atonement, and the Wrath of the Lamb

The book of Revelation, also known as the Apocalypse (based on the first word that appears in its text—Ἀποκάλυψις), cannot be limited in genre to "apocalyptic," although it certainly is that too. Just a few verses into the narrative, two additional words occur that expand the categories guiding readers' thoughts—"prophecy" / τῆς προφητείας (Rev 1:3) and (by implication) "letter," since the book anticipates a "reader" / ἀναγινώσκων (1:3) and "hearers" / οἱ ἀκούοντες (1:3) of what is to be sent "to seven churches" / ταῖς ἑπτὰ ἐκκλησίαις (1:4). Before engaging Revelation's atonement language, a few preliminary remarks about the Apocalypse's three-fold genre are in order, the bulk of which relate to apocalyptic and prophecy (but only in broad summary form).[1]

APOCALYPTIC AND APOCALYPSES
Inasmuch as this project depends primarily on the text of the Apocalypse, the first matter of concern is the word "apocalyptic." Ernst Käsemann certainly heightened awareness of "apocalyptic" in the mid-twentieth century. As part of the so-called "New Quest of the Historical Jesus," Käsemann created something of a stir in the scholarly world with his publication (later translated into English) of "The Beginnings of Christian Theology"[2] in which he posited that the fundamental message about Jesus found in the New Testament is that early Jewish Christians understood Jesus expressly in terms of Jewish apocalyptic. To say the least, his essay sparked renewed interest in apocalyptic that produced a flurry of scholarship that continues to this day.

Mitchell G. Reddish is clearly on target about apocalyptic:

> Apocalyptic thought apparently arose within Judaism following the sixth
> century Babylonian exile of the Jewish people. Although the book of
> Daniel is the only complete example of an apocalypse in the Hebrew
> Bible, other passages contain ideas that are either apocalyptic or similar
> to apocalyptic thought. Examples would include Zechariah 9–14, Ezekiel
> 38–39, and Isaiah 24–27. Apocalyptic literature flourished within
> Judaism between the third century BC and the second century AD. At
> least fourteen nonbiblical Jewish apocalypses were produced during this
> time.[3]

In *The Crucifixion: Understanding the Death of Jesus Christ*, "The Apocalyptic War: *Christus Victor*," Fleming Rutledge acknowledges that "[t]here
is widespread mystification about the strange word 'apocalyptic.'"[4] Yet since
apocalyptic language is found in biblical texts across the Old and New
Testaments, as well as related noncanonical texts, common themes emerge
that are pivotal for understanding texts like Revelation. Consequently, in
1979 the Society of Biblical Literature settled on the following working
definition:

> "Apocalypse" is a genre of revelatory literature with a narrative framework,
> in which revelation is mediated by an otherworldly being to a human
> recipient, disclosing a transcendent reality which is both temporal,
> insofar as it envisages eschatological salvation, and spatial, insofar as it
> involves another, supernatural world.[5]

Along the same lines, Frederick J. Murphy, who has written widely on
Revelation, has suggested,

> Apocalypses project experience onto a cosmic screen, using all the
> resources at their disposal, including elements from their own religious
> traditions as well as from their broader environment. The result is imagi-
> native literature, which uses symbolic language to evoke aspects of reality
> that are beyond powers of literal description.[6]

In his breakthrough theological work *Theology of Hope*, Jürgen
Moltmann articulated four themes characteristic of apocalyptic. First, apocalyptic is deterministic in nature—matters are settled from the beginning
with history being the setting for the unfolding plan. Second, apocalyptic

involves the history of the world (not just God's people). Third, apocalyptic does not envision the overcoming of evil by good but the separation of good and evil. And fourth, judgment is an immutable fate, not something that can be averted.[7] Whether or not Revelation meets satisfactorily any or all of these criteria, Moltmann's summary is instructive about this genre and the degree to which this New Testament document fits it. To be sure, in some capacity it contains within it most, if not all, of these characteristics. The theological point being made by apocalyptic as a genre, in broad terms, is that the world is so inexorably corrupt that only divine intervention can fix it.

Gregory K. Beale has aptly acknowledged as well that John of Revelation "has utilized three genres of apocalyptic, prophecy, and epistle in composing the book."[8] Moreover, Beale concludes that the "word 'apocalypse' in 1:1 is a direct allusion to Daniel 2, where the word is used of the prophetic revelation communicated from God to the prophet Daniel (see again on 1:1). In this sense, Revelation is best seen as fitting into the genre of OT prophetic-apocalyptic works, especially that of Ezekiel, Daniel, and Zechariah."[9] Beale is in agreement with most commentators on Revelation, and those of the Society of Biblical Literature, that Revelation does not fit exclusively into the framework of the working definition of apocalyptic alone. Michelle Fletcher's essay, "Apocalypse Noir: How Revelation Defined and Defied a Genre," suggests that "[a] radically different perspective is required if we are to move forward in our understanding of Revelation and apocalyptic/apocalypse . . . ."[10] She focuses, in particular, on the dialectic of "revealing and concealing" with Revelation's penchant for "exaggeration/selecting/side-lining/signaling." In other words, Revelation defies strict apocalyptic categorization although it "is not lacking apocalyptic features compared to other apocalypses. Rather, the features it has are different."[11] Prophecy and epistle are important categories as well that John utilized in conveying his message.

Recognized apocalyptic documents, however, do contain a number of distinct features. In particular, these texts acknowledge an interaction of two worlds—the heavenly and the earthly—the divine and the human. Prevailing in the interaction in Revelation is the heavenly with God ultimately triumphing. As Revelation 21 points out, God is the architect of something new (Rev 21:1-5, cf. particularly 21:5a—"Behold I am making all things new" / Ἰδοὺ καινὰ ποιῶ παντα) in the aftermath of a number of local and global cataclysms that are described throughout the book. In fact, the anticipated new things about which John speaks are also found

characteristically in other apocalyptic texts like those of Ezekiel, Isaiah,
Daniel, and Zechariah in the biblical tradition.

Apocalyptic as a medium of communication also includes a number of
distinguishable literary characteristics. In short, readers do not encounter
conventional prose narrative; rather, they discover a book filled with signs,
visions, and images of stock apocalyptic language. As a first rule of interpretation, readers must avoid confusing the "sign" with the "signified." In
many ways John's Gospel (chapters 1–11 as the Book of Signs), while not
apocalyptic, illustrates well this lesson. For example, in the Gospel there
are terms like *light, darkness, birth, water, bread,* and *life,* all of which are
signs pointing to an intended meaning not necessarily obvious on the
surface. To take any of these signs literally is to miss their meaning entirely.
Nicodemus of John 3, for example, is portrayed as the classic literalist
who did not understand what it meant to be "born again." He reasoned
the natural impossibility of entering a second time into his (most likely
deceased) mother (John 3:4) for a second birth. John's point is that only
a proper differentiation of the sign from the signified allows a reader to
understand that there is birth, and that there is "birth" beyond the physical
birth implied in the word "born."

Revelation, to be sure, requires a similar approach if it is to be understood. John could hardly have made this point more clearly than he does in
the opening verse of the Apocalypse. In it he said, "The revelation of Jesus
Christ, . . . and he *signified*[12] [emphasis added] by sending his messenger
to his servant John" / Ἀποκάλυψις Ἰησοῦ Χριστοῦ,... καὶ ἐσήμανεν
ἀποστείλας διὰ τοῦ ἀγγέλου τῷ δούλῳ αὐτοῦ Ἰωάννῃ (Rev 1:1). His
means of "signification" is by use of apocalyptic and prophetic words in
the epistolary format that he employs. In each of the genres he uses, he
engages signs as means of communicating his revelation. The cognate
σημεῖον ("sign") of the verb form ἐσήμανεν ("he signified") mentioned
in 1:1 appears in Revelation 12:1, 3; 13:13, 14; 15:1; 16:14; and 19:20 as
well, no doubt as a reminder to readers not to confuse the sign with the
signified. John, of course, uses signs everywhere in Revelation even when
he does not use the word "sign" / σημεῖον or "signify" / σημαίνω to alert
the hearer or reader.[13]

The Apocalypse also includes dualistic characteristics—good vs. evil—
as well as transcendent emphases alongside immanent ones. It recognizes
the qualitative difference between God and man. While it tends to be
pessimistic about this world as it presently is, it is optimistic about God's
coming intervention to right the wrongs of it. As such, it has eschatological

hope. And while concerned with theodicy, it maintains unshakable belief in God to right the wrongs of the world despite the present evil in the world.

It uses multiple media for its presentation, including visions of heaven and earth, a journey to and from heaven, and something of a last testament or farewell speech alongside surveying history in which it places what is happening now within the greater context of world events. To carry out its purpose it employs figurative language, often giving bodily form to evil and good. There are prayers and songs, including a chorus of twenty-four elders. Numbers figure prominently as well. There are fractions of incompleteness (1/2 hour; 1/3; 1/4; 3 1/2 years); there are whole numbers like 4 denoting the world and wholeness alongside 5 (human's number—with 5 human "digits"), 6 (which is one number larger than man but one number less than 7), 7 (the number of fullness and completion) that is God's number/divine/totality (see 7 spirits; 7 churches; 7 lampstands; 7 stars; 7 seals; 7 thunders (not elaborated); 7 trumpets; 7 plagues; and 7 unnumbered doxologies—1:5-6; 4:1-11; 5:8-14; 7:11-17; 12:11-17; 12:10-12; 15:1-5; 19:1-8);[14] there is 10 (and its multiples) denoting completeness; and, finally, 12 (and its multiples) equating wholeness/fullness (24 elders; 12 tribes; 144,000; 12 pearled gates).

Likewise, there are colors: pale green=death; dark green=life; white=purity/conquering; red=war; black=famine; gold=value and worth; bronze=strength; scarlet=immorality. Animals are prominent as well, representing human beings or human qualities (good or bad). There is the Lamb=Jesus (with seven horns and seven eyes=divinity); frogs=evil (like the plague of the Old Testament); eagle/vulture=bearer of bad news like locusts, monster beasts of land and sea with the Dragon=evil parodies of the four good "living creatures," and there is the slain Lamb.[15]

Of importance regarding apocalyptic is Richard J. Bauckham's observation that "John's visions, however, are not historical narrative but vehicles of the cosmic significance of historical events, and for this reason they often resemble the images of myth, while retaining the historical reference that genuine myths lack."[16] For instance, and of importance to this project (see chapters 4 and 5 below), it is as Bauckham says:

The serpent or the Dragon, Revelation's symbol for the primeval source of evil in the world, the devil (12:3–9), is a good example of a symbol with strong biblical roots (Gen 3:14-15; Isa. 27:1) which Revelation evokes, but also with wide cultural resonances in the minds of contemporary readers, owing to its prominence in pagan mythology and religion.

[These symbols] . . . do not create a purely self-contained aesthetic world with no reference outside itself, but intend to relate to the world in which the readers live in order to reform and to redirect the readers' response to that world. However, if the images are not timeless symbols, but relate to the "real" world, we need also to avoid the opposite mistake of taking them too literally as descriptive of the "real" world and of predicted events in the "real" world. They are not just a system of codes waiting to be translated into matter-of-fact references to people and events. Once we begin to appreciate their sources and their rich symbolic associations, we realize that they cannot be read either as literal descriptions or as encoded literal descriptions, but must be read for their theological meaning and their power to evoke response.[17]

These revelatory keys, which are expanded in great detail in any of the critical commentaries on Revelation, provide a brief introduction to understanding the symbolic language that John uses and will be assumed in the expositions found in the balance of this work.

PROPHECY

Besides the apocalyptic characteristics of Revelation, its prophetic capacities have been rightly identified as well. Bauckham notes that prophecy is something "intended to be read aloud in the context of Christian worship, and this claim to be a prophecy is confirmed by the epilogue to the book (cf. 22:6-7, which echoes 1:1-3, and especially 22:18-19)."[18] He continues with the observation that "[v]irtually all we know about John, the author of Revelation, is that he was a Jewish Christian prophet. Evidently he was one of a circle of prophets in the churches of the provinces of Asia (22:6), and evidently he had at least one rival: the Thyatiran prophetess whom he considers a false prophet (2:20)."[19] Moreover, since prophets prophesied in worship settings, this apocalyptic-prophecy was written to be read as a letter to the seven congregations.

Bauckham acknowledges two kinds of prophecy—oracles spoken in the name of God or Christ and reports of visions. The following points are informative:

We should certainly not doubt that John had remarkable visionary experiences, but he has transmuted them through what must have been a lengthy process of reflection and writing into a thoroughly literary creation which is designed not to reproduce the experience so much as to communicate the meaning of the revelation that had been given him.

Certainly Revelation is literary work designed for oral performance (1:3), but as a complex literary creation, dense with meaning and allusion, it must be qualitatively different from the spontaneous orality of most early Christian prophecy.[20]

M. Eugene Boring appropriately qualifies the concept of prophecy. He indicates,

In our modern culture "prophecy" is often understood as "prediction of the future," and this is a valid understanding of the word in many modern contexts. A fundamental misunderstanding of biblical prophecy occurs, however, when it is equated with "predicting the future." . . . The prophets of the Old Testament did in fact sometimes make predictions, both of this-worldly historical events (e.g., Isa. 7:1–8:15, the Syro-Ephraimite war) and of the final victory of God at the end of history (e.g., Isa. 2:2-4; 9:2-7; 11:1-9) . . . . but it is a fundamental misunderstanding of Old Testament prophecy to regard it as essentially "prediction."[21]

Instead of the exclusively predictive nature of prophecy that some suppose, Hebrew Scriptures make clear that "[p]rophets were not predictors of historical events of the distant future but were inspired interpreters of historical events through which their hearers were living."[22] Moreover,

John served as prophetic interpreter of events for his congregations in two ways: (1) He declared the meaning of the historical events through which they were living and Christian responsibility within it . . . [and] (2) John continued to interpret the meaning of the event of the initial appearance of Jesus, giving it new interpretations and giving to Jesus new Christological titles which were meaningful ways to understand the significance of the Christ event in John's time . . . .[23]

Prophets also served God's purposes strategically as harbingers for change; namely they called the people of God to repentance. David Hill's work on *New Testament Prophecy* provides valuable insights on how Revelation functions prophetically.[24] Likewise, Boring notes that "[a] prophet is an immediately inspired spokesman for the (or a) deity of a particular community, who receives revelations which he is impelled to deliver to the community."[25] In other words, a prophet is one who "speaks before" as in one who foretells present and future events of the judgment or salvation of

God and as such is one who stands before, as a member of, and speaks or writes to a community of people the unique word received from God.

Because a prophet receives the message immediately, a prophet is distinguished from the proclaimer or teacher who expounds upon words received from a past authority. Revelation as prophecy is concerned more with the content than with the characteristic qualifiers of a prophet. What is clear, however, from the common thread that runs through the prophets of the Old Testament and Jesus, is suffering, rejection, and death. John fits this category himself as a prophet since he is exiled on Patmos as "your brother and partner in tribulation" / ὁ ἀδελφὸς ὑμῶν καὶ συγκοινωνὸς ἐν τῇ θλίψει (Rev 1:9).

The New Testament elsewhere reveals that prophets sometimes use apocalyptic speech (Mark 13:24-27; Luke 10:18) and that prophets some-times do not use apocalyptic speech (Mark 13:9-12; Acts 11:28). Elisabeth Schüssler Fiorenza, following J. Panagapoulos, suggests five functions of prophecy: (1) eschatological, (2) addresses a specific concrete situation, (3) contains a revelatory word of the resurrected Lord, (4) includes para-clesis for the church, and is (5) multidimensional in form.[26] Bauckham adds one additional item to this list: New Testament prophecy is in conti-nuity with the Old Testament in that it discerns the contemporary situation (how things look both from the worldly situation and from the heavenly realm), it predicts how God's ultimate purpose is related to the contempo-rary situation, and it evokes a response on the hearers' parts leaving room for human freedom and avoiding fatalism.[27] Prophecy does not predeter-mine the outcome.

John, as prophet, while never quoting the Old Testament directly, calls upon it in unique Christian prophetic fashion to declare the judgment and salvation of God. Prophecy always has as its message the theme of repen-tance for the people of God and the possible aversion of judgment. In fact, "repent" as a verb occurs eleven times in Revelation (2:5—two times; 2:16; 2:21—two times; 2:22; 8:3; 8:19; 9:20; 9:21; 16:9; 16:11), each speaking to the historical context of the people of God.

Last, but not least, is the affirmation found in Revelation 19:10b that the key prophet of Revelation (and the Christian faith) is Jesus. As the verse says, "For the testimony of Jesus is the spirit of prophecy" / ἡ γὰρ μαρτυρία Ἰησπῦ ἐστιν τὸ πνεῦμα τῆς προφητείας.

EPISTLE

Added to the apocalyptic-prophecy of John is his letter or epistolary style. The familiar "Grace to you and peace" / χάρις ὑμῖν καὶ εἰρήυη of 1:4 is reminiscent of a number of Paul's Epistles that begin similarly.[28] Moreover, the name of the author "John" / Ἰωάννης and the recipients "to the seven churches in Asia" / ταῖς ἑπτὰ ἐκκλησίας ταῖς ἐν τῇ Ἀσίᾳ round out the letter format. Stephen S. Smalley reminds readers that "[l]etters were well-established forms of instruction in Greek literature before the Christian era . . . ; and the New Testament epistles are descendants of this means of teaching. The didactic content of Revelation seems to be cast in a similarly epistolary form."[29]

Revelation 1:4-5a serve as an epistolary *Praescriptio* (Prescript) accompanied by the standard internal elements of *Superscriptio* (Superscript)—"John" / Ἰωάννης, *Adscriptio* (Addressees)—addressed "to the seven churches in Asia" / ταῖς ἑπτὰ ἐκκλμσίαις ταῖς ἐν τῇ Ἀσίᾳ, and *Salutatio* (Greeting)—of "grace and peace to you" / χάρις ὑμῖν καὶ εἰρήνη. Beale credits J. Ramsay Michaels who observed that Revelation is "'mixed' and unique: If a letter, it is like no other early Christian letter we possess. If an apocalypse, it is like no other apocalypse. If a prophecy, it is unique among prophecies."[30] So this apocalyptic-prophecy was inspired by God and told to John: "What you see write in a book and send it to the seven churches" / Ὃ βλέπεις γράψον εἰς βιβλίον καὶ πέμψον ταῖς ἑπτὰ ἐκκλησίαις (Rev 1:11).

John's conclusion has epistolary qualities as well. Craig R. Koester notes,

> Revelation has features of a letter . . . . The Pauline letters were usually dictated to a scribe (Rom 16:22) and sometimes included Paul's name and final comments in his own hand (1 Cor 16:21-24; Col 4:18; 2 Thess 3:17; Phlm 17; cf. Gal 6:11). By way of analogy, Revelation concludes with Jesus' verbal signature. Third, like the name of a witness at the end of an official document, Jesus' name attests to the truth of what is said.[31]

Reddish's summary is helpful:

> Finally, Revelation operates impressionistically rather than logically. John attempted to convey his message through imagination, symbols, and metaphors. The reader should remember that this is revelatory literature, presented as visions. It is not tightly organized, rational arguments. For

the modern reader to analyze and dissect the work, instead of experiencing it, is to do an injustice to the work. We should avoid the temptation to impose too rigid a structure or order on John's writing.[32]

With these briefly identified preliminary remarks in place, John's means of communicating his view of atonement in Revelation will hopefully be easier to follow.

ATONEMENT: SACRIFICE AND THE WRATH OF THE LAMB, PROPITIATION AND EXPIATION, AND RANSOM

As a second step toward arriving at the meaning of Jesus' death on the cross (specifically Revelation's understanding of it), theologians and biblical scholars customarily reach back to Christianity's predecessor Judaism, the Hebrew sacrificial system, and its emphasis on either (or both) propitiation or expiation as background material for the meaning of atonement and sacrifice. In the case of Revelation, the Paschal (Passover) Lamb of Judaism is also significant. Although it was not originally viewed in any sense as expiatory for taking away sin, Paul in 1 Corinthians 5:7 noted that "Christ, our paschal lamb, has been sacrificed" / τό πάσχα ἡμῶν ἐτύθη Χριστός prompting Raymond E. Brown to observe that within "the concept of the Paschal lamb, the function of taking away the world's sin could easily be fitted."[33] Granted that Revelation acknowledges the redemptive capacity of the Lamb's death, what does that mean? What does John conclude was accomplished when he says "you purchased (or ransomed) to God by your blood those from every tribe and tongue and people and nation" / ἠγόρασας τῷ θεῷ ἐν τῷ αἵματί σου ἐκ πάσης φυλῆς καὶ γλώσσης καὶ λαοῦ καὶ ἔθνους (Rev 5:9)?

Sacrifice[34] and the Wrath of the Lamb

In the first place, the role of sacrifice was quite important in Judaism and in the early Christian tradition. It certainly informs John's understanding of the death of Jesus in Revelation. Fleming Rutledge understands this well, and in her book *The Crucifixion: Understanding the Death of Jesus Christ* she includes a significant chapter on "The Blood Sacrifice." Her emphasis falls on the "enduring importance" of the "motif of Christ's blood, as derived from the New Testament . . . ."[35] This powerful metaphor, she notes, defies the "[l]iteral-mindedness [that] is the enemy of vital biblical interpretation."[36] She acknowledges that the "salient point was that God, knowing that the Israelites could not come near him as they were in their guilt, provided the means for them to live in his presence . . . . The spilled blood of the animal . . . was the means of obtaining remission of sin."[37] Genesis 9:4 and Deuteronomy 12:23 come quickly to mind with their emphasis on life being in the blood.

Loren L. Johns explores "Atonement and Sacrifice in the Book of Revelation" and makes the following astute observation:

> [O]ne of the problems with using atonement terminology is its lack of precision. Does Revelation even have a theology of the atonement? It depends on what one means by atonement. Although the death of Christ in Revelation is central to its theology and clearly salvific, the book's primary focus is on how evil is conquered and how God's reign is established on earth, not on how sin is dealt with forensically in putting humanity into right relationship with God.[38]

In other words, the significance of Jesus' death as an atoning sacrifice for an individual's sin is something that must be deduced rather than something that can be discovered by examination of any explicit statements found in Revelation.

As David E. Aune states,

> While it is likely that the figure of the Lamb in Revelation must be understood at least in part on the basis of OT sacrificial ritual, it is not at all clear which type of sacrifice is primarily in view, for sheep or lambs were used as sacrificial victims in several different types of sacrifice in the OT and early Judaism.[39]

For instance, Johns points out that "two lambs were sacrificed every day as a burnt offering in the *Tamid* (the daily offering). However, this daily burnt offering never carried with it any atoning significance. The Passover lamb was a type of peace offering [שְׁלָמִים] (*šelāmîm*), which had nothing to do with atonement."[40] He notes Aune's general agreement with Gary A. Anderson that

> it seems apparent that the historical *realia* of the Israelite sacrificial cult . . . do not provide anything more than a general context in which the metaphor of the slaughtered Lamb whose blood somehow effects redemption can be understood. The sacrificial features of the Lamb of

Revelation are primarily a textual phenomenon with only very loose associations with actual cultic practice.[41]

Anderson argues as well that "the act of sacrifice serves to purge or purify something rather than to remove sin."[42] He further suggests that once the temple was destroyed, while sacrifice still had a place, it served only theoretically in the atonement theology of Rabbinic Judaism.[43] Lesley R. DiFransico traces how the Hebrew Bible develops the metaphorical concept of sins being washed away. By using the "Conceptual Metaphor Theory" of George Lakoff and Mark Johnson, DiFransico explores this expression in five passages found in three specific texts: Isaiah 1; 4; Jeremiah 2; 4; and Psalm 51. Sin in these places is seen as a bloodstain (in Isa 1:15; 4:4), as filth (in Jer 4:14), and as impurity (in Ps 51). Her study acknowledges the variety of usages found in Hebrew Scripture for responding to the problem of sin. She notes that only later in the tradition is washing away of sin found, particularly in the rituals at Qumran, which later most likely influenced first-century Jewish and subsequent Christian practices.[44]

Johns observes that twelfth-century "Maimonides famously systematized the sacrificial system as no one before or since. Nevertheless, he was capable of being quite critical of the whole system. In any case, 'burnt-offerings and sacrifice . . . are of secondary importance.'"[45] To be sure, the Bible's metaphorical capacity is at work in the language of blood sacrifice and atonement. More correctly, as Rutledge points out, metonymy or synecdoche (the use of one idea for another, or the part for the whole)[46] are better and more descriptive terms that should be embraced when seeking to understand Revelation's intention.

Johns quite plausibly concludes,

> It is impossible to speak of atonement and sacrifice without some underlying understanding of how God saves—and from what. The word sacrifice is often associated [by Christians] with Anselm's satisfaction theory of the atonement—and for good reason. Anselm saw humanity as owing a debt that it could not pay. Humanity was atoned when Jesus' death "expiated" humanity's sin. The analogy in the immediate background was the sacrificial system, with which nearly everyone in the Greco-Roman world, whether Jew or Gentile, would have been familiar, though less so in Anselm's day. So the relationship between sacrifice and Anselm's satisfaction theory is a natural one.[47]

Does, however, the sacrificial system inform an understanding of the relationship between the blood of the sacrifice and the life implied in the blood of the sacrificial victim? That question prompted significant discussion at the close of the nineteenth and opening of the twentieth century. What is at stake is whether or not there is any connection between the sacrificial life of Jesus[48] and his particular life being representative or perhaps substitutionary. Moreover, should atonement be limited just to his blood irrespective of his life? James Denney rightly challenged such a restrictive understanding,[49] and Rutledge concurs, that there can be no "dividing the life from the death, the blood offered from the blood shed."[50] All of which is to say, the life and the blood are one and the same, so much so that they cannot be separated: "The miracle of Christ's sacrificial death is that the priest and the victim have become one."[51]

Need such a conclusion imply that the wrath of God towad sin is appeased in a satisfactory manner through the shed blood of sacrifice, namely in Jesus' death on the cross? More specifically, does John's atonement language in Revelation support any notion of a blood sacrifice as being essential for appeasing the wrath of God? To answer the question, the following exploration of the word "wrath" found in Revelation proves instructive.[52] The word "wrath" makes more than a few appearances in the Apocalypse. In fact, John actually uses the words "wrath" (ὀργή) and "anger" (θυμός) a number of times and does so interchangeably.[53] Aune points out that in classical Greek θυμός is used of the inner emotion of anger while ὀργή is used of an external expression. Never mind their classical usage, in both the LXX and Revelation they are used interchangeably.[54]

English translations only occasionally distinguish the two. In fact, John uses ὀργή and θυμός ("wrath" and "anger") when referring to the Lamb (6:16—"of the wrath of the lamb" / τῆς ὀργῆς τοῦ ἀρνίου) and God (11:18—"your wrath came" / ἦλθεν ἡ ὀργη σου) and the Lamb and God (6:17—"their wrath" / τῆς ὀργῆς αὐτῶν). He does the same in referring to the cup of wrath (14:10—"in the cup of his wrath" / ἐν τῷ ποτηρίῳ τῆς ὀργῆς αὐτοῦ). Referring to God again, both words appear in 16:19—"the cup of the wine of the fury of his wrath" / τὸ ποτή-'ριον τοῦ οἴνου τοῦ θυμοῦ τῆς ὀργῆς αὐτου and in 19:15—"the wine of the fury of the wrath of God almighty" / τοῦ οἴνου του θυμοῦ τῆς ὀργῆς του θεοῦ τοῦ πάτοκράτορος. John uses θυμός only when referring to the Dragon (12:12—"having great fury" / ἔχων θυμὸν μέγαν), and he does the same when referring to Babylon (14:8—"of the wine of the fury of her immorality" / τοῦ οἴνου τοῦ θυμοῦ τῆς πορνείας

αὐτῆς). Moreover, John uses θυμός when referring to God in 15:1—
"the fury of God" / ὁ θυμός τοῦ θεοῦ, and he does the same in 15:7—
"of the fury of God" / τοῦ θυμοῦ τοῦ θεοῦ. As for the "bowls of wrath,"
only 16:1 uses the word "wrath" / θυμός referring to God. The subsequent
seven bowls mentioned respectively in 16:2, 3, 4, 8, 10, 12, and 17 use
simply "bowls" without the qualifying word "wrath" / θυμός. In 18:3 John
mentions Babylon (the harlot) and the nations being drunk on the "wine
of her angry immorality" / τοῦ οἴνου τοῦ θυμοῦ τῆς πορνείας αὐτης—
a phrase identical to that in 14:8.

Strikingly, for all of its uses, not once does Revelation ever indicate that
either God's or the Lamb's wrath is in any way directed toward or related to
divine propitiation. Moreover, God's wrath is never described as meted out
against the Lamb. In fact, the "wrath of the Lamb" (τῆς ὀργῆς τοῦ ἀρυίου)
in Greek grammatical structure is always possessive genitive or genitive of
source, but is is never objective genitive. That is, the Lamb is always the
one acting and is never the object of God's wrath. As such its meaning is
unrelated in a propitiatory sense of atonement, besides having nothing to
do with any specifically identified sacrificial offering.

Of the things said about the Lamb of God in Revelation, surely none is
more perplexing than the expression "wrath of the Lamb" / τῆς ὀργῆς τοῦ
ἀρυίου (6:16). The mere thought of a lamb conjures anything but anger
or aggression. Caird must be right when he notes that the "wrath of the
Lamb" can hardly be anything other than "a deliberate paradox, by which
John intends to goad his readers into theological alertness."[55]

There is an ironic twist at work when the slain Lamb of Revelation 5:6,
9, 12 is likewise known as the wrathful Lamb of 6:16 and 6:17 (see also
"God's wrath" in 14:10 where the "Lamb" is present as witness to the one
"tormented with fire and sulfur" / βασανιοθήσεται ἐν πυρὶ καὶ θείῳ).
John is perhaps informed by the image found in 1 Enoch 89–90 where
the lamb is identified as a conquering warrior.[56] The irony, however, of a
conquering lamb is equally direct in Revelation 19:11-21 where the rider
on the white horse "wears a garment dipped in blood" / περιβεβλημένος
ἱμάτιον βεβαμμένον αἵματι (19:13) and also "he treads the winepress of
the fury of the wrath of God Almighty" / αὐτὸς πατεῖ τὴν ληνὸν τοῦ οἴ
νου τοῦ θυμοῦ τῆς ὀργῆς τοῦ θεοῦ τοῦ πατοκράτορος (19:15).[57] To help
the reader understand this seemingly curious relationship, John previously
identified the slain Lamb of 5:9 as likewise "the Lion of the tribe of Judah"
/ ὁ λέων ὁ ἐκ τῆς φυλῆς Ἰούδα in 5:5. The connotation of a lion, across
both biblical and non-biblical literature, is consistently one of strength,

power, and aggression, certainly not one of passivity. In fact, Bauckham cites the example of 4 Ezra 11–12 where the lion is to "conquer the eagle, the symbol of the fourth world-empire."[58] He even says that "[a]t Revelation 5:5-6 John is introducing the sea-beast's conqueror: the Lion of Judah who appears as a Lamb . . . , [and in so doing] John forges a new symbol of conquest by sacrificial death, which is essentially a new symbol."[59] Surely, as Caird points out,

> It is almost as if John were saying to us at one point after another: "Wherever the Old Testament says 'Lion,' read 'Lamb.'" Wherever the Old Testament speaks of the victory of the Messiah or the overthrow of the enemies of God, we are to remember that the gospel recognizes no other way of achieving these ends than the way of the Cross.[60]

Bauckham acknowledges as much in his further affirmation that "Christ's suffering witness and sacrificial death are, in fact . . . the key event in God's conquest of evil and establishment of his kingdom on earth . . . . God is related to the world not only as the transcendent holy One, but also as the slaughtered lamb."[61] In contrast to notions of a future, Davidic Messianic warrior and war, the

> Messiah Jesus does not win his victory by military conquest, and those who share his victory and his rule are not national Israel, but the international people of God. But still it is a victory over evil won not only in the spiritual but also in the political sphere against worldly powers in order to establish God's kingdom on earth.[62]

Taking a slightly different tack than Caird, but with virtually the same outcome, Bauckham points out,

> The portrayal of Jesus' death in these terms was already familiar in Christian tradition, but by placing the image of the sacrificial victim alongside those of the military conqueror, John forges a new symbol of *conquest* by sacrificial death. Insofar as 5:5 expresses Jewish hopes for messianic conquest by *military violence*, 5:6 replaces those hopes; and insofar as 5:5 evokes narrowly nationalistic expectations of Jewish triumph over the Gentile nations, 5:6 replaces this expectation . . . . Jesus the Messiah has already defeated evil by sacrificial death. He [h]as [sic] won a victory, but by sacrifice, not military conflict, and he has delivered God's people, but they are from all nations, not only Jews.[63]

Donald Guthrie maintains that "[s]ince the Lamb is presented as one who has been slain, there can be no question that the sacrificial lamb must be in mind . . . . In spite of some objections that the Lamb of God in this passage is not expressed in sacrificial terms, it is difficult to see how the removal of sin by a lamb could be understood in any other terms than in terms of sacrifice."[64] What kind of sacrifice John understands the Lamb to be is of great importance to the Apocalypse and is at the heart of Revelation's emphasis throughout.

Certainly, the enigma in the juxtaposed "Lamb standing as having been slain" / ἀρνίον ἑστηκὸς ὡς ἐσφαγμένον (5:6) and "wrath of the Lamb" / τῆς ὀργῆς τοῦ ἀρνιου (6:16) is at once obvious. Is the Lamb self-sacrificial and self-giving, or is he only temporarily so until he has had his fill of opposition and then becomes wrathful himself? This question did not escape the notice of A. T. Hanson, whom Caird summarizes:

> The wrath of God in the Revelation, as elsewhere in the Old and New Testaments, represents not the personal attitude of God towards sinners, but an impersonal process of retribution working itself out in the course of history; that the Lamb is at all times a symbol to be understood with reference to the Cross, so that the Cross itself is both the victory of God and the judgment of the world; and that therefore the wrath of the Lamb must be interpreted as "the working out in history of the consequences of the rejection and crucifixion of the Messiah." The two premises of this argument are, I believe, sound, and their soundness will be demonstrated as we follow the course of John's visions . . . . It seems probable therefore that, whenever John speaks of Christ as the Lamb, he thinks of him not as the dispenser but as the bearer of the world's judgment.[65]

Caird clearly understands that the wrath of God, as Revelation presents it, cannot be something meted out against the Lamb by God for the purpose of satisfying God's fury at human sinfulness. That would be contrary to God's character, something that Revelation avoids saying. Moreover, his conclusion dispenses of the notion that the Lamb becomes as angry (or perhaps angrier) as those who opposed him were angry during their time on earth. Further, "[t]here is no need to find a place in John's theology for any concept of the wrath of the lamb, since it is not a phrase which he uses *propria persona*, but one which he puts on the lips of the terrified inhabitants of the earth. It has its source not in the true nature of Christ, but in the tragic and paranoiac delusion to which they have surrendered themselves."[66]

Boring contributes to the matter with his own observation that John introduces an "exquisitely paradoxical phrase," placing "before the imagination of his hearer-readers both the terror of the coming judgment and the glad tidings that the judge is the One who has already paid the supreme penalty in behalf of the world. Though it is no less wrath for being so, the wrath is 'the wrath of the Lamb.'"[67]

Guthrie says,

> It is significant that although very little is said in this book about the death of Christ and its interpretation, . . . [i]t is clearly not accidental that in this vivid pictorial way the centrality of the cross is so presented. The method of conquest is so totally alien to the use of force that it serves as an object lesson. Conquest by sacrifice must be seen as a viable alternative. In the end at the coming of Christ victory is achieved without a fight, God establishes His rule through the powerful agency of His Son.[68]

Having echoed these thoughts himself, Bauckham is somewhat paradoxical when he suggests that the language of conquering is used of three stages of Christ's work: he conquered in his death and resurrection (3:21; 5:5), his followers will conquer in the time before the end (12:11; 15:2), and he will conquer at the *parousia* (17:14). If, as he says, "The decisive victory has in fact already been won by Christ [then] [h]is followers are called to continue the battle in the present. The final victory still lies in the future."[69] To be sure, Bauckham is employing the well-known language of "already/not yet" inaugurated eschatology popularized by Oscar Cullmann[70] and George E. Ladd[71] in relation to C. H. Dodd's "realized eschatology."[72] Bauckham is surely a devotee of the former two.

Of interest to this study is that despite John's use of "wrath of God" language, he never suggests that God's wrath is "satisfied" in any sense by the death of the Lamb, or in any death for that matter. To the degree that wrathful language is applied in any capacity toward God's satisfaction, that notion is something artificially introduced into the Apocalypse. In fact, Johns departs from Beale's position on this matter. He states,

> And Gregory Beale concludes that the Lamb's death is best understood as a removal of the divine wrath barring entrance to God's presence by means of the Lamb bearing that wrath himself as a penal substitute for his people. This notion is based on the OT sacrificial background, especially the Day of Atonement, where the sacrificial animal is a representative penal substitute for Israel.[73]

Where, in other words, in Revelation does Beale find such a suggestion of removal of divine wrath through a penal substitute?

The nearest thing to this idea may be found in Revelation 14:10—"in the cup of his wrath" / ἐν τῷ ποτηρίῳ τῆς ὀργῆς αὐτοῦ. In this text the Lamb is identified as present as witness to the one "tormented with fire and sulfur," but is that tantamount to the Lamb either bearing the wrath of God or in any sense being a substitute recipient of it? The meaning of this text, as Boring suggests, is that this

> language does not function to give an objective picture of what shall in fact happen to God's enemies, the outsiders. To even ask whether Revelation "teaches" eternal punishment for the damned is to misconstrue the book as a source of doctrines, to mistake the pictures for propositions . . . ; it functions to warn insiders, who ponder the question "Is it such a terrible thing to participate in Roman worship?" [he] answers, "More terrible than you can imagine!"[74]

While Martyn Smith expends a brief part of a chapter (titled "Biblical Violence") addressing what he identifies as divine violence in Revelation 14, his overall concern is to depart from more recent modernist, feminist, or pacifist agendas that he concludes are anti-biblical.[75] He finds Miroslav Volf's thinking more acceptable. He says, "Volf's self-stated intention is not, therefore, to demonstrate that God's violence is unworthy of God, but rather that it is beneficial to humans."[76] Smith affirms,

> In a similar, but less stark assertion, we therefore present God as One who is ontologically love, but crucially is both capable and willing to use and utilize extrinsic violence, even when this is against his best intention and desire when this is required; in the majority of biblical instances this will especially be manifest for his soteriological purposes.[77]

His theological observations noted, the relationship between sacrifice and the wrath of the Lamb is hardly one that validates anything propitiatory. Johns's conclusion, along with that of others, is that "[e]ven the so-called 'sin' offering . . . was not primarily about the expiation of sin. Indeed, this offering sometimes purified when sin was not even in view."[78] Purification, from all accounts, was at the heart of the sacrificial system. And the need for purification came to be extended beyond just the personal grievances that the people of God brought upon themselves by their disobedience to God or by their offenses one to another.

Not coincidentally, purification did become a broader concern for the Hebrew people including how they perceived that God would deal with his (and their) enemies, the unclean unbelievers who were outside the covenant. Jewish apocalyptic developed its own militant strain of theology for addressing this problem. John, however, departs strategically from his Jewish apocalyptic predecessors that anticipated, in another ironic twist of imagery, a lamb turned militant that would one day come with violence to destroy evil.[79] John's Revelation turns that notion on its head. He may, in fact, have had 2 Maccabees in mind since the death of the martyrs is what "brings to an end the wrath of the Almighty that has justly fallen on our whole nation" (2 Macc 7:37-38). At any rate, the martyred Lamb, depicted as a "Lamb standing as having been slain" / ἀρνίον ἑστηκὸς ὡς ἐσφαγμένον (5:6; 13:8), is not one who slays anyone (see below chapter 2, "19:13" and "19:15").

Such a notion of self-sacrifice envisioned in a slain lamb as beneficial to the people of God was, for the most part, quite foreign in Jewish circles of the first century (2 Macc 7:37-38 being an exception). Rutledge even suggests that "John the Baptist had no conception of a suffering, dying Messiah."[80] What Revelation reveals instead of the militant lamb of Jewish apocalyptic is a lamb of suffering like the Suffering Servant (see the lamb imagery of Isaiah 53) as well as the Paschal lamb mentioned in 1 Corinthians 5:7 by Paul as having been "sacrificed." John clearly places emphasis in a different place than the sacrificial lamb as appeasement of a wrathful God.

Johns, who concurs with this conclusion, depends largely on the research of Sophie Laws for a proper understanding of sacrificial language in Revelation. Based upon her observations, he says,

> Revelation took care to avoid a sacrificial interpretation of the death of Christ. As Sophie Laws and others have pointed out, the Seer consistently uses the Greek word *sphazô* [σφάζω] to speak of the Lamb as having been slaughtered, or murdered, rather than *thyô* [θύω], the word that would normally have been used when speaking of ritually "sacrificing" an animal . . . . Though all animal sacrifice involved slaughter, not all slaughter involved sacrifice. *Sphazô* [σφάζω] means to kill or to slaughter . . . . Once in Revelation it refers to the killing or murder of people (6:4). Twice it refers to the slaughter of God's people in martyrdom (6:9; 18:24).

> In none of these cases is the slaughter considered expiatory, reducing
> the possibility that the rhetorical force of the slaughter of the Lamb in
> Revelation is primarily expiatory.[81]

Careful commentators, therefore, avoid emphasizing too precisely anything about sacrificial atonement in Revelation that is not specifically stated in the text. For instance, Martin Rist says,

> This concept of the saving power of blood, its efficacy in washing
> away sins, is found quite generally in all old sacrificial systems of
> religion . . . . Accordingly, just as by the blood of the Passover lamb the
> first-born of the Jews were saved from death, so the blood of Jesus Christ,
> the new Passover Lamb that was slain, will preserve his first-born, the
> faithful Christians from final destruction and death.[82]

While Rist is surely right, is there any degree of emphasis in John's understanding of the Lamb's sacrifice that is either expiatory or propitiatory?

Propitiation and Expiation

In many ways C. H. Dodd's 1935 publication of *The Bible and the Greeks*[83] turned atonement thinking away from the idea of sacrifice as propitiation (to appease God's wrath) and toward expiation (to cleanse or cover sin) instead, a move that continues to have influence today.

The timing of Dodd's work roughly coincided with that of Gustaf Aulén's 1931 classic *Christus Victor* that acknowledged that it is God in Christ whose death on the cross was "a victory over the devil"[84] that is at the heart of atonement, not propitiation or expiation. In Christian history, however, the *Christus Victor* understanding of the death of Jesus was eclipsed by Anselm of Canterbury's eleventh-century theory of atonement when he advocated for "a deliverance from the guilt of sin; and, above all, . . . an 'objective' Atonement, according to which God is the object of Christ's atoning work, and is reconciled through the satisfaction made to His justice."[85] Aulén not only challenged Anselm's *Cur Deus Homo*'s[86] view but also countered the position of Peter Abelard (*Sic et Non*[87]) as well whose "'subjective' doctrine of the atonement . . . explains the atonement as consisting essentially of a change taking place in men rather than a changed attitude on the part of God."[88] Aulén's classical alternative posits that the "central theme is the idea of the Atonement as a Divine conflict and victory; Christ—*Christus Victor*—fights against and triumphs over the evil powers of the world, the 'tyrants' under which mankind is in bondage and suffering, and in Him God reconciles the world to Himself."[89] In short, atonement in the New Testament, as Aulén identifies it, is soteriology whereby "a complete change in the situation, a change in the relation between God and the world"[90] has occurred.

J. Denny Weaver's book *The Nonviolent Atonement* has taken up Aulén's *Christus Victor* work and identifies it as "virtually an extended, multifaceted statement of the *Christus Victor* image."[91] Johns, however, rightly criticizes Aulén for having "almost completely ignored the book of Revelation in his survey of the New Testament theology of atonement."[92] Weaver does provide a partial chapter in which he offers a summary overview of the Apocalypse's *Christus Victor* theme. Johns's chapter on "Atonement and Sacrifice in the Book of Revelation" pays tribute to Weaver yet pushes well beyond him. He says "that both atonement and sacrifice (or sacrificial) are slippery words that require careful definition and qualification."[93] Indeed, after examining atonement and sacrifice in Revelation, Johns concurs in part with Aulén that "while Christ's death is uniquely salvific, it is also exemplary—a model for believers to follow. Insofar as Revelation supports a theory of the atonement, it clearly supports a narrative *Christus Victor* model over Anselm's satisfaction theory."[94]

Dodd's work, referred to above, seems to have had such thinking in its sights as well. Never mind the fact that it led to a significant shift in thinking; modern English translations, aware of the challenges brought against his interpretation of the word ἱλαστήριον (*hilasterion*), often simply use the expression "sacrifice of atonement," or something similar, without qualifying the meaning of it. Rather than approving the word "propitiation" (found in the King James Version of the Bible at Rom 3:25), Dodd's principal argument was that while pagan Greek thought understood ἱλαστήριον (*hilasterion*) as propitiatory, the Hebrew word כַּפֹּרֶת (*kapporeth*) on which ἱλαστήριον (*hilasterion*) in Greek translations is based is better translated "to cleanse," "to remove," "to cover" (translated less often as "a place where mercy is found"), or "to provide means for forgiveness," not "appease the wrath of God." Only some years later in 1955 did Leon Morris offer a challenge to Dodd when he took up the matter in his *The Apostolic Preaching of the Cross*. Morris's argument proceeded ostensibly from an exegesis of Romans 3:25 in which his detailed word study countered Dodd in confirming that ἱλαστήριον (*hilasterion*), when properly understood, does in fact include a sense of the appeasement of God's wrath.[95]

Dodd's thesis seems to stand or fall on whether or not the Hebrew word כַּפֹּרֶת (*kapporeth*) (translated with the Greek term ἱλαστήριον—*hilasterion*) consistently meant "to cleanse, cover, or remove."[96] Morris came to conclude otherwise. Making his work more commendable was the detailed exploration done by David Hill in *Greek Words and Hebrew Meanings: Studies in the Semantics of Soteriological Terms*. In it he included other Septuagint texts, classical Greek texts, and a number of deutero-canonical writings overlooked by Dodd that in fact use the word ἱλαστήριον (*hilasterion*) in a propitiatory sense.[97]

Certainly, the propitiatory or expiatory nature of atonement[98] continues to produce discussion and debate with scholars somewhat divided between the two: to cleanse, remove, or cover sin (expiation) or to appease the wrath of God (propitiation) toward sinners. Some, as various translations suggest, have (cautiously) taken a neutral position in choosing to translate ἱλαστήριον in Romans 3:25 along the lines of "the means for forgiveness" without landing on either side of the expiatory or propitiatory divide. A sampling of English translations that hold on to propitiation are King James Version, American Standard Version, New American Standard Version, Judean & Authorized Version, J.B. Phillips, and James Moffatt. Those that use expiation are Revised Standard Version and New English Bible. Other examples include Living Bible—"take away those sins"; Goodspeed—"sacrifice of reconciliation"; New International Version—"sacrifice of atonement"; New Living Translation—"satisfy God's anger"; Good News for Modern Man—"the means by which men's sins are forgiven"; and New Revised Standard Version—"sacrifice of atonement."

Long before the contemporary debates about atonement, John Calvin, quoting Augustine's comments on John's Gospel, contributed to this matter:

> For it was not after we were reconciled to him through the blood of his Son that he began to love us. Rather, he loved us before the world was created, that we also might be his sons along with his only-begotten Son—before we became anything at all. The fact that we were reconciled through Christ's death must not be understood as if the Son reconciled us to him that he might begin to love those whom he hated. Rather, we have already been reconciled to him who loves us, with whom we were enemies on account of sin. The apostle will testify whether I am speaking the truth: "God shows his love toward us in that while we were yet sinners Christ died for us" [Rom 5:8]. Therefore, he loved us even when we practiced enmity toward him and committed wickedness. Thus in a marvelous and divine way he loved us even when he hated us.[99]

Contemporary defenders of the propitiatory idea find an advocate in
C. K. Barrett's conclusion that "expiation has, as it were, the effect of
propitiation: the sin that might justly have excited God's wrath is expiated
(at God's will) and therefore no longer does so."[100] Alongside Barrett is
J. I. Packer, whose book *Knowing God* declared a distinct difference between
pagan and Christian propitiation: "In paganism, man propitiates his gods,
and religion becomes a form of commercialism and, indeed, of bribery. In
Christianity, however, God propitiates his wrath by his own action. He set
forth Jesus Christ . . . to be the propitiation of our sins."[101]

In essence, those who stress the idea of propitiation do so because it
specifically addresses the aspect of the atonement that in their estimation
deals with God's wrath toward sin. On the other hand, critics of this view
state that seeing the atonement as appeasing God is more of a pagan idea
that makes God seem selfishly cruel rather than genuinely loving. Johns's
conclusion is that "[i]n each of these cases, the controlling context for
understanding the meaning of Christ's death in Revelation seems to be
orthodox theology, rather than the book of Revelation itself."[102] He draws
his conclusions based on the results of the following analysis:

> In none of these cases is the slaughter considered expiatory, reducing the
> possibility that the rhetorical force of the slaughter of the Lamb in Reve-
> lation is primarily expiatory. However, unlike [ἀποθνῄκω] ("murder"),
> [σφάζω] may have some ritual overtones. If so, this would lend some
> credence to the argument of Marc Bredin that John understands the
> death of Jesus to challenge the mimetic desire at work in the sacrificial
> system. At the very least, John's use of the word slaughter for both the
> death of Jesus and the death of the saints implies some kind of participa-
> tion of the latter in the shed blood of Jesus.[103]

Johns further points out that the word "atonement," if used to describe
what Revelation has in mind, does not necessarily include any expiatory
or propitiatory connotations, since such notions in reality are foreign to
the text.[104] He rightly states that only some Old Testament sacrifices were
considered expiatory to begin with, but that both the burnt offering and
the Passover Lamb were not for atonement.[105] Rather than being expiatory, "[t]he Passover lamb was a type of peace offering [שלמים], which had
nothing to do with atonement."[106]

The Apocalypse never suggests per se either a propitiatory or expiatory[107] function of the "Lamb slain from the foundation of the world" / τοῦ

ἀρνίου τοῦ ἐσφαγμένου ἀπὸ καταβολῆς κσομου (Rev 13:8). In truth, the meaning of the death of the Lamb is left specifically unstated by John relative to either an objective or a subjective understanding of atonement.

Ransom

Revelation, as noted thus far, does not use propitiatory or expiatory language, rather John uses "purchase" ("ransom" or "redemption" / ἀγοράζω) language. The following is a cursory review of John's general use of "ransom" language for atonement. In the first place, he uses the word "loosed" or "freed" in 1:5b: "to the one who loves us and loosed/feed us from our sins by his blood" / Τῷ ἀγαπῶντι ἡμᾶς καὶ λύσαντι ἡμᾶς ἐκ τῶν ἁμαρτιῶν ἡμῶν ἐν τῷ αἵματι αὐτοῦ. This verse anticipates the fuller expression that John will provide in 5:9 that "you were slain and you purchased/ransomed to God by your blood those from every tribe and tongue and people and nation" / ἐσφάγης καὶ ἠγόραοας τῷ θεῷ ἐν τῷ αἵματι σου ἐκ πάσης φυλῆς καὶ γλώσσης καὶ λαοῦ καὶ ἔθνους (Rev 5:9). While the words "you were slain" (ἐσφάγης) and "you purchased/ ransomed" (ἠγόρασας) will receive additional attention below in chapter 3, they receive necessary remarks at this point.

Early in the doxology (Rev 1:1-6) Revelation 1:5 not only sets the stage for who Jesus is but also provides an initial acknowledgment of his redemptive work. He is "Jesus Christ, the faithful witness, the firstborn from the dead, and the ruler of the kings of the earth" / Ἰησοῦ Χριστοῦ, ὁ μάρτυς ὁ ποτός, ὁ πρωτότοκος τῶν νεκρῶν καὶ ὁ ἄρχων τῶν βαοιλέων τῆς γῆς. He is likewise the "one who loved us and freed/loosed us from our sins by his blood" / Τῷ ἀγαπῶντι ἡμᾶς καὶ λύσαντι ἡνᾶς ἐκ τῶν ἁμαρτιῶν ἡμῶν ἐν τῷ αἵματι αὐτοῦ. While the word "freed" or "loosed" (λύσαντι) has superior manuscript support, there is minor attestation for a textual variant "washed" (λούσατι[108]), which Ladd rightly points out has minimal theological difference from "loosed," yet he (along with most scholars) prefers the text that is based on the earliest Greek manuscripts.[109]

John's point in making such a statement in the introductory doxology of the Apocalypse is to establish both the identity of the Lamb (as he is further qualified in 5:6, 9) and the implications of the Lamb's blood (called "his blood" / αἵματι αὐτοῦ in 1:5b). Boring has summarized John's conclusion clearly:

> that Christian existence is not innocent existence but forgiven existence; he knows that forgiveness came, as in the Old Testament sacrificial

conceptuality, only at the cost of life (cf. e.g., Heb. 8-10, esp. 9:22). Like the Old Testament, John does not think that "blood" has any saving efficacy as a substance; it represents "life." Jesus is praised because he set us free from sin by giving himself, his life, for us.[110]

John has drawn undoubtedly from the Christian tradition in this impressive hymn found in Revelation 1:5-6. In particular, the verb λύω is an active verb associated with redemption rather than forgiveness. "Loosing" and "freeing" are redemptive terms about which Elisabeth Schüssler Fiorenza has written with clarity. She notes that the Lamb of God is worthy to assume eschatological reign for three reasons: (1) The Lamb was slain—that is—the Lamb was slaughtered in a similar capacity as the Paschal lamb.[111] (2) The Lamb has purchased people for God like that of a "purchasing agent." As such, the nature of the purchase was like what would be paid for prisoners of war. These prisoners, as Revelation indicates, were ransomed by the Lamb. And this Lamb was like someone from their home country who bought their freedom for them and secured their return to their homeland.[112] To be sure, this liberation sounds remarkably like the release of Israel from slavery in Egypt in connection with the exodus and the Paschal lamb—which is precisely John's point. In this case, as was so with the exodus, the Paschal lamb had no substitutionary connotation, but rather there is an association with the redemptive liberation of the Israelites from bondage. "This interpretation of *agorazein* [ἀγοραζεῖν]," she states, "is supported by Rev 14:4, where it is said that the 144,000 on the Mount Zion are purchased from mankind (in v. 3 from the earth) as the first fruits (*aparchē*) [ἀπαρχὴ] for God and the Lamb."[113] And, finally, (3) the Lamb brought the prisoners of war back home for a purpose: he "made us a kingdom priests to God" / ἐποίησεν ἡμβᾶς βασιλεία, ἱερεῖς τῷ θεῷ.[114] What Fiorenza rightly avoids saying is more than what the text allows. Who is paid is not the question answered in this text. That the Lamb has in fact ransomed the prisoners[115] by his blood is without doubt John's point.

In a similar way, Bauckham concurs with Fiorenza. He states, "That Revelation's image of the Lamb refers to the lamb sacrificed at the Passover is clear especially from 5:9-10. There it is said that by his blood the Lamb has 'ransomed' a people and made them 'a kingdom and priests serving our God.'"[116] He continues this line of reasoning by connecting it to the covenant at Sinai of Exodus 19. The point of the Exodus account is that God ransomed his people from Egyptian slavery to become his people. Thus Revelation "treats the blood of the Lamb as the price of redemption,

. . . [and] . . . really goes beyond the role which the blood of the Passover
Lamb played in the Exodus (cf. Exod. 12:12, 23)."[117] Nevermind that the
Passover lamb was not a part of Jewish expectation of a new exodus; in
Revelation 5:6, 9 John clearly alludes to the Passover lamb as well as to the
Suffering Servant of Isaiah 53:7, both portrayed as a sacrificial lamb. In
other words, the death of Jesus in Christian understanding was considered
redemptive and Jesus was linked to the Lamb as "the new exodus motif."[118]

More specific, as Johns has indicated, is that in

> biblical thought, sacrifice was much broader theologically than expia-
> tion. This is even more obviously the case in the Greco-Roman religions.
> In the Old Testament, only some sacrifices were considered expiatory.
> Sacrifice was the central feature of worship in Israelite religion. The burnt
> offering was prominent in Israel's theology and practice of sacrifice, but
> expiation was not the focus of burnt offering, and the lamb was not the
> primary offering of expiation. In other words, lamb was not an obvious
> symbol for expiation in the sacrificial cult. There were other sacrifices
> for which sin was not at issue. For instance, the peace offerings included
> the thank offering, the free will offering, and the votive offering, none of
> which had anything to do with atonement.[119]

Bauckham reminds readers as well that "[t]he central image in this complex
[of Christ's victory] is that of Jesus himself as the Passover Lamb (first introduced at 5:6, 9-10). That Revelation's image of the Lamb refers to the lamb
sacrificed at the Passover is clear especially from 5:9-10. There it is said that
by his blood the Lamb has 'ransomed' a people and made them 'a kingdom
and priests serving our God.'"[120]

CONCLUSION

By using apocalyptic, prophetic, and epistolary media, John proceeds to
articulate how God uses the atoning death of the Lamb to ransom his
followers and how that self-sacrificial death is best expressed through the
counterintuitive expression "wrath of the lamb." This expression does not
denote either a propitiatory or an expiatory understanding of sacrifice but
embodies instead God's means of ransoming or purchasing his people. To
whom the ransom is paid is not of concern to John so much as is the defeat
of the perpetrator of murder against the Lamb (see chapter 5 below).

George E. Ladd states,

> Why in the providence and purpose of God it must be that the Lion of the tribe of Judah can only win his final victory over his foes by first filling the role of the slain lamb is not explained. In ordinary Christian thinking, we are primarily concerned with the cross as the place where Jesus bore our sins and accomplished atonement for sinners. John's emphasis is that only by virtue of Jesus' sacrifice as the Lamb of God can he fill the role of the messianic King and bring human history to its denouement in the Kingdom of God.[121]

While Ladd has touched on the heart of the matter of Jesus as the Lamb of God, John never speaks of Jesus actually bearing humanity's sin. His conclusions about atonement rest in another place. What John does say is that the Lamb was slain by the evil powers of his day, and, as a consequence of his death, God uses it as a means of victory over evil. This emphasis he develops throughout The Apocalypse to which we turn below.

Notes

1. For an expanded treatment of these components in Revelation see any of the commentaries that are referenced throughout.

2. Ernst Käsemann, "Die Anfänge christlicher Theologie," ZThK 57 (1960): 162–85, published in English as "The Beginnings of Christian Theology," *Journal for Theology and Church* 6, ed. Robert W. Funk (New York, 1969): 17–46.

3. Mitchell G. Reddish, *Revelation*, Smyth & Helwys Commentaries (Macon GA: Smyth & Helwys, 2001) 6.

4. Fleming Rutledge, *The Crucifixion: Understanding the Death of Jesus Christ* (Grand Rapids MI: Eerdmans, 2015) 348.

5. J. J. Collins, "Introduction: Towards the Morphology of Genre," *Semeia* 14 (1979): 9.

6. Frederick J. Murphy, "Introduction to Apocalyptic Literature," *The New Interpreter's Bible*, vol. 7, ed. Leander Keck (Nashville: Abingdon, 1996) 7.

7. Jürgen Moltmann, *Theology of Hope: On the Ground and the Implications of a Christian Eschatology* (London: SCM, 1967) 133–34.

8. G. K. Beale, *The Book of Revelation: A Commentary on the Greek Text*, The New International Greek Testament Commentary, ed. I. Howard Marshall and Donald A. Hagner (Grand Rapids MI: Eerdmans, 1999) 37.

9. Ibid.

10. Michelle Fletcher, "Apocalypse Noir: How Revelation Defined and Defied a Genre," *The Book of Revelation: Currents in British Research on the Apocalypse*, ed. Garrick V. Allen, Ian Paul, and Simon P. Woodman, in *Wissenschaftliche Untersuchungen zum Neuen Testament* (Tübingen: Mohr Siebeck, 2015) 115.

11. Ibid., 133.

12. See chapter 4 below for an extended treatment of the word σημαίνω.

13. More about "sign" and "signified" will be found in chapter 5.

14. Rome, of course, is known for its seven hills: Aventine Hill (*Aventinus*); Caelian Hill (*Cælius*); Capitoline Hill (*Capitolinus*); Esquiline Hill (*Esquilinus*); Palatine Hill (*Palatinus*); Quirinal Hill (*Quirinalis*); Viminal Hill (*Viminalis*).

15. Bits and pieces of this imagery will appear in greater detail in chapters 3, 4, and 5 below, and the exposition of Rev 12 provided there, as they inform John's perspective on the death of the "male child" (12:5—υἱόν, ἄρσεν) that when born is devoured by the Dragon (12:4—ἵνα ὅταν τέκῃ τὸ τέκνον αὐτῆς καταφάγῃ).

16. Richard Bauckham, *The Climax of Prophecy: Studies on the Book of Revelation* (Edinburgh: T&T Clark International, 1993) 186.

17. Richard J. Bauckham, "The Figurae of John of Patmos," in Ann Williams, ed., *Prophecy and Millenarianism: Essays in Honour of Marjorie Reeves* (London: Longman, 1980) 116–21; in revised form: chapter 6 ("The Lion, the Lamb and the Dragon") in Bauckham, *The Climax of Prophecy*.

18. Richard J. Bauckham, *Theology of the Book of Revelation*, New Testament Theology, ed. James D.G. Dunn (Cambridge: Cambridge University Press, 1993) 1.

19. Ibid., 2.

20. Ibid., 3–4.

21. M. Eugene Boring, *Revelation*, Interpretation (Louisville KY: John Knox, 1989) 23–24.

22. Ibid., 24.

23. Ibid., 26.

24. David Hill, *New Testament Prophecy* (London: Marshall, Morgan & Scott, 1979).

25. M. Eugene Boring, "What Are We Looking For? Toward a Definition of the Term 'Christian Prophet,'" *Boring Seminar SBL Papers* 2 (1973): 142.

26. J. Panagopoulos, "Prophecy in the Early Church: Its Character and Function," *Prophetic Vocation* (Brill: Leiden, 1977) 1–32.

27. Bauckham, *Theology of the Book of Revelation*, 159–64.

28. See Rom 1:7; 1 Cor 1:3; 2 Cor 1:2; Gal 1:3; Phil 1:2 as examples.

29. Stephen S. Smalley, *The Revelation of John: A Commentary on the Greek Text of the Apocalypse* (Downers Grove IL: InterVarsity, 2005) 26, provides a summary of the epistolary details.

30. J. Ramsay Michaels, *Interpreting the Book of Revelation* (Grand Rapids MI: Baker, 1992) 30, 31–32.

31. Craig R. Koester, *Revelation: A New Translation with Introduction and Commentary*, The Anchor Yale Bible (New Haven: Yale University Press, 2014) 856.

32. Reddish, *Revelation*, 22.

33. Raymond E. Brown, *The Gospel According to John* (New York: Doubleday, 1966) 62.

34. The word "sacrifice" has been given a great deal of attention by René Girard. See James G. Williams, ed., *The Girard Reader* (New York: Crossroad, 1996) for a collection of Girard's work. In particular, Girard believed that sacrifice reaches back to primitive practices of "scapegoating" whereby human vengeance came to be a controlled practice—the victimization of the scapegoat. He saw in the New Testament, however, an overturning of the old scapegoating practices of the sacrificial system in Jesus' innocent death. In other words, once Jesus is seen to be truly innocent, a scapegoat "theology" can no longer be relied on to restore peace. Only as humanity withdraws from violence of any kind (scapegoating included) will there be an avoidance of apocalyptic disaster that is otherwise inevitable. God, in Jesus, has become a victim (clearly innocent) in order to reveal that he is on the side of the victim and not the perpetrator of violence against anyone, least of all against the innocent man Jesus. Girard, however, did very little with the book of Revelation aside from seeing it as validating violence based more on traditional apocalyptic rather than what Revelation actually suggests in the slain Lamb.

35. Rutledge, *The Crucifixion*, 233.

36. Ibid., 234.

37. Ibid., 236.

38. Loren L. Johns, "Atonement and Sacrifice in the Book of Revelation," *The Work of Jesus Christ in Anabaptist Perspective: Essays in Honor of J. Denny Weaver*, ed. Alain Epp Weaver and Gerald J. Mast (Telford PA: Cascadia, 2008) 135. Johns continues in the essay his studies associated with his dissertation. See Loren L. Johns, *The Lamb Christology of the Apocalypse of John: An Investigation into Its Origins and Rhetorical Force* (Tübingen: Mohr Siebeck, 2003).

39. David E. Aune, *Revelation 1–5*, Word Biblical Commentary (Dallas: Word, 1997) 372.

40. Johns, "Atonement and Sacrifice in the Book of Revelation," 131.

41. Ibid, quoting Aune, *Revelation 1–5*, 373.

42. Gary A. Anderson, "Sacrifice and Sacrificial Offerings (Old Testament)," in *Anchor Bible Dictionary*, ed. David Noel Freedman (New York: Doubleday, 1992) 879.

43. Johns, "Atonement and Sacrifice in the Book of Revelation," 131.

44. Lesley R. Defransico, *Washing Away Sin: An Analysis of the Metaphor in the Hebrew Bible and its Influence* (Leuven, Belgium: Peeters, 2016).

45. Johns, "Atonement and Sacrifice in the Book of Revelation," 325–26. He cites the reference in Moses Maimonides, *The Guide for the Perplexed*, translated from the Original Arabic Text (New York: Dover Publications); Anderson, "Sacrifice," 5.871; and Jacob Neusner et al., *The Encyclopedia of Judaism* (New York: Continuum, 1999) 2.532. For a more thorough and appreciative consideration of Maimonides' theology of sacrifice, see Josef Stern, *Problems and Parables of Law: Maimonides and Nahmanides on Reasons for the Commandments (Ta'Amei Ha-Mitzvot)* (Albany: State University of New York Press, 1989).

46. Rutledge, *The Crucifixion*, 237.

47. Johns, "Atonement and Sacrifice in the Book of Revelation," 135.

48. Rutledge, *The Crucifixion*, 237–38, footnote 14. She summarizes well the argument to this end made by Vincent Taylor and B. F. Westcott that the emphasis was exclusively on the life in the blood and not the death. She wisely distances herself from those who take such a path because of their personal disdain for violence, never mind the broader testimony of the Bible.

49. James Denney, *The Death of Christ and The Atonement and the Modern Mind* (Edinburgh: T and A Constable, 1903) 309–34.

50. Rutledge, *The Crucifixion*, 238.

51. Ibid., 254. Rutledge draws from the testimony of the book of Hebrews in arriving at this conclusion.

52. Anthony T. Hanson, *The Wrath of the Lamb* (London: SPCK, 1957) 159–80, provides a chapter called "The Wrath in the Apocalypse."

53. Christopher C. Rowland, "The Book of Revelation," *The New Interpreter's Bible*, vol. 12, ed. Leander Keck (Nashville: Abingdon, 1998) 675–76.

54. David Aune, *Revelation 6–16*, Word Biblical Commentary (Dallas: Word, 1998) 834.

55. George B. Caird, *The Revelation of St. John the Divine* (New York: Harper and Row, 1966) 90.

56. Mitchell G. Reddish, "Martyr Christology in the Apocalypse," *Journal for the Study of the New Testament* 33 (1988): 88.

57. See below "Dressed in a Garment Dipped in Blood" and "The Winepress of the Fury of the Wrath of God," 19:13 and 19:15.

58. Bauckham, *The Climax of Prophecy*, 182.

59. Ibid., 183.

60. Caird, *The Revelation of St. John the Divine*, 75.

61. Bauckham, *Theology of the Book of Revelation*, 64.

62. Ibid., 68.

63. Bauckham, *The Climax of Prophecy*, 215.

64. Donald Guthrie, "The Lamb in The Structure of the Book of Revelation," *Vox Evangelica* 12 (1981): 69.

65. Caird, *The Revelation of St. John the Divine*, 91–92; Anthony T. Hanson, *The Wrath of the Lamb* (London: SPCK, 1957) 159–80.

66. Ibid., 92.

67. Boring, *Revelation*, 127.

68. Guthrie, "The Lamb in the Structure of the Book of Revelation," 69.

69. Bauckham, *Theology of the Book of Revelation*, 70.

70. Oscar Cullmann, *Christ and Time*, trans. Floyd V. Filson (Philadelphia: Westminster, 1951).

71. George E. Ladd, *Jesus and the Kingdom* (New York: Harper and Row, 1964).

72. C. H. Dodd, *Apostolic Preaching and Its Developments* (New York: Harper and Row, 1964).

73. Johns, "Atonement and Sacrifice in the Book of Revelation," 134, references G[regory] K. Beale, *The Book of Revelation: A Commentary on the Greek Text*, The New International Greek Testament Commentary, ed. I. Howard Marshall and Donald A. Hagner (Grand Rapids MI: Eerdmans, 1999) 660.

74. Boring, *Revelation*, 127.

75. Martyn John Smith, *Divine Violence and the Christus Victor Atonement Model: God's Reluctant Use of Violence for Soteriological Ends* (Kindle e-book, loc 6130). Smith challenges John Macquarrie's views often in this work as he engages Macquarrie's works: "Demonology and the Classic Idea of Atonement," Pts. 1 and 2, *Expository Times* 68/1 (October 1956): 3–6 and (November 1956): 60–63; *God-Talk: An Examination of the Language and Logic of Theology* (London: SCM, 1967); *Jesus Christ in Modern Thought* (London: SCM, 1990); *Paths in Spirituality* (London: SCM, 1972); *Principles of Christian Theology* (London: SCM, 1977); and *The Scope of Demythologizing: Bultmann and His Critics* (London: SCM, 1960).

76. Smith, *Divine Violence and the Christus Victor Atonement Model*, loc 6130; cf. Marislov Volf, *Exclusion and Embrace: A Theological Exploration of Identity, Otherness, and Reconciliation* (Nashville: Abingdon, 1996) 303. John Christopher Thomas and Frank D. Macchia, *Revelation*, New Horizons New Testament Commentary (Grand Rapids: Eerdmans, 2016) 433, take up the matter of violence ("The Sovereign God at War") with Macchia concluding with Barth's Jesus is Victor through grace rather than Volf's emphasis on God's justice that includes resistance against evil.

77. Smith, *Divine Violence and the Christus Victor Atonement Model*, loc 6152.

78. Johns, "Atonement and Sacrifice in the Book of Revelation," 131.

79. See 1 Enoch 90 and the Testament of Joseph for militant lambs that have horns.

80. Rutledge, *The Crucifixion*, 256.

81. Johns, "Atonement and Sacrifice in the Book of Revelation," 132.

82. Martin Rist, *The Revelation of St. John the Divine*, The Interpreter's Bible, vol. 12, ed. George A. Buttrick (Nashville: Abingdon, 1957) 370.

83. C.H. Dodd, *The Bible and the Greeks* (London: Hodder and Stoughton, 1935) 93.

84. Gustaf Aulén, *Christus Victor: An Historical Study of the Three Main Types of the Idea of the Atonement*, trans. A.G. Hebert (New York: MacMillan, 1969) 2.

85. Ibid.

86. Saint Anselm, *Cur Deus Homo*, trans. Sidney N. Deane (Fort Worth: Richard D. McCormack, 2005).

87. Peter Abelard, *Sic et Non: A Critical Edition*, ed. Blanche B. Boyer and Richard McKeon (Chicago: University of Chicago Press, 1976).

88. Aulén, *Christus Victor*, 2.

89. Ibid., 4.

90. Ibid., 6.

91. J. Denny Weaver, *The Nonviolent Atonement* (Grand Rapids MI: Eerdmans, 2001) 20.

92. Johns, "Atonement and Sacrifice in the Book of Revelation," 125, footnote 3.

93. Ibid.

94. Ibid., 126.

95. Leon Morris, *The Apostolic Preaching of the Cross* (Grand Rapids MI: Eerdmans, 1955) 155.

96. Dodd, *The Bible and the Greeks*, 93.

97. David Hill, *Greek Words and Hebrew Meanings: Studies in the Semantics of Soteriological Terms* (Cambridge: Cambridge University Press, 1967).

98. Hanson, *The Wrath of the Lamb*, 181–201, surveys the propitiatory/expiatory matter in his chapter "The Wrath of the Lamb in Christian Doctrine."

99. John Calvin, *Institutes of the Christian Religion*, trans. Ford Lewis Battles and ed. John T. McNeil, Library of Christian Classics, vol. 1 (Philadelphia: Westminster, 1960) II.16.4.

100. C. K. Barrett, *A Commentary on the Epistle to the Romans*, Harper's New Testament Commentaries (New York: Harper and Row, 1957) 77–78.

101. J. I. Packer, *Knowing God* (Downers Grove IL: InterVarsity, 1973) 207.

102. Ibid.

103. Johns, "Atonement and Sacrifice in the Book of Revelation," 132.

104. Ibid., 135.

105. Ibid., 130.

106. Ibid., 131.

107. Johns, "Atonement and Sacrifice in the Book of Revelation," 133 says, "More recently, John and Gloria Ben-Daniel [*The Apocalypse in the Light of the Temple: A New Approach to the Book of Revelation* (Jerusalem: Beit Yochanan, 2003)] developed an interest in cultic life and thought and wrote a book that pushes the Old Testament sacrificial cult for all its worth as a key to understanding the book of Revelation. For the Ben-Daniels, the blood of the Lamb in Revelation 'has a profound expiatory effect.' The book of Revelation is for them an elaborate liturgy of atonement in which Satan is the scapegoat Azazel, yet the martyrdom of the saints is part of the heavenly liturgy that eventuates in atonement for the world."

108. While some manuscripts have λούω ("washed") instead of λύω ("loosed" or "freed"), textual evidence is superior for the latter. See Bruce M. Metzger, *A Textual Commentary on the Greek New Testament: A Companion Volume to the United Bible Societies' Greek New Testament* (3rd ed.), 662.

109. George E. Ladd, *A Commentary of the Revelation of John* (Grand Rapids MI: Eerdmans, 1972) 26.

110. Boring, *Revelation*, 77.

111. Elisabeth Schüssler Fiorenza, *The Book of Revelation: Justice and Judgment* (Philadelphia: Fortress, 1985) 73.

112. Ibid., 74

113. Ibid.

114. Ibid.

115. See Stanislas Lyonnet, "The Terminology of Redemption," in *Sin, Redemption and Sacrifice: A Biblical and Patristic Study* (Rome: Biblical Institute, 1970) 61–184; Dale Martin, *Slavery as Salvation: The Metaphor of Slavery in Pauline Christianity* (New Haven: Yale University Press, 1990) 63; and Stephen Finlan, *The Background and Content of Paul's Cultic Atonement Metaphors* (Atlanta: Society of Biblical Literature, 2004) 166.

116. Bauckham, *Theology of the Book of Revelation*, 70–71.

117. Ibid., 71.

118. Ibid.

119. Johns, "Atonement and Sacrifice in the Book of Revelation," 130.

120. Bauckham, *Theology of the Book of Revelation*, 70–71.

121. Ladd, *Commentary of the Revelation of John*, 87.

CHAPTER 2

Revelation's Supporting Atonement Language: Throne, Temple, and Altar

In a number of relevant passages John develops his atonement theme through use of a variety of related, similar, and sometimes dissimilar terms. To be sure, neither the English word "atonement" nor its Greek equivalents are found anywhere in Revelation. Moreover, the word "sacrifice" (θυσία) never appears in the book either. Other familiar terms like "redemption" (ἀπολύτρωσις; λύτπωσις) and "expiation" (ἱλαστήριον) are also absent from the Apocalypse. These lacunae notwithstanding, John uses other metaphors and images (consistent with his style) around which his understanding of atonement coalesces. Nevertheless, commentators on Revelation do refer with frequency to the sacrificial death of the Lamb by use of these related terms and images. What these terms mean and how they function in Revelation are anticipatory of John's overall meaning of atonement and contribute significantly to the goal of this project.

Of strategic importance to John is his use of the word "altar" / θυσιαστήριον. He uses this word eight times (6:9; 8:3—twice; 8:5; 9:13; 11:1; 14:18; 16:7) and means by this term "the *place* where sacrifice is made" similar to "the LXX where it occurs over four hundred times . . . [for] altar."[1] In Revelation 8:3 (twice); 8:5; and 9:13 it refers to the altar of incense, while in 6:9; 11:1; and 16:7 it refers to the altar of burnt offerings, and, finally, in 11:1 and 14:18 it refers to sanctuary. Only once, in 11:1, does the altar refer to the earthly temple where both "temple" / ναός (3:12; 7:15; 11:1, 19; 14:15, 17; 15:5, 6, 8; 16:1; 16:17; 21:22) and "altar" / θυσιαστήριον appear together. These "temple" and "altar" texts require some engagement, with some passages receiving more attention than others, as they inform John's emerging atonement theology.

The following is a list of terms and phrases that are associated with atonement as they appear in Revelation. For the sake of convenience, this chapter will address throne, temple, and altar, while chapter 3 will examine the balance of these terms and phrases: "faithful witness (or "martyr") / ὁ μάρτυς ὁ ποτός (1:5a); "loosed (or freed) us from our sins by his blood" / λύσαντι ἡμᾶς ἐκ τῶν ἁμαρτιῶν ἡμῶν ἐν τω αἵματι αὐτοῦ (1:5b); "the Tree of Life" / τοῦ ζύλου τῆς ζωῆς (2:7); "ones who have not soiled their garments" / ἃ οὐκ ἐμόλυναν τὰ ἱμάτια αὐτῶν (3:4); "thus the one who conquers will be robed in white garments, and his name will not be erased from the book of life" / ὁ νικῶν οὕτως περιβαλεῖται ἐν ἱματίοις λευκοῖς, καὶ οὐ μὴ ἐζαλείψω τὸ ὄνομα αὐτοῦ ἐκ τῆς βίβλου τῆς ζωῆς (3:5); "white garments" / ἱματίοις λευκοῖς (3:18; 4:4); "lamb standing having been slain" / ἀρνίον ἑοτηκὸς ὡς ἐσφαγμένον (5:6); "because you were slain and purchased for God by your blood" / ὅτι ἐσφάγης καὶ ἠγόρασας τῷ θεῷ ἐν τῷ αἵματι σου (5:9); "white robes" / οτολή λευκή (6:11; 7:9); "these were dressed in white robes" / Οὗτοι οἱ περιβεβλημένοι τὰς οτολὰς τὰς λευκὰς (7:13); "washed them in the blood of the lamb" / ἐλεύκαναν αὐτὰς ἐν τῷ αἵματι τοῦ ἀρνίου (7:14), "and they conquered him by the blood of the lamb" / καὶ αὐτοὶ ἐνίκησακ αὐτὸν διὰ τὸ αἷμα τοῦ ἀρνίου (12:11); "in the lamb's book of life who had been slain from the foundation of the world" / ἐν τῷ βιβλίῳ τῆς ζωῆς τοῦ ἀρνίου τοῦ ἐσφαγμένου ἀπὸ καταβολῆς κσομου (13:8); "these were purchased (or ransomed) from men as firstfruit to God and to the lamb" / οὗτοι ἠγοράσθησαν ἀπὸ τῶν ἀνθρώπων ἀπαρχὴ τῷ θεῷ καὶ τῷ ἀρνίῳ (14:4); "whose name is not written in the book of life from the foundation of the world" / ὧν οὐ γέγραπται τὸ ὄνομα ἐπὶ τὸ βιβλίον τῆς ζωῆς ἀπὸ καταβολῆς κόσμου (17:8b); "fine linen, pure and bright" / βύσσινον λαμπρὸν καθαρόν(19:8); "garment dipped in blood" / περιβεβλημένος ἱμάτιον βεβαμμένον αἵματι (19:13); "clothed in pure white linen" / ἐνδεδυμένοι βυσσινον λευκὸν καθαρόν (19:14); "and another book was opened, which is [the book] of life" / καὶ ἄλλο βιβλίον ἠνοίχθη, ὅ ἐστιν τῆς ζωῆς (20:12b); "and anyone not found having been written in the book of life, was thrown into the lake of fire" / καὶ εἴ τις οὐχ εὑρέθη ἐν τῇ βίβλῳ τῆς ζωῆς γεγραμμένος, ἐβλήθη εἰς τὴν λίμνην τοῦ πυρός. (20:15); "the ones having been written in the Lamb's book of life" / οἱ γεγραμμένοι ἐν τῷ βιβλίῳ τῆς ζωῆς τοῦ ἀρνίου (21:27); and "Blessed are those who wash their robes" / Μακάριοι οἱ πλύνοντες τὰς στολὰς αὐτῶν (22:14). These expressions are found scattered across Revelation, some of which will be clustered together for exploration below.

THRONE

Alongside the "temple" and "altar" is the related word "throne" / θρόνος, which in the Apocalypse appears forty-seven times, and as Aune has noted, in six heavenly scenes: (1) 4:2–6:17; (2) 7:9-17; (3) 11:15-19; (4) 14:1-5; (5) 15:2-8; and (6) 19:1-8.[2] To this list should also be added three additional scenes: when John says, "And I saw thrones" / Καὶ εἶδον θρόνους (20:4), when Satan was chained in the abyss for 1,000 years; the "great white throne" / θρόνον μέγαν λευκὸν of 20:11-15; the new heaven and new earth and "the one who sat upon the throne" / ὁ καθήμενους ἐπὶ τῷ θρόνῳ (21:5), as well as the crystal river "flowing out of the throne of God and the Lamb" / ἐκπορευόμενον ἐκ τοῦ θρόνου τοῦ θεοῦ καὶ τοῦ ἀρνίου (22:1, 3). The latter "throne" references of 20:11-15 and 21:5 will be addressed below in the section "The Book of Life (of the Lamb)" Revelation 3:5; 13:8; 17:8b; 20:12b; 20:15; 21:27.

At every juncture in Revelation, God's throne denotes "divine control . . . exercised over the world's affairs: including its suffering."[2] Inasmuch as the Lamb comes to share the throne of God, "the Lamb also shares the sovereignty of God."[4] A closely related enthronement is that of "the souls who had been beheaded [martyred] for their testimony to Jesus and for the word of God" / τὰς ψυχὰς τῶχ πεπελεκιομένων διὰ τὴν μαρτυρίαν Ἰησοῦ καὶ διὰ τὸν λόγον τοῦ θεοῦ (20:4). Because of their martyrdom "judgment was given to them" / κρίμα ἐδόθη αὐτοῖς (20:4). Clearly the basis of their judgment and enthronement is death, the death of the Lamb that modeled for them and led them to embrace their own deaths as martyrs (cf. 14:4). The atoning result of their sacrifice is at once evident in their being pictured seated on thrones in the presence of God. Only because they have been purified, however, can they abide God's presence, a point that John emphasizes by mentioning "they washed their robes and made them white in the blood of the lamb" / ἔπλυναν τὰς οτολὰς αὐτῶν καὶ ἐλεύκαναν αὐτάς ἐν τῷ αἵματι τοῦ ἀρνίου (Rev 7:14). The only way that they can be in God's presence is that they have been purified, just as 22:4 confirms: "and they will see his face, and his name [will be] upon their foreheads" / καὶ ὄψονται τὸ πρόσωπον ἀτοῦ, καὶ τὸ ὄνομα αὐτοῦ ἐπὶ τῶν μετώπων αὐτῶν (echoing Matt 5:8: "blessed are the pure in heart, for thy will see God" / μακάριοι οἱ καθαροὶ τῇ καρδίᾳ, ὅτι αὐτοὶ τὸν θεὸν ὄψονται).

Beale recognizes that forty-two of the forty-six times that thrones are mentioned, they are heavenly except three times when they refer to Satan or the beast's throne. These data prompt him to conclude that these are heavenly thrones on which the martyrs sit in 20:4.[5] These martyrs are enthroned alongside God which "[i]n Revelation [identifies] judgment [a] s consistently ascribed to God (Rev 14:7; 16:5, 7; 20:12-13) and Christ (19:11)."[6] Their identity, according to the majority of commentators, is "all the faithful . . . treating the martyrs as emblematic of the whole church."[7]

John's references to thrones and the ones who sit on them contribute to his atonement theology—that the sacrificial Lamb not only shares the throne of God but is also the means for his followers to have a place in the heavenly entourage because they have been made clean.

TEMPLE

In developing his understanding of atonement, John uses the word "temple" / ναός (3:12; 7:15; 11:1, 19; 14:15, 17; 15:5, 6, 8; 16:1; 16:17; 21:22) and the word "altar" / θυσιαστήριον (6:9; 8:3—twice; 8:5; 9:13; 11:1; 14:18; 16:7). Since the altar is located within the temple or tabernacle,[8] these terms are interconnected.

3:12; 7:15

The first mention of "temple" / ναός is found in 3:12 in the Son of Man's message to the Philadelphians. John refers specifically to the heavenly temple in which faithful ones will be rewarded metaphorically to become a "pillar in the temple of my God" / οτῦλον ἐν τῷ ναῷ τοῦ θεοῦ μου. Elsewhere he says "for the Lord God Almighty is the temple" / ὁ γὰρ κύριος, ὁ θεός, ὁ παντοκράτωρ, ναὸς αὐτῆς ἐστιν (21:22), "and is the Lamb" / καὶ τὸ ἀρνίον (21:22). John's meaning is that the people of God will be with God as reward for having "kept my word of patient endurance" during "the hour of trial that is coming on the whole world" (3:10). Later, in 7:15 the redeemed 144,000 are likewise identified as such because of the "blood of the lamb" (cf. 7:14 and "Blood of the Lamb" below), and they have a permanent dwelling place with God "day and night within his temple" / ἡμέρας καὶ νυκτὸς ἐν τῷ ναῷ αὐτοῦ (7:15). Believers have a permanent dwelling place and are able to endure during times of trial because of the Lamb around whom everything revolves in the Apocalypse.

11:1-2

John's next mention of the "temple" occurs in 11:1-2 where he combines it with the word "altar" / τὸ θυσιαστήριον. In fact, the temple, the altar, and the worshipers, John says, are all to be "measured." The "court outside the temple" / τὴν αὐλὴν τὴν ἔξωθεν τοῦ ναοῦ (11:2), however, is not to be measured. This measuring, from virtually all commentators' perspectives, draws on Ezekiel 40:3 where a man (angel?) "proceeds to measure the eschatological temple."[9] With John's previous communication about the temple still in mind, as noted in 3:12, his metaphorical intentions remain. While he need not mean the identical thing in both places, his general use of metaphor is likely the case. Aune's summary of the various positions relative to this sometimes enigmatic text is helpful and his conclusion most plausible. He says that the view

> most widely held among modern interpreters is that the temple of God is not a literal building but, together with the altar and the worshipers, represents the Christian community who worship God, while the court outside the temple and the holy city refer to the outer life of the Church, the vulnerability of the people of God to suffering and death.[10]

Koester concurs yet offers an additional observation. He says,

> Where Daniel pictured the temple being trampled, Ezekiel envisioned its restoration. Yet where Ezekiel saw an angel use a reed to measure the court around the temple (Ezek 40:3-8; 41:8; 42:16-20), John is told not to measure the outer court, since it is given over to the nations. The result is that Rev 11:1–2 combines aspects of Daniel and Ezekiel in a new way in order to portray a temple that is both threatened and preserved.[11]

John's use of the phrase often translated "leave out" (11:2) is actually a more forceful expression than translations sometimes indicate. The words are indeed "cast outside" / ἔκβακε ἔξωθεν. Aune acknowledges that John's meaning is figurative in terms of "'exclude' rather than 'cast out.'"[12] Yet arguments abound on all sides of this issue,[13] with the general meaning of the passage, whether "cast outside" or "leave out," being something that is unprotected and subject to assault.

Undoubtedly spiritual preservation is in John's mind, since he cannot mean physical protection only to describe the two witnesses (11:3) mentioned in the attending verses as physically killed by the beast (11:7). Moreover, since the earthly Jerusalem temple and its altar were likewise destroyed by the Romans in 70 CE, by analogy, the metaphorical altar of the temple is also subject to destruction. That is, believers may lose their lives (they have in fact done so) as 6:9 states (cf. 2:13 and Antipas).

In other words, those who are measured are protected spiritually, as in eternally protected against any onslaught, but they are nevertheless subject to physical attack, even martyrdom as a result of their witness (cf. 6:10). By this metaphorical temple and its altar, John may in fact mean something like Paul's analogy that "your body is the temple of the Holy Spirit within you, which you have from God" / τὸ σῶμα ὑμῶν ναὸς τοῦ ἐν ὑμῖν ἁγίου πνεύματός ἐστιν, οὗ ἔχετε ἀπὸ θεοῦ (1 Cor 6:9). John's use of the singular "cast outside and do not measure it" / ἔκβαλε ἔξωθεν, καὶ μὴ αὐτὴν μετρήσῃς may relate to an individual's body that is subject to attack and death.

Certainty about these concerns, although lacking, does not diminish the implications of John's understanding of atonement. One may reasonably conclude that the worshipers and the two witnesses who give their lives as a result of their "prophesying" (11:6) is at the heart of the matter. They have indeed given their lives in sacrifice on the "altar" even if the beast has taken their lives from them. There is no indication, of course, who the recipient of this sacrifice is but only an affirmation of the witnesses having had their lives taken from them by the beast. These events contribute accordingly to John's developing understanding of atonement—that martyrdom has its place in God's plan as well.

11:19

The blowing of the seventh trumpet (11:15) happens to "introduce the period of the end (9:7)."[14] In v. 19 the temple is identified as "the temple of God in heaven" / ὁ ναὸς τοῦ θεοῦ ὁ ἐν τῷ οὐρανῷ accompanied by the ark of the covenant, as well as some apocalyptic signs.[15] This heavenly dwelling place of the presence of God, as all references to it indicate, includes for the first and only time in the Apocalypse the "ark of his covenant" / ἡ κιβωτὸς τῆς διαθήκης αὐτοῦ (11:19). Aune acknowledges that "the ark is never mentioned as part of the sacred furnishings of the heavenly temple," yet he concludes that "the throne could serve as a heavenly counterpart to the ark."[16] The First Testament's understanding of the ark was

> (a) as the extension or embodiment of the presence of Yahweh, a coun-
> terpart to the divine soul (cf. e.g., Num. 10:35-36; I Sam. 6:3, 5, 8, 20);
> (b) as a war palladium of Israel's amphictyony in the days before the
> monarchy (I Sam. 4); (c) as a container, whether of a fetish stone from
> a sacred place like Sinai, as some of the older scholars thought, or of the

two tables of the Decalogue . . . ; (d) as a portable throne for the invisible presence of Yahweh.[17]

By all accounts, Caird's observation is on target: "The earthly ark had stood in the Holy of holies of Solomon's temple . . . . What he [John] sees is the heavenly archetype of which the earthly was but a copy (Exod. xxv.40; cf. Heb. viii. 5). But like its copy the heavenly ark stands in the inner sanctuary of the temple."[18] The appearance of the ark at the blowing of the seventh trumpet "signals not only judgment but also God's gracious presence with his redeemed community and his provision of grace by atonement."[19]

The fact that the "temple of God is opened in heaven" / ἠνοίγη ὁ ναὸς τοῦ θεοῦ ὁ ἐν τῷ οὐρανῷ is a previously unheard of thought since the ark was synonymous with God's holy presence and always avoided by sinful people except the high priest on *Yom Kippur*. Only on the Day of Atonement, blood was sprinkled on the mercy seat (Lev 16:14-16) to which only the high priest had access. The picture that John presents means that the world as it had been known has certainly come to an end and a new day has been inaugurated. Truly "God's dwelling is with men, and he will dwell with them, and they will be his people, and God himself will be with them" / ἡ σκηνὴ τοῦ θεοῦ μετὰ τῶν ἀνθρώπων, καὶ οκηνώσει μετ᾽ αὐτῶν, καὶ αὐτοὶ λαοὶ αὐτοῦ ἔσονται, καὶ αὐτός ὁ θεὸς μετ᾽ αὐτῶν ἔσται (21:3).

The simultaneity of "the rewarding of your servants" / δοῦναι τὸν μισθὸν τοῖς δούλοις σου of 11:18 and the temple being opened seems evident by John's use of "and" / Καὶ to introduce 11:19. The reward of being in the presence of God happens only because of the atonement of the Lamb, the ultimate fulfillment of that for which the annual Day of Atonement was anticipatory. The impressiveness of this vision is clear. Since only on the Day of Atonement did the priest enter the holy of holies, and since John pictures the "sanctuary opened" / ἠνοίγη ὁ ναὸς for all to see, surely "God's presence [is] in their midst, assuring them that their sins are forgiven and that God's covenant stands firm."[20] Without atonement having occurred, no sinful person could survive being in the presence of holy God. Only because of the cleansing and purifying accomplished by the Lamb are believers sustained in God's presence.

14:15, 17 (8:3, 5)

In the gory scene depicted in Revelation 14:14-20, John envisions the harvest of the earth,[21] as it sometimes is called, and "the great winepress of the wrath of God" / τὴν ληνὸν τοῦ θυμοῦ τοῦ θεοῦ τὸν μέγαν. With the Lamb as the governing principle for understanding this scene, the subsequent arguments below, despite a number of disagreements, seem to point to one conclusion.

As the narrative develops, John says that "another angel came out of the temple" / ἄλλος ἄγγελος ἐξῆλθεν ἐκ τοῦ ναοῦ (14:15) to encourage the "one like a son of man" / ὅμοιον υἱὸν ἀνθρώπου (14:14) to commence the harvest (14:15-16). The angel's place of origin, the temple, is of interest to this study and is instructive as it "indicates that he comes from the presence of God . . . ."[22] Since this son of man is immediately identified as seated on "a white cloud" / νεφέλη λευκή (14:14), just as the son of man was noted as "coming with the clouds" / ἔρχεται μετὰ τῶν νεφελῶν in 1:7, there seems little doubt that this one is Jesus. The parallel to Daniel 7:13-14 is also in John's view making all of these considerations, once collected together, point to the Lamb who is in a place of judgment and authority.

Similarly, in the adjacent scene (14:17-20), John says that "another angel came out of the temple in heaven" / ἄλλος ἄγγελος ἐξῆλθεν ἐκ τοῦ ναοῦ τοῦ ἐν τῷ οὐρανῷ (14:17), and he was directed by yet "another angel [that] came out from the altar" / ἄλλος ἄγγελος ἐκ τοῦ θυσιαστηρίου (14:18) to commence with the grape harvest. The latter angel, moreover, "has authority over fire" / ὁ ἔχων ἐξουσίαν ἐπὶ τοῦ πυρός (14:18). Not coincidentally, earlier in Revelation 8:3-5 John mentions an "angel who filled the censer from the fire of the altar" / ὁ ἄγγελος τὸν λιβανωτόν,καὶ ἐγέμιοεν αὐτὸν ἐκ τοῦ πυρὸς τοῦ θυσιαστηρίου. These scenes bear similarity to Isaiah 6:6 where "one of the seraphim had in his hand a burning coal that he took with tongs from the altar" / ἐν τῶν σεραφιν, καὶ ἐν τῇ χειρὶ εἶχεν ἄνθρακα, ὃν τῇ λαβίδι ἔλαβεν ἀπὸ τοῦ θυσιαστηρίου. In Isaiah "the seraph touches the prophet's mouth with a coal from the altar and pronounces that his guilt is removed and his sin forgiven."[23]

Because the burning altar coals are the means for consuming offerings, the connection to sacrificial or incense offerings must be in John's thinking. Commentators, however, have long debated whether the harvests in question are sacrifices of believers,[24] judgment of unbelievers,[25] or perhaps as Bauckham suggests a combination of both, with the first (grain harvest of believers) being positive and the second (grape harvest of unbelievers) being negative.[26] The grain harvest of the biblical and classical tradition certainly has both positive and negative (Homer, Il. 11.67–71; Jer 9:22)[27] precedent with the positive being the more dominant view (Sir 7:3; John 4:36-38; Gal 6:8).[28] The vintage harvest, however, has had primarily judgment connotations as in Isaiah 18:5; 24:13. Alongside harvest language in these scenes is the "sickle" / τὸ δρέπανόν, which may be either a positive instrument of peace or a negative instrument of violence.[29] The sum total of these factors does not point decisively in one direction or another. Caird, however, says, "Harvest and vintage are described in too close parallelism to be regarded as symbols for contrary realities . . . ."[30]

Of course, given John's penchant for inverting themes and images, past precedents do not always hold sway over present meaning for him. The emerging picture of blood running "horse-bridle deep for 1600 stadia" / ἄχρι τῶν χαλινῶν τῶν ἵππων ἀπὸ σταδίων χιλίων ἑξακοσίων (14:20) leads Koester to see a parallel to

> an eschatological battle, when sinners will slay each other "until a stream shall flow with their blood" and a "horse shall walk through the blood of sinners up to his chest; and the chariot shall sink down up to its top" (1 En. 100:1-3; cf. 4 Ezra 15:35-36) . . . Revelation transforms this battle imagery by treating it as a comment on the vineyard imagery that preceded it. Just as the stream flowing from a winepress shows how much juice the grapes contained, the stream of blood shows how much violence the vineyard of earth contained. In this vision the earth's violence, or "blood," has reached a horrific level. The river reveals how much blood the earth contains, showing the need for God's judgment against it.[31]

His comments are surely on the right path; yet rather than the grape harvest being a picture of God's judgment, it may be reasonably understood as a delineation of the collective blood of the saints that God uses to accomplish his purposes similarly as he has used the blood of the Lamb (cf. 7:14; 12:11). For John it is the Lamb's blood, and by extension that of the Lamb's followers (and the prophets before them), that accomplishes the universal goal of redemption. Aune says that "with the blood of the lamb" / αἵματι τοῦ ἀρνίου is "metonymy for the death of Christ or more particularly the atoning death of Christ."[32] That granted, and given that the Son of Man is connected to the harvest, the means of his harvest is arguably by his own blood. What is perplexing is how the one "with sharp sickle in hand" / ἐν τῇ χειρὶ αὐτοῦ δρέπανον ὀξύ (14:14) who does the harvesting could likewise be the one being harvested. Is this character possibly an angel[33] like the one in Revelation 10:1 since "another angel" / ἄλλος ἄγγελος is mentioned in 14:15? Or if this one is the Son of Man (the Christ), then why would an angel command him (Rev 14:15)? This question is answered by acknowledging that angels are God's messengers; hence the one commanding is God. Moreover, if the Son of Man's coming is "for judgment,"[34] that judgment need not be construed as retribution[35] but may be a positive ingathering.

Aune insists that the mention of "angel over fire" / ἐπὶ τοῦ πυρός contributes to John's description of a judgment scene.[36] There may, though, be another available option. It is possible that the harvests in question represent by analogy sacrificial offerings, and as such suggest that it is believers whose own deaths serve the plan of God just as the death of the Lamb did. John appears to have anticipated as much with his preliminary statement to this scene—"Blessed are those who die in the Lord from now on. Yes indeed says the spirit, that they may rest from their labors, for their deeds follow them" / Μακάριοι οἱ νεκροὶ οἱ ἐν κυρίῳ ἀποθνῇσκοντες ἀπ᾽ ἄρτι. ναί, λέγει τὸ πνεῦρμα, ἵνα ἀναπαήσονται ἐκ τῶν κόπων αὐτῶν, τὰ γὰρ ἔργα αὐτῶν ἀκολουθεῖ μετ᾽ αὐτῶν (14:13). Their final deed is their life-giving sacrifice. Caird certainly thinks that this is John's intention. He states,

> By his juxtaposition of the two symbols, and by the parallelism of language which so clearly converts them into a unit of imagery, John has achieved yet another rebirth of images, and has found a way of telling his friends that Christ, who turned the Cross to victory and the four horsemen into angels of grace, can transform even the shambles of martyrdom into a glorious harvest-home.[37]

While commentators are mute on the following point, there is perhaps a Eucharistic connection being implied with the "grain harvest" / ὁ θερισμός (14·15), located as it is alongside the "harvested grapevines of the earth" / ἐτρύγησεν τὴν ἄμπελον τῆς γῆς (Rev 14:18). Should it be that grain is analogous with the bread of the Eucharist, and that the grapes of the grapevines point to the wine of the Eucharist, John may be picturing in his uniquely communicative style that believers are like Jesus whose broken body and shed blood are in view in these images. Certainly, John does not mention the Eucharist in any direct way elsewhere in the Apocalypse, granted that some have seen allusions to it in 3:20[38] and 19:9.[39] In the former the language, "I will eat with him" / δειπνήσω μετ᾽ αὐτοῦ, and in the latter "the marriage supper of the Lamb" / τὸ δεῖπνον τοῦ γάμου τοῦ ἀρνίου, would be hard-pressed to fit unambiguously into a Eucharistic scheme. Should it be that John is alluding to the Eucharist, then a harvest of believers as martyrs, as Caird argues, is in view.

What one concludes about "the great wine press of the wrath of God" / τὴν ληνὸν τοῦ θυμοῦ τοῦ θεοῦ τὸν μέγαν has great bearing on the meaning of this otherwise macabre scene. In the section below ("Loosed/ Purchased" and "His/Slain Lamb's Blood") where 14:4 is addressed, we conclude that the redeemed believers (5:9; 14:4) "follow the Lamb wherever he goes" / οὗτοι οἱ ἀκολουθοῦντες τῷ ἀρνίῳ ἀρνίῳ ὅπου ἂν ὑπάγῃ. That is, they are indeed "a kingdom, priests to his God and Father" / βασιλείαν, ἱερεῖς τῷ θεῷ καὶ πατρὶ αὐτοῦ[40] whose duty and identity lead them to do what the Lamb has done—lay down their lives sacrificially. These followers of the Lamb are identified as both "firstfruits to God and the Lamb" / ἀπαρχὴ τῷ θεῷ καὶ τῷ ἀρνίῳ (14:4) and "blameless" or "without blemish" / ἄμωμοί (14:5), which in Jewish tradition of first fruits included grain, grapes, and other crops (Exod 34:22; Num 13:20). These firstfruits apply to "the whole nation of Israel redeemed from Egypt 'holy to the Lord, the first of his harvest.'"[41]

Closely related to this discussion is the location "outside of the city" / ἔξωθεν τῆς πόλεως at which the wine press is trodden. Koester, after surveying scholarly opinion, concludes that "the city can better be understood as a metaphor for the believing community (cf. Rev 11:2), just as the vineyard is a metaphor for the earth and the sickle and winepress are metaphors for judgment."[42] Caird, building on the temple and altar language of 14:15,17, and 18, directly states that "the great martyrdom is the sacrifice offered to God by the royal house of priests,"[43] who are all believers (cf. Rev 1:6). Most important from the perspective of atonement, how God receives the sacrifice is not indicated as an expiatory or propitiatory offering.

15:5, 6, 8

The scene in Revelation 15 proceeds from the conclusions of "the great winepress of the wrath of God" / τὴν ληνὸν τοῦ θυμοῦ τοῦ θεοῦ τὸν μέγαν (14:19). The liturgical setting of "singing the song of Moses the servant of God and the song of the lamb" / ᾄδουσιν τὴν ᾠδὴν Μωϋσέως τοῦ δούλου τοῦ θεοῦ καὶ τὴν ᾠδὴν τοῦ ἀρνίου (15:3) pictures the redeemed people of God (those who were part of the "harvest of the earth" and "the winepress of God") celebrating victoriously. They rejoice, as Boring points out, even though "the final victory is not yet realized (on earth) but is already accomplished and celebrated in heaven, the ultimately real world, and thus can be celebrated in this world . . . ."[44]

John's use of "temple" language in 15:5, 6, and 8 (two times) as "the temple of the tent of witness" / ὁ ναὸς τῆς σκηνῆς τοῦ μαρτυπίου, "of the

temple" / τοῦ ναοῦ, "the temple was filled with smoke of the glory of God"
/ ἐγεμίσθη ὁ ναὸς καπνοῦ ἐκ τῆς δόξης τοῦ θεοῦ, and "the temple" /
τὸν ναὸν appear respectively) means that all earthly events happen under
the auspices of heavenly oversight and with divine permission and direction. The "opened temple of the tent of witness" / ἠνοίγη ὁ ναὸς τῆς
σκηνῆς τοῦ μαρτυρίου (15:5) that John saw, like all temple references in
the Apocalypse, are, as Koester states, "a single entity, rather than a structure with two parts. It is where God is enthroned (Rev 7:15), and it houses
the incense altar and ark of the covenant (6:9; 8:3; 11:19)."[45] Thus, it is
from God's presence that the seven angels with the seven plagues originate
to reveal the content of the plagues.

Smalley observes that the phrase "the temple of the tent of witness"
/ ὁ ναὸς τῆς σκηνῆς τοῦ μαρτυρίου (15:5) that John uses only here in
Revelation "may include . . . the 'witness to (or by) Jesus,' since he fulfills
in himself the covenantal requirements of the Father."[46] The angels that
come forth from the temple do so as God's messengers to reveal from yet
another vantage point God's consistent plan. The result of the forthcoming
"seven bowls of the wrath of God" / τὰς ἑπτὰ φιάλας τοῦ θυμοῦ τοῦ
θεοῦ (15:6) has already been revealed in 15:4. John says, "All nations shall
come and worship before you, because your righteous judgments have been
revealed" / πάντα τὰ ἔθνη ἥξουσιν καὶ προσκυνήσουιν ἐνώπιόν σου,
ὅτι τὰ δικαιώματά σου ἐφανερώθησαν (15:4). Caird raises an appropriate question about this conclusion to God's plan:

> Those scholars who think that John held out no hope of repentance
> for the heathen world are embarrassed by the martyrs' confidence, and
> have to argue that in this context fear and do homage indicate not a true
> conversion but only an awed submission to power. We have already seen
> that this interpretation will not do for the two earlier passages in which
> John has used these expressions (xi. 13; xiv. 7). When the angel of the
> gospel calls on men to fear God, do him homage, and worship him, we
> cannot seriously believe that he is inviting them to do something which
> will make not an iota of difference in their eternal destiny.[47]

The fact that "no one is able to enter the temple until the seven plagues
of the seven angels have been completed" / οὐσεις ἐδύνατο εἰσελθεῖν εἰς
τὸν ναὸν ἄχρι τελεσθῶσιν αἱ ἑπτὰ πληγαὶ τῶν ἑπτὰ ἀγγέλων (15:8b)
connects well to the "temple filled with the smoke of God's glory and his
power" / ἐγεμίσθη ὁ ναὸς καπνοῦ ἐκ τῆς δόξης τοῦ θεοῦ καὶ ἐκ τῆς

δυάμεως αὐτοῦ (15:8a). In other words, although John has described the ultimate heavenly celebration in 15:2-4, he digresses until he has delineated an additional piece of the redemptive puzzle. The sum total of human evil that has been filling up "the seven golden bowls of the wrath of God" / τὰς ἑπτὰ φιάλας τοῦ θυηοῦ τοῦ θεοῦ (16:1, 2-21) must yet be disclosed and addressed. While the ultimate outcome is clear, the smoke of the temple means that there are some remaining details that need to be cleared away before the full picture will be in view. Once that happens, and John addresses a few additional matters, "they will [finally] see his face" / ὄψονται τὸ πρόσωπον αὐτοῦ (22:4).

Before the "seven bowls of the wrath of God" / ἑπτὰ φιάλας χρυσᾶς γεμούσας τοῦ θυηοῦ τοῦ θεοῦ (16:1) of Revelation 16 are pictured as poured out, they are first mentioned in the summary verse 15:7. As Beale recognizes, there is a recapitulation at work in the bowl scenes that "complement and round out the portrayal of divine wrath in the seals and trumpets. It is in the fuller presentation of punishment in the bowls that it can be said that God's wrath has been completely expressed . . . ."[48] The bowl plagues that originate from the temple and throne of God speak to the unfolding divine plan, a significant piece of which is the death of Jesus, and, hence, atonement.

16:1; 16:17 (8:3, 5)

In the seven bowl plagues revealed in Revelation 16, in 16:1 and 16:17, John mentions the word "from the temple" / τοῦ ναοῦ and "out of the temple, from the throne" / τοῦ ναοῦ ἀπὸ τοῦ θρόνου respectively. His use of "temple" in these two places reaches back to 15:5, 6, and 8 (see above).

Since John reports, "I heard a great voice out of the temple" / ἤκουσα μεγάλης φωνῆς ἐκ τοῦ ναοῦ, this voice is undoubtedly that of God coming from the temple. The connections among the heavenly entourage mentioned in Revelation 15 and 16 (angels, one of the four living creatures, and God) emanating from the temple identify one of John's four usages of temple: the temple in Jerusalem (11:1-2); the temple as metaphor for the people of God (3:12); the heavenly temple (7:15; 11:19—2 times; 15:5, 6, 8—2 times; 16:1, 17); and the presence of God as a temple in the New Jerusalem (21:22—2 times).[49] Certainly, here John intends the heavenly temple.

Each of the seven angels summarily "pours out his bowl" / ἐξέχεεν τὴν φιάλην αὐτοῦ (16:2, 3, 4, 8, 10, 12, 17) "of the wrath of God" /

τοῦ θυμοῦ τοῦ θεοῦ. Above we discussed the synonym "wrath of the Lamb" (see "Sacrifice and the Wrath of the Lamb") that John here relates to it. A couple of interconnections are also at play in the "bowl" / τὴν φιάλην language that John uses (introduced in 15:7) along with the "altar" / τοῦ θυσιαστηρίου of 16:7. The "bowl" was the vessel identified in Exodus 27:3 for carrying ashes of offerings and sacrifices from the altar that John mentions as the containers, which are "golden bowls filled with incense, which are the prayers of the saints" / φιάλας χρυσᾶς γεμούσας θυμιαμάτων, αἵ εἰσιν αἱ προσευχαὶ τῶν ἁγίων (5:8). A similar term, "censer" / τόν λιβανωτόν, appears in Revelation 8:3, 5 associated with the "smoke of the altar [that] ascended with the prayers of the saints" / ἀνέβη ὁ καπνὸς τῶν θυμιαμάτων ταῖς προσευχαῖς τῶν ἁγίων. In the censer that contained smoke and prayers of the people, John pictures an angel "mix it with fire of the altar, and cast it to the earth" / ἐγέμισεν αὐτὸν ἐκ τοῦ πυρὸς τοῦ θισιαστηρίου, καὶ ἔμαλεν εἰς τὴν γῆν (8:5) to commence the blowing of the seven trumpets. This image of destruction being returned to the earth in the de-creation that the seven trumpets depict is similar to the bowls of wrath recapitulated in Revelation 16.

In 16:1-21 the seven bowls, when poured out, bring judgment upon the earth similar to that of the seven trumpets. The second and third bowls (Rev 16:4-7) specifically mention blood (vv. 4 and 6), recalling both the third trumpet (Rev 8:10-11) and the plague on the Nile of Exodus 7:17-21. What remains unmentioned is the contents found in any of the bowls, other than that they are "seven bowls of the wrath of God" / τὰς ἑπτὰ φιάλας τοῦ θυμοῦ τοῦ θεοῦ. John's prior mention of God's wrath is in 15:7 preceded by 15:1, both of which have 14:19 and "the great winepress of the wrath of God" / τὴν ληνὸν τοῦ θυμοῦ τοῦ θεοῦ τὸν μέγαν in mind. This image surfaces again when "he will tread the winepress of the wine of the fury of the wrath of God almighty" / αὐτὸς πατεῖ τὴν ληνὸν τοῦ οἴνου τοῦ θυμοῦ τῆς ὀργῆς τοῦ θεοῦ τοῦ παντοκράτορος (19:15). Each of these scenes share the common theme of God's wrath with "wine" imagery, no doubt alluding to the blood implied in the color of wine.

In terms of "wine" / οἶνος, John uses this word eight times (6:6; 14:8, 10; 16:19; 17:2; 18:3, 13; 19:15) (see chapter 3, "Dressed in a Garment Dipped in Blood" and "The Winepress of the Fury of the Wrath of God" 19:13 and 19:15). John also uses the word "cup" / ποτήριον four times (14:10; 16:19; 17:4; 18:6) and "winepress" / ληνός three times (14:19, 20; 19:15). An exploration of these images reveals both direct and indirect connections to blood, particularly the blood of the saints. The only two

exceptions are when the third seal is opened in 6:6 and in 18:3 when, as
the latter reveals, wine is listed as no longer available in the fallen city of
Babylon the Great. In 6:6 John refers to wine in reference to the black horse
of famine associated with war brought on by the white and red horsemen.
Wine there does not relate to blood, but instead, as "do not harm the oil
and the wine" / τὸ ἔλαιον καὶ τὸν οἶνον μὴ ἀδικήσῃς suggests, seems
always to be the case, as Rist says that "[l]uxuries were accessible; necessities
were coming to be beyond reach."[50]

In 14:8 John mentions "wine" / τοῦ οἴνου and in 14:10 both "wine" /
τοῦ οἴνου and "cup" / τῷ ποτηρίῳ. In both cases Babylon, introduced for
the first time (and as an alias for Rome[51]), and those connected to the beast
that represents her, are associated with her fall since "she [is the one] who
made all the nations drink the wine of her angry immorality" / ἣ ἐκ τοῦ οἴ
νου τοῦ θυμοῦ τῆς πορνείας αὐτῆς πεπότικεν πάντα τὰ ἔθνη. Her fall
is likewise mentioned in 16:19 where "Babylon the great [reaching back to
14:8] was remembered before God who gave her the cup of the fury of his
wrath" / Βαβυλὼν ἡ μεγάλη ἐμνήσθη ἐνώπον τοῦ θεοῦ δοῦαι αὐτῇ τὸ
ποτήριον τοῦ οἴνου τοῦ θυμοῦ τῆς ὀργῆς αὐτοῦ. What this wine and
cup represent is borne out in the imagery of the vintage in Revelation 14.

In particular, when the symbol of the vintage is added to "the cup"
/ τῷ ποτηρίῳ and "blood" / τοῦ αἵματος of Revelation, a conglomerate
is formed. In 14:18, 19 "drinking the wine of the wrath of God which
is poured unmixed in the cup of his wrath" / πίεται ἐκ τοῦ οἴνου τοῦ
θυμοῦ τοῦ θεοῦ τοῦ κεκερασμένου ἀκράτου ἐν τῷ ποτηρίῳ τῆς ὀργῆς
αὐτοῦ (14:10) is later combined with 17:2 where "the ones who dwell
on the earth are drunk on the wine of her immorality" / ἐμεθύθησαν οἱ
κατοικοῦντες τὴν γῆν ἐκ τοῦ οἴνου τῆς πορνείας αὐτῆς. She is the
same woman of 17:4 with a "golden cup in her hand full of abominations
and impurities of her immorality" / ποτήριον χρυσοῦν ἐν τῇ χειρὶ αὐτῆς
γέμον βδελυγμάτων καὶ τὰ ἀκάθαρτα τῆς πορνείας αὐτῆς from which
"the woman was drunk with the blood of the saints and with the blood
of the martyrs of Jesus" / τὴν γυναῖκα μεθύουσαν ἐκ τοῦ αἵματος τῶν
ἁγίων καὶ ἐκ τοῦ αἵματος τῶν μαρτύρων Ἰησοῦ (17:6). Moreover, John
further describes the collapse of the city (woman) "because all the nations
have drunk from the wine of her angry immorality" / ὅτι ἐκ τοῦ οἴνου τοῦ
θυμοῦ τῆς πορνείας αὐτῆς πέπτωκαν πάντα τὰ ἔθνη (18:3). She, appropriately, receives a double mixture as John says, "Give back to her as she has
given, and give double the double according to her deeds: in the cup that
she mixed mix it double" / ἀπόδοτε αὐτῇ ὡς καὶ αὐτὴ ἀπέδωκεν, καὶ

διπλώσατε τά διπλᾶ κατὰ τὰ ἔργα αὐτῆς· ἐν τῷ ποτηρίῳ ᾧ ἐκέρασεν κεράσατε αὐτῇ διπλοῦν (18:6). Ultimately the city is doomed because she "had found in her the blood of the prophets and the saints and all who have been slain on earth" / ἐν αὐτῇ αἷμα προφητῶν καὶ ἁγίων εὑρέθη καὶ πάντων τῶν ἐσφαγμένων ἐπὶ τῆς γῆς (18:24).

These details yield a picture of the bowls of wrath of Revelation 16 being filled with the blood of the saints of all the ages, including the blood of the Lamb, as well as that of the prophets of old. These bowls, as the "seven final plagues" / πληγὰς ἑπτὰ τὰς ἐσχάτας (15:1), are filled to running over with the collective, accumulated blood of the saints. John undoubtedly sees the world having reached its worst and finally having arrived at its tipping point. With each consecutive bowl having been filled and tipped over to spill its blood, the world's evil perpetrators receive in kind what they have given throughout the ages with the result that they "blasphemed the name of God . . . and they did not repent and give him the glory" / ἐβλασφήμησαν τὸ ὄνομα τοῦ θεοῦ . . . , καὶ οὐ μετενόησαν δοῦναι αὐτῷ δόξαν (16:9). The emerging picture is that what evil has done throughout the ages comes back upon itself. A. T. Hanson states it clearly: "The wrath-sin process brings its own dreadful interest; . . . We may therefore sum up John's use of θυμός, οἶνος, and ποτήριον by claiming that when he uses these words, he is *always* referring to the wrath process as worked out in history . . . ."[52] The same way that it will happen to the woman in 18:6, it is described as having happened in the bowl plagues.

The end result of the bowls being poured out prompted John to write, "It is finished" / Γέγονεν (16:17). To be sure, this saying is reminiscent of Jesus' dying words on the cross. There, Jesus, said, "It is finished, and when he bowed his head he gave up the spirit" / ὁ Ἰησοῦς εἶπεν· Τετέλεσται, καὶ κλίνας τὴν κεφαλὴν παρέδωκεν τὸ πνεῦμα (Jn. 19:29). Koester, however, points out that

> [c]ompletion is indicated by the Greek word *gegonen* in the third person singular: "It is done"; yet the completion of these plagues does not mean that God's purposes have been fully realized. The end comes only in the new creation, where Revelation uses the plural *gegonan* to announce that "all is done," because God makes all things new (Rev 21:6). Interpreters sometimes link God's statement "it is done" to Jesus saying "it is finished" on the cross (John 19:30) . . . , but there is little to suggest such a connection.[53]

God, as only the divine can do, lets evil do its worst until, as sometimes is said, "what goes around comes around." After a thorough investigation of the divine passive in Revelation, Bauckham notes,

> We should probably not think of the majority of judgments in Revelation as special divine interventions. They are simply the regular evils of human history, escalated over the course of the three septenaries to exceptional proportions . . . . That God does not prevent such things, that God leaves humanity to the consequences of its ways, is a form of judgment.[54]

Hanson anticipated Bauckham's conclusion with his own: "The wrath of God is the punishment of God, and the punishment of God is what he permits us to inflict on ourselves."[55] Jacques Ellul concurs "that we must clearly take account of the fact that the judgment of God takes place in the direction established by man himself. In some way, God let the act of men develop: it is in this sense, and in this sense only, that 'our acts judge us'. . . . But God lets the work of man bear its own fruits: and that is the judgment. Man suffers the consequences of that which he has done."[56]

John ultimately sees the end as a great seismic disaster (16:18) echoing the earthquake of the sixth seal (6:12-17), and the sixth trumpet, but this one is more globally cataclysmic than the fall of "the tenth of the city" / τὸ δέκατον τῆς πόλεως (11:13). He also pictures the end of the world from the vantage point of the fall of "the great city" / ἡ πόλις ἡ μεγάλη (16:19) about which he will say more in Revelation 17–18 and even more in Revelation 19–20.

In terms of wrath, John's atonement imagery of temple, blood, bowls of incense, wine and winepress, cup, and God's wrath all point consistently to the redemption theme that he will articulate strategically with a set of different images in Revelation 12. In the details examined thus far, God's wrath is not directed in any sense at the Lamb, although his redemptive purpose is working itself out.

What John is describing in these bowls of wrath is even better understood after an examination of the sixth bowl of 16:12-16. From this vantage point, John pictures the end of the world as a great battle. This plague is patterned after the drying up of the Red Sea (Exod 14:21-22; Rev 16:12a) and also echoes the drying up of the River Euphrates (Rev 16:12b) described in Isaiah 44:27-28 that allowed Cyrus the Persian to enter Babylon and defeat it, prompting the eventual release of God's people from captivity. Of special interest is Cyrus in this story, in particular the fact that God used a pagan king to attack another pagan kingdom. That is, God used the ambition of pagan King Cyrus, who supposed that he was building his own kingdom, to accomplish not so much his but God's purposes.

This is a familiar theme among the prophets (cf. especially Hab 1-3 where he challenged why God would use an eviler power than his own people to accomplish his purposes). The coming "of the kings from the east" / τῶν βασιλέων τῶν ἀπὸ ἀνατολῆς ἡλίου (Rev 16:12c) to the River Euphrates happened at the eastern boundary of civilization during the Roman period. Those people had a well-known fear that Nero would return, leading the Parthians against the Roman Empire.[57] John provides a picture here of an evil power coming against the existing evil empire. Since he has spoken symbolically about Babylon throughout his book, mention of the Euphrates here (where ancient Babylon was located) draws attention back to Babylon. He previously identified Babylon symbolically as the "Great City" / τῆς πόλεως τῆς μεγάλης (Rev 11:8a), "which is called spiritually Sodom and Egypt where also the Lord was crucified" / ἥτις καλεῖται πνεματικῶς Σόδομα καὶ Αἴγυπτος, ὅπου καὶ ὁ κύριος αὐτῶν ἐσταυρώθη (11:8b). "Babylon the great" is found in 16:19; 17:5; 18:2; 18:10, 21 as well, and in each of these references speaks to the symbolic meaning of Babylon. The Euphrates, therefore, must not be connected to a literal river running through Iraq, Syria, and Turkey.[58]

At the center of this approaching army are the Dragon, Beast, and False Prophet with unclean spirits like frogs (Rev 16:13). The Dragon, Beast, and False Prophet all speak with "foul/unclean spirits like frogs" / πνεύματα τρία ἀκάθαρτα ὡς βάτραχοι in contrast to the Son of man who has a "sword" of truth in his mouth (1:16; 2:12; 19:21). The "unclean" frog-like spirits suggest the deception with which they speak. These "frogs" are reminiscent of the second Exodus plague (Exod 8:2–11), which, when recalling that frogs are also counted among the unclean animals (Lev 11:9-12, 41-47), and the sounds made by frogs, brings to mind what should be considered "meaningless croaking."[59] The evil empires seem incessant in their constant calls to war. Meanwhile, conspicuously absent are the people of God in this war. That John identifies a "trinity" of evil makes the image more potent. They are "demonic spirits performing signs" / πνεύματα δαιμονίων ποιοῦντα σημεῖα (16:14) with the intention to deceive the kings. Their intent is clear when the connection with the second beast of 13:13 who deceived men and women is made. By this time their reach is global, to the "kings of the whole world" / τοὺς βασιλεῖς τῆς οἰκουμέμης ὅλης. In other words, evil has become universal and is all-pervasive by the time John describes this bowl that is filled to running over with wrath.

From every indication, evil will not rest until it destroys all or is itself destroyed. The goal of this evil triumvirate is destruction through war, which John calls "the great day of God the almighty" / τῆς ἡμέρας τῆς μεγάλης τοῦ θεοῦ τοῦ παντοκράτορος (16:14). This expression occurs in 19:19 and 20:8 as well with this scene depicting a war of evil against evil, while in 19:19 and 20:8 the scene describes evil warring against the rider of the white horse and the camp of the saints respectively. This battle is the same as that of 6:12-17; 11:7-10; 19:11-21; and 20:7-10. In the remarkable vision that John reveals here, the focus is on the destruction that evil brings upon other evil; namely, evil from beyond the eastern borders is pictured coming against Rome who was the first century's symbol of all that opposed God.

While the image of 11:7-10 focuses on the destruction of believers by the "beast of the bottomless pit, 19:11-21 and 20:7-10 both focus on the battle as between evil and good. John, in each of these war scenes, describes things from a different vantage point. While evil supposes that it is gathering to win its final battle, in reality God uses the evil beyond the civilized world to destroy the evil of so-called civilized Rome, the Great City that has become incurably corrupt. John pictures the "City" as "the woman drunk with the blood of the saints and the blood of the witnesses/martyrs of Jesus" / τὴν γυναῖκα μεθύουσαν ἐκ τοῦ αἵματος τῶν ἁγίων καὶ ἐκ τοῦ αἵματος τῶν μαρτύρων Ἰησοῦ (Rev 17:6).

Such a reading is consistent with the six other plagues that are poured out on unbelievers. The "seven bowls of the wrath of God" / τάς ἑπτά φιάλας τοῦ θυμοῦ τοῦ θεοῦ (16:1) are indeed the grand collection of evil that, once the bowls are full, comes back to plague the perpetrators. The Lamb's blood and the saints' blood are all part of what plagues the world and what comes forth "out of the temple" / ἐκ τοῦ ναοῦ (16:1), where the blood has been collecting (in sacrifice) throughout the ages (see also below "Altar" 6:9-11), and finally fills the bowls to running over.

21:22

The final mention of the word "temple" appears in Revelation 21:22 where John says that "I did not see a temple in it, for the Lord, God, the Almighty, is its temple, and the Lamb" / ναὸν οὐκ εἶδον ἐν αὐτῇ, ὁ γὰρ κύριος, ὁ θεός, ὁ παντοκράτωρ, ναὸς αὐτῆς ἐστιν, καὶ τὸ ἀρνίον. That is, the work of redemption having been completed, the previous symbols that speak of God's work are all recapitulated into one—which is three—the Lord, the Almighty, the Lamb.

Altar
6:9

John's first mention of "altar" / θυσιαστήριον occurs in 6:9 at the opening of the fifth seal following the four colored horses. About the altar he says, "I saw under the altar the souls who had been slain" / εἶδον ὑποκάτω τοῦ θυσιαστηρίου τὰς ψυχὰς τῶν ἐσφαγμένων. Certainly, altars were well known in both the biblical and pagan world. Koester says, "Revelation envisions a heavenly sanctuary with a single altar for sacrifice and prayer. This differs from Israel's tabernacle and temples, which had two altars: one for incense within the sanctuary and another for burnt offering."[60] He summarizes scholarly opinion that is split between the altar in Revelation 6:9 as being either "the altar of burnt offering" or "the altar of incense."[61] The function of the altar is here identified with sacrifice, namely of martyred souls.

In particular, the martyrs are specified as "souls of the ones slain because of the word of God and the witness which they had" / τὰς ψυχὰς τῶν ἐσφαγμένων διὰ τὸν λόγον τοῦ θεοῦ καὶ διὰ τὴν μαρτυρίαν ἣν εἶχον (6:9). The connection of the altar with slain martyrs speaks to how differently John views the death of believers than the senseless death of others who are casualties of war during the rampage of the four horsemen that he saw. The result of the evil horsemen's actions is much death at the hands of these riders on a white horse with a bow, a red one with a sword, a black one with famine, and a pale green one with death. Koester agrees with Wisdom 3:6 that the martyrs' "location under the altar shows that God receives those who are slaughtered on account of their witness."[62] They stand and die as testimony of their faithfulness to God's alternative plan for this world.

The war horses so well described by John have run amuck in human history. As they have done their deadly deeds, they have left in their wake nothing but carnage. While believers have not always been singled out for murder by the war machines (although sometimes they have been) that have romped throughout the ages, believers have been caught in the crossfire as collateral damage and are counted among "the one-fourth of the earth" / τὸ τέταρτον τῆς γῆς (6:8) that have died. The martyrs described in 6:9

as being "beneath the altar" / ὑποκάτω τοῦ θυοιαστηρίου and crying for God's justice are addressed below in 6:11 ("White/Washed Robes").

8:3-5
See above "Temple," 16:1, 17.

9:13

The altar about which John writes in 9:13 appears like Judaism's altars, which Exodus 27:2 says have four horns. This one is a "golden altar" / τοῦ θυσιαστηρίου τοῦ χρυσοῦ from which John says "I heard the voice of one of the horns" / ἤκουσα φωνὴν μίαν ἐκ τῶν κεράτων.[63] The golden altar in the Old Testament tabernacle was for incense.

The voice that John hears speaking may be either the collective voices of the martyrs, if this use of altar reaches back to 6:9, 11 (see below "White/ Washed Robes" 6:11) and 8:3-5 (see above "Temple" 16:1, 17). If this is not John's meaning, then this voice is the representative angel associated with the altar, or, as Edmondo Lupieri suggests, is the altar itself speaking.[64] Since the unleashed monsters pictured in this vision "kill one-third of humankind" / ἀπεκτάνθησαν τὸ τρίτον τῶν ἀνθρώπων (9:18), believers are certainly included in this number that John mentions. Undoubtedly more blood of the saints is spilled during this onslaught similar to the ones associated with the four colored horses. Although repentance is God's goal in allowing these horrors to fall on humanity, "the ones that were not killed by these plagues did not repent of their deeds" / οἳ οὐκ ἀπεκτάνθησαν ἐν ταῖς πληγαῖς ταύταις, οὐδὲ μετενίησαν ἐκ τῶν ἔργων (9:20), no "they did not repent" / οὐ μετενόησαν (9:21).

Occasionally in the evils that humans do to each other, especially in war times, there is an ownership of the atrocities with recompense, and sometimes requisite repentance. John makes clear that of all the horrors done on earth that he is describing in this sequence, none are more heinous than those that humans do one to the other. He could hardly mean less since he describes "their faces as men's faces, and they have hair as women's hair" / τὰ πρόσωπα αὐτῶν ὡς πρόσωπα ἀνθρώπων, καὶ εἶχον τρίχας ὡς τρίχας γυναικῶν (9:7-8). The result of these horrors is the same in all instances: people die because people are sinfully power hungry, and such sinful people often kill. Nevertheless, God's patience and permission in allowing evil men and women to kill is a recognition of God's way in the world. God allows humans their freedom while using even human tragedy in some cases to lead to change.

CONCLUSION

John's use of throne, temple, and altar moves the reader closer to understanding the role that blood and death play in Revelation. The Lamb's ascendency to the throne denotes the place of authority from which God has decreed and has allowed for both the death of the Lamb and the death of the Lamb's followers. The self-sacrifice to which the Lamb submits himself by his blood and death is God's counterintuitive means of winning victory in a world turned violent. Because of their deaths the Lamb and his followers all sit in righteous judgment over the events that happen both in heaven and on earth. These events are the deeds and means that God has used to declare his redemptive ways in the world.

The temple, both earthly and heavenly, is God's metaphorical dwelling place and residence of the altar. Angels, messengers, and people are pictured as coming and going with frequency to and from the temple and its altar carrying out the plan of God. While the heavenly temple is a place of eternal security and protection, it is also the location from which divine instruction comes. Of course, attending to the temple and its altar are divinely appointed priests who have been elected to sacrificial service in God's redemptive plan.

John's emphasis on the altar reminds believers that their deaths, like the death of the Lamb, do serve a purpose even if that purpose is not always evident in the moment. The sum total of the collective blood of the saints that has filled the bowls of wrath mentioned in 16:1, 17 (see above "Temple" 16:1, 17) will one day reach its full complement. Once "their fellow servants and their brothers [and sisters] should be complete who were about to be killed as even they had been" / πληρωθῶσιν καὶ οἱ σύνδουλοι αὐτῶν καὶ οἱ αιδελφοὶ αὐτῶν οἱ μελλοντες ἀποκτέννεσθαι ὡς καὶ αὐτοί (Rev 6:11—see below chapter 3 "White/Washed Robes" 6:11), then God's atoning plan will have arrived at another of its goals—evil's self-destruction—which is presaged by John's account of the defeat of the Dragon (see chapter 5 below).

11:1
See above "Temple," 11:1-2.

14:18
See above "Temple," 14:15, 17.

Notes

1. David Aune, *Revelation 6–16*, Word Biblical Commentary (Dallas: Word, 1998) 405.

2. David Aune, *Revelation 1–5*, Word Biblical Commentary (Dallas: Word, 1997) 278.

3. Stephen S. Smalley, *The Revelation of John: A Commentary on the Greek Text of the Apocalypse* (Downers Grove IL: InterVarsity, 2005) 114–15.

4. David Aune, *Revelation 17–22*, Word Biblical Commentary (Dallas: Word, 1998) 1177.

5. G. K. Beale, *The Book of Revelation: A Commentary on the Greek Text*, The New International Greek Testament Commentary, ed. I. Howard Marshall and Donald A. Hagner (Grand Rapids MI: Eerdmans, 1999) 999.

6. Craig R. Koester, *Revelation: A New Translation with Introduction and Commentary*, The Anchor Yale Bible (New Haven: Yale University Press, 2014) 772.

7. Ibid., 773, for a list of commentators.

8. The world σκηνή / "tabernacle" is mentioned in Revelation only at 21:3 where its focus is on "dwelling" with God, not the wilderness institution.

9. Aune, *Revelation 6–16*, 603.

10. Ibid., 597. He includes the following names in support of this conclusion: Behm, Allo, Lohse, Sweet, Mounce, Beagley, Boring, and Bauckham.

11. Koester, Revelation, 494–95, qualifies this point: "John's vision transforms the temple, the altar, and those who worship there into an image for the Christian community (Note on 11:1). Revelation has already said that faithful people are to be pillars in the temple (naos) of God (3:12), and this idea is now given expanded visual form. Thus far, the scenes of true worship (proskynein) have been centered in heaven (4:8-11; 5:8-14; 7:9-12), where an altar stands before God's throne (6:9; 8:3, 5; 9:13; 14:18; 16:7), which is in the celestial temple (14:15; 15:5). The congregations of Jesus' followers are the earthly counterpart. Their community is God's temple on earth, where true worship takes place and the redeemed serve as priests (1:6; 5:10)."

12. Aune, *Revelation 6–16*, 607.

13. Ibid.

14. George E. Ladd, *A Commentary of the Revelation of John* (Grand Rapids MI: Eerdmans, 1972) 160.

15. Beale, *The Book of Revelation*, 618, identifies these signs of "lightning, sounds, thunders, earthquake, and great hail" as "indicator of the last act of judgment (so 4:5; 8:5; 16:18; see on 8:5b)."

16. Aune, *Revelation 6–16*, 678.

17. G. Henton Davies, "Ark of the Covenant," *The Interpreter's Dictionary of the Bible A-D*, ed. George A. Buttrick (Nashville: Abingdon, 1962) 222–23.

18. George B. Caird, *The Revelation of St. John the Divine* (New York: Harper and Row, 1966) 144.

19. Beale, *The Book of Revelation*, 619.

20. Caird, *The Revelation of St. John the Divine*, 144.

21. Heikki Räisänen, "Revelation, Violence, and War: Glimpses of a Dark Side," William John Lyons and Jorunn Økland, eds., *The Way the World Ends? The Apocalypse of John in Culture and Ideology* (Sheffield: Sheffield Phoenix, 2009) 155–56, cites that the text of the *Battle Hymn of the Republic*, composed by Julia Ward Howe during an early phase of the American civil war in 1862, was based on this text.

22. Ladd, *Commentary on the Book of Revelation*, 200.

23. Gene M. Tucker, "The Book of Isaiah: Introduction, Commentary and Reflections," *The New Interpreter's Bible*, vol. 6, ed. Leander E. Keck (Nashville: Abingdon, 2001) 103.

24. Caird, *Revelation of Saint John the Divine*, 190–95; M. Eugene Boring, *Revelation*, Interpretation (Louisville KY: John Knox, 1989) 169–72.

25. Beale, *The Book of Revelation*, 770–784.

26. Richard Bauckham, *The Climax of Prophecy: Studies on the Book of Revelation* (Edinburgh: T&T Clark International, 1993) 283–96; Smalley, *Revelation of John*, 372, suggests that "the scene is salvific judgment; the harvester is the royal judge, and not a warrior," as he presents the variety of options, pp. 372–75.

27. Koester, *Revelation*, 625.

28. Ibid.

29. Ibid., 624.

30. Caird, *Revelation of Saint John the Divine*, 191.

31. Koester, *Revelation*, 626. He provides a thorough summary of commentators who take a variety of positions relative to the harvest of the earth on pages 628–29.

32. Aune, *Revelation 6–16*, 475.

33. Martin Kiddle, *Revelation of St. John*, The Moffatt New Testament Commentary (New York: Harper & Brothers, 1940) 277, thinks so.

34. G.R. Beasley-Murray, *The Book of Revelation*, New Century Bible Commentary (Grand Rapids MI: Eerdmans, 1974) 229.

35. Robert Mounce, *The Book of Revelation*, New International Commentary on the New Testament (Grand Rapids MI: Eerdmans, 1977) 279.

36. Aune, *Revelation 6–16*, 845–46. Also, Beale, *The Book of Revelation*, 775, notes that "in twenty-three of twenty-four Apocalypse occurrences 'fire' [πῦρ] depicts judgment."

37. Caird, *Revelation of Saint John the Divine*, 194.

38. Ibid., 58; and Beale, *The Book of Revelation*, 309.

39. Christopher C. Rowland, "The Book of Revelation," *The New Interpreter's Bible*, vol. 12, ed. Leander Keck (Nashville: Abingdon, 1998) 587, sees a link between the meal of 3:20 and 19:9, but makes no Eucharistic connections.

40. See also Rev 1:6—βασιλείαν, ἱερεῖς τῷ θεῷ καὶ πατρὶ αὐτοῦ

41. Beale, *The Book of Revelation*, 743.

42. Koester, *Revelation*, 625.

43. Caird, *Revelation of Saint John the Divine*, 194.

44. Boring, *Revelation*, 173–74.

45. Koester, *Revelation*, 645.

46. Smalley, *Revelation of John*, 390.

47. Caird, *Revelation of Saint John the Divine*, 198–99. Bauckham, *Climax of Prophecy*, 283–337, differs with Caird and offers detailed reasoning for concluding that the grain harvest is positive (of believers) and the grape harvest is negative (of unbelievers). He sees a transfer of dominion rather than a conversion of the nations (330).

48. Beale, *Book of Revelation*, 788.

49. Aune, *Revelation 6–16*, 877.

50. Rist, *The Revelation of St. John the Divine*, 413.

51. Edmondo, F. Lupieri, *A Commentary on the Apocalypse of John*, trans. Marian Poggi Johnson and Adam Kamesar (Grand Rapids MI: Eerdmans, 1999) 224.

52. Anthony T. Hanson, *The Wrath of the Lamb* (London: SPCK, 1957) 164.

53. Koester, *Revelation*, 661–62.

54. Richard Bauckham, "Judgment in the Book of Revelation," *The Book of Revelation: Currents in British Research on the Apocalypse*, ed. Garrick V. Allen, Ian Paul, and Simon P. Woodman, in *Wissenschaftliche Untersuchungen zum Neuen Testament* (Tübingen: Mohr Siebeck, 2015) 62.

55. Hanson, *Wrath of the Lamb*, 198.

56. Jacques Ellul, *Apocalypse: The Book of Revelation*, trans. George W. Schreiner (New York: Seabury, 1977) 184.

57. Beale, *Book of Revelation*, 830.

58. Ibid., 832.

59. Ibid.

60. Koester, *Revelation*, 398.

61. Ibid.

62. Ibid., 399.

63. Ibid., 466, identifies the manuscripts that say the heavenly altar has four horns (025 046 1006; cf. ESV, NAB, NRSV), but many others omit the number four ($\mathfrak{P}$47 ℵ1 A 027; cf. NET, NIV).

64. Lupieri, *Apocalypse of John*, 164.

CHAPTER 3

Revelation's Other Atonement Metaphors

While John's fullest expression of the meaning of the death of Jesus is found about midpoint of Revelation (Rev 12:1-12), he sets the stage for his comments there through a number of intervening verses, those about the "throne, temple, and altar" (see chapter 2) included. In fact, John uses a variety of words and images that are associated with blood atonement or its effect: "lamb" / ἀρνίον (28 times), "blood" / αἷμα (5 times when referring to the "lamb"), "loosed/freed" / λύω (1 time), and "purchased/bought/ redeemed" / ἀγοράζω (2 times). The connection between "blood" and "the Lamb" is obvious as well as that to which both blood and the Lamb relate.

In the third bowl of wrath (and the second bowl—16:3) mentioned in 16:4-7, John includes blood images that are visited on the earth like the first Exodus plague (Exod 7:17-21). This bowl also echoes the third trumpet (Rev 8:10-11) yet is comprehensive and not limited in scope like that of the third trumpet. Koester suggests, "The vision inverts religious customs from John's world; that is, those who have typically poured out libations to the gods of the empire now have God's anger poured out on them."[1] Beale concludes that the bowls of wrath are a paralleled recapitulation of the seven trumpets.[2]

In this case the collective blood of the saints spills from its overflowing second bowl back onto the earth causing "the rivers and fountains of water" / τοὺς ποταμούς καὶ τὰς πηγὰς τῶν ὑδάτων to "become blood" / ἐγένετο αἷμα (16:4). Those who have followed the Lamb by suffering and dying like he did see their blood serve God's plan as well. As 16:6-7 notes, "because the blood of the saints and the prophets was poured out, and blood was given to them to drink, you are worthy. And I heard the altar saying: Yes, Lord, God, The Almighty, true and right are your judgments" / ὅτι αἷμα ἁγίων καὶ προφητῶν ἐξέχεαν, καὶ αἷμα αὐτοῖς δέδωκας πεῖν· ἄξιοί εἰσιν. καὶ ἤκουσα τοῦ θυσιαστηρίου λέοντος Ναί, κύριε, ὁ θεός, ὁ παντοκράτωρ, ἀληθίαι καὶ δίκαιαι αἱ κρίσεις σου makes clear that this is John's intention.

Note, again, that it is the blood of the Lamb and the saints that works in an active sense in these scenes without reference to God's propitiatory or expiatory satisfaction. John's atonement thinking is otherwise.

"MARTYR/WITNESS": 1:5A

Of related interest to atonement language is John's use of the word "martyr" (ὁ μάρτυς). While this word takes on a different connotation later in Christian history, inasmuch as the book of Revelation declares that its message is "from Jesus Christ, the faithful witness/martyr, the firstborn from the dead" / ἀπὸ Ἰησοῦ Χριοτου, ὁ μάρτυς ὁ ποτός, ὁ πρωτότοκος τῶν νεκρῶν (1:5), the meaning of "witness" or "martyr" (ὁ μάρτυς) is important. Beale suggests,

> Consequently, *marturia* ("witness," and its related word group) is probably not a technical term in the Apocalypse for "martyr." Nevertheless, the word group is used repeatedly in conjunction with the deaths of Christians (in addition to 1:5 and 2:13, cf. 1:9; 11:7; 17:6) in order to show that faithful Christian witness brings suffering, a typical trait also of OT prophets (cf. Luke 11:47–51).[3]

Koester, in part, echoes Beale:

> The Greek word *martys* is not yet a technical term for one who dies for the faith; instead, witness involves attesting to the truth where the truth is disputed. John was relegated to Patmos because of his witness (1:9). For others, witness culminates in death, as in the case of Jesus, Antipas (2:13), and the two witnesses later in Revelation (11:3-10; cf. 6:9; 12:11; 17:6). Yet witness is not simply dying. Attesting to the truth can provoke the opposition that leads to death, 'but witness cannot simply be equated with death (6:9; 12:11).[4]

The above granted, language of "witness" does evoke something of a courtroom scene and that of a judicial proceeding, full explanation forthcoming later in Revelation 12:7-11. Because Jesus bore faithful witness to God before both a Jewish (Sanhedrin) and a Roman (Pilate's) "court," he died and became "the firstborn from the dead" / ὁ πρωτότοκος τῶν νεκρῶν (1:5). Such language surely anticipates at some level Revelation

12:7-9 (which we will address in greater detail in chapters 4 and 5) and the combat scene pitting "Michael and his angels fighting against the Dragon" / ὁ Μιχαὴλ καὶ οἱ ἄγγελοι αὐτοῦ τοῦ πολεμῆσαι μετὰ τοῦ δράκοτος, and more impressively the presence of "Satan" / ὁ Σατανᾶς in that text as "the one who accuses our brothers before God day and night" / ὁ κατη-ʹγωρ τῶν ἀδελφοῶν ἡμῶν, ὁ κατηγορῶν αὐτοὺς ἐμώπιον τοῦ θεοῦ ἡμῶν ἡμέρας καὶ νυκτός (Rev 12:10).

Caird makes the right observation about this matter in his comments on Revelation 12:7-11. The Satan, he says, "holds an appointment as accuser or prosecutor in the lawcourt of God. His task is to arraign men before the bar of the divine justice."[5] Even more specific to the language of "martyr/witness" (ὁ μάρτυς) is the means of victory that John describes in Revelation 12:11: "and they conquered him [The Satan] by the blood of the Lamb and by the word of their testimony ("witness" or "martyrdom"), and they loved not their lives even unto death" / καὶ αὐτοὶ ἐνίκησαν αὐτὸν διὰ τὸ αἷμα τοῦ ἀρνίου καὶ διὰ τὸν λόγον τῆς μαρτυρίας αὐτῶν, καὶ οὐκ ἠγάπησαν τὴν ψυχὴν αὐτῶν ἄχρι θανάτου. The latter clause certainly qualifies John's meaning—that martyrdom (both the Lamb's and believers') should be included as the means for victory.

Ladd's comment speaks to the question about martyrdom very well: "The answer is that every disciple of Jesus must be in principle a martyr and be ready to lay down his life for his faith. Jesus himself taught that more than once that those who would follow him must be ready to take up their cross (Mark 8:4; Matt 10:38), and the cross is nothing less than an instrument of death."[6] Victory is clearly expressed through the laying down of life. Just how God receives this sacrifice, and to what end, is addressed more clearly in Revelation 12.

"Loosed/Purchased" and "His/Slain Lamb's Blood"

Revelation 1:5b-6 and 5:6, 9-10 stand in parallel to each other with the latter qualifying the former in significant ways. The first mention of sin, and the blood of Jesus Christ as the means of freedom from sins, is found in Revelation 1:5b. That John takes up this matter in the opening doxology of The Apocalypse is no minor detail, never mind, as Johns points out, that "only once in Revelation (1:5) is there a reference to believers' sins being atoned by the blood of Christ."[7] Similarly, at a strategic interlude in Revelation 14 (see below "14:4"), John revisits his earlier emphasis on those who were ransomed by the Lamb.

1:5b-6

The word "loosed" / λύσαντι (or "freed") that John uses is suggestive.
What he intends by this word may only be understood in terms of the
relationship it has with "loves" / ἀγαπῶντι and "made" / ἐποίησεν that
are found in 1:5b and 1:6 on either side of "loosed" / λύσαντι (or "freed"),
and the word "purchased" / ἠγόρασας (or "ransomed") found in 5:9. In
fact, Fiorenza has pointed out that in 1:5b and 1:6 these are "three pred-
icative statements" that are reminiscent of the early Christian "baptismal
tradition."[8] That Christ's love is now with them and that Christians are
now free from their sins by the blood of Christ both anticipate that the
redeemed are part of a "kingdom, priests to God" / βασιλείαν, ἱερεῖς τῷ
θεῷ (Rev 1:6). Of particular interest is the middle phrase "loosed (or freed)
us from our sins by his blood" / λύσαντι ἡμᾶς ἐκ τῶν ἁμαρτιῶν ἡμῶν ἐν
τῷ αἵματι αὐτοῦ. Ladd reminds readers that the "Greek idiom here in turn
reflects a Hebrew idiom, so that . . . 'he has freed us from our sins at the
price of his blood'"[9] is John's meaning. That is, "[t]he sacrifice of Christ on
his cross was the cost of loosing men from bondage to their sins."[10]

As for the word "loosed" / λύσαντι (or "freed"), Koester's observations
are on target:

> The verb *lyein* (released) was used for forgiving sins, though without
> reference to sacrifice (Isa 40:2; Sir 28:2; Job 42:9). Christ's blood was
> more commonly identified with words for ransom, which were similar
> in form and indicate both release, as in Rev 1:5, and purchase, as in 5:9
> (*lytroun*, 1 Pet 1:19; *lytrōsis*, Heb 9:12; *apolytrosis*, Rom 3:24-25; Eph
> 1:7). Instead of "released" (*lysanti*, 𝔓18 ℵ A C 1611 2050 2329), some
> manuscripts read "washed" (*lousanti*, P 1106 1841 1854 2053 2062;
> cf. NJB, NRSVfn). The concept of washing in the blood of the Lamb
> appears elsewhere (*plynein*, 7:14; 22:14), but "released" has better manu-
> script support . . . .[11]

While John clarifies the implications of the sacrificial action a bit later
in Revelation 5:9-10 (see below), by inclusion of the word "purchased" /
ἠγόρασας (or "ransomed") he has introduced to the Apocalypse the sure
message that "liberation from our sins is obviously of crucial importance,
though he [John] does not specify in precisely what sense Christ's blood
frees us from them."[12]

Nevertheless, commentators are agreed that Christ's love is demonstrated through his "loosing/freeing" / λύσαντι blood to the end that those

who are freed are likewise "made" / ἐποίησεν priests in his kingdom. Aune points out that "'to free someone from sin,' occurs only here in the NT and in the Apostolic Fathers. λύειν means 'to release, rescue' in the literal sense of setting free from being tied up . . . . Thus, . . . (5.9), . . . God is the new owner, λύειν and ἀγοράζειν are virtually synonymous."[13] To be sure, as Christopher Rowland states,

> There has been much debate over the background to the imagery. The juxtaposition of buying/redeeming/loosing, blood, and a lamb suggests a Passover context, in which deliverance is effected for the children of Israel by the blood of a lamb, bringing deliverance from the angel of death and facilitating the process of liberation from Egypt (Exod 12:22-23, 31). As the hymn in v. 9 suggests, the death of The Lamb—who is no passive victim but one who was a faithful witness (1:5 NRSV)—has brought about release. The Lamb's death has "made them to be a kingdom and priests serving our God, they will reign [assuming that the future rather than the present tense is the earlier reading] on earth" (v. 10).[14]

Beale, therefore, appropriately asks, "But how is the paradox of 'conquering through suffering' to be understood more precisely?" While his answer is on the right path, he says more than the text truly allows. He says that "Christ himself overcame by maintaining his loyalty to the Father through suffering and finally death (cf. 1:5) . . . . He willingly submitted to the unjust penalty of death, which was imposed on him ultimately by the devil. As an innocent victim he became a representative penal substitute for the sins of his people."[15] Suggestions of a penal substitute, however, reflect more of the theological tradition than what Revelation actually verifies.

In other words, Jesus' sacrificial death means that "he reigned as king ironically by conquering death and sin through the defeat at the cross and subsequent resurrection (1:5)."[16] John expresses his meaning of a reigning king who conquers through his own defeat in the perplexing picture of the slain Lamb (5:6, 9) juxtaposed with the lion of the tribe of Judah (5:5). This pairing "constitutes [for John] the most impressive rebirth of images he anywhere achieves."[17] What, therefore, is the relationship among these related yet disparate concepts?

5:6, 9-10

In Revelation every mention of freeing or loosing and the blood of Christ has the slain Lamb in mind. At Revelation 5:6 John introduces "the Lamb"

/ ἀρνίον for the first of twenty-eight times that it is found in the Apocalypse. While ἀρνίον "is diminutive in form and although one should
probably not translate it as a diminutive ("little lamb" or "lambkin"), it
probably does serve to underline its vulnerability. In the Septuagint, *arnion*
[ἀρνίον] is used only of lambs that symbolize vulnerability, whereas *amnos*
[ἀμνός] is used almost exclusively of sacrificial lambs."[18] However, as Beale
notes, "by the first century ἀρνίον ("lamb") no longer had a diminutive
nuance . . . . On the other hand, if the diminutive nuance is still held, it
intensified the contrast between the powerful lion image of OT prophecy
and the fulfillment through the little, apparently powerless lamb."[19]

Bauckham concurs and points out,

> The word "Lamb," referring to Christ, occurs 28 (7 X 4) times. Seven of
> these are in phrases coupling God and the Lamb together (5:13; 6:16;
> 7:10; 14:4; 21:22; 22:1, 3). Four is, after seven the symbolic number
> most commonly and consistently used in Revelation. As seven is the
> number of completeness, four is the number of the world. . . . The 7 X
> 4 occurrences of "Lamb" therefore indicate the worldwide scope of his
> complete victory.[20]

Aune has done yeoman's work unpacking the particulars of the Lamb as
either a metaphor for leader or for sacrifice. He leaves no stone unturned
in surveying the broad literature on either of these metaphorical references.
Having addressed all things related to the two, he concludes (following
Dodd) that "it is not necessary to choose between these two possibilities,
for it seems clear that the author of Revelation has fused both of *these*
associations together in the single figure of the Lamb (Dodd, *Interpretation*, 232)."[21] What we see is the result of "the earthly ministry of Jesus as
a suffering servant of God (cf. Matt 11:2-6=Luke 7:18-23). The central
dramatic scene of this vision segment is the cosmic sovereignty that the
Lamb is revealed to possess . . . ."[22]

In the first place, inasmuch as "the lion of the tribe of Judah has
conquered" / ἐνίκησεν ὁ λέων ὁ ἐκ τῆς φολῆς Ἰούδα, Rowland clarifies
the matter: "The identification of Christ with the Lamb, made throughout
the book, suggests that an act of witness, at great cost, has turned the world
upside down. The victim is shown to be in the right, and the demonstration of that witness shakes the fabric of the cosmos and its institutions to
the core."[23] Truly by "juxtaposing the two contrasting images [Lion of the
Tribe of Judah and the sacrificial Lamb], John has forged a new symbol of

conquest by sacrificial death . . . . The Messiah has certainly won a victory, but he has done so by sacrifice and for the benefit of people from all nations (5:9)."[24] Of course, Bauckham suggests, "Who or what it is that the Lamb has conquered is not expressed (cf. 3:21) (though it is probable that we should see the defeat of Satan by Michael, depicted in 12:7-9, as a symbol of the Lamb's victory). The object of conquest is left undefined in chapter 5 so that the victory should be boundless in scope."[25]

Moreover, Bauckham acknowledges that since the

> blood of the Lamb as the price of redemption . . . goes beyond the role which the blood . . . played in the exodus (Exod 12;12, 23) [then] . . . John alludes not only to the Passover lamb, but also to Isaiah 53:7, where the suffering Servant is portrayed as a sacrificial lamb. He may well have connected this verse with the new exodus language of Deutero-Isaiah and seen the Suffering Servant of Isaiah 53 as the Passover lamb of the new exodus. In any case, it is the central role which the death of Jesus played in the Christian understanding of redemption which accounts for the centrality of the Lamb to Revelation's use of the new exodus motif.[26]

Charles E. Hill sees a connection between sin as a debt that has to be paid off and the bondage of imprisonment that is related to it. He may be forcing Revelation, however, to suggest that "by the price of his blood, has [Christ] rendered to God the acceptable payment which has liberated us from our bondage to sin and death."[27] Such a notion implies that it is to God to whom the payment of blood was made, something that Revelation does not say. John T. Carroll and Joel B. Green avoid saying what Revelation does not say. In their chapter on "The Death of Jesus in Hebrews, 1 Peter, and Revelation," they acknowledge Jesus' death as victory[28] as well as being redemptive, focusing on John's "purchased" language (ἠγόρασας) without indicating to whom the price was paid. They place emphasis most appropriately on "how universal dominion comes into being not through coercive force but through the Lamb's faithful witness unto death."[29]

That God is the subject to whom the purchase price is paid can hardly be the case given that "you [the Lamb] ransomed us *for God* [emphasis added] in your blood [not to God] those from every tribe, tongue, people, and nation" / ἠγόρασας τῷ θεῷ ἐν τῷ αἵματί σου ἐκ πάσης φυλῆς καὶ γλώσσης καὶ λαοῦ καὶ ἔθνους (5:9). Moreover, 14:4 (which parallels this text) says that "these have been ransomed from mankind as firstfruits *for God and for the Lamb* [emphasis added]" / οὗτοι ἠγοράσθησαν ἀπὸ τῶν ἀνθρώοων ἀπαρχὴ τῷ θεῷ καὶ τῷ ἀρνιῷ. Aune points out, "The passive suggests that God is the one who did the purchasing (the passive of divine activity), though the price is not specified. In Rev 5:9c, of course, the price is 'by your blood,' i.e., by your death."[30]

Even so "the new Passover Lamb has been slaughtered and he has ransomed a people for God."[31] The word "slaughtered" / ἐσφαγμένον that John uses to describe the Lamb (5:6, 9, 12; 13:8) has been explored carefully by Koester, who identifies "three dimensions of meaning": vulnerability, deliverance, and atonement.[32] Bauckham summarizes the matter similarly himself. He acknowledges,

> When the slaughtered Lamb is seen "in the midst of" the divine throne in heaven (5:6; cf. 7:17), the meaning is that Christ's sacrificial death *belongs to the way God rules the world.* The symbol of the Lamb is no less a divine symbol than the symbol of "the One who sits on the throne." . . . But if God is not present in the world as "the One who sits on the throne," he *is* present as the Lamb who conquers by suffering . . . . Moreover, Christ's presence (walking among the lampstands: 1:13; 2:1) with his people who continue his witness and sacrifice is also God's presence.[33]

To these two images—"the Lamb standing as having been slain" / ἀρνίον ἐστηκός ὡς ἐσφαγμένον (5:6) and "the one who sits on the throne" / τοῦ καθημένου ἐπὶ τοῦ θρόνου (5:7)—is added a third that is "the Lion of the tribe of Judah" / ὁ λέων ὁ ἐκ τῆς φυλῆς Ἰούδα (5:5). This trilogy of terms captures well the Apocalypse's understanding of God: God is simultaneously all three. Most likely John intends something else as well with the positioning of these three, not the least of which is that in the heavenly scene one always sees the "One who sits on the throne" / τοῦ καθημένου ἐπὶ τοῦ θρόνου (5:7) ("the one on the seat of judgment") by looking through the slain Lamb. Likewise, the "One who sits on the throne" (on the judgment seat) sees everything and everyone always as well by looking through the slain Lamb. Aune makes this point himself with his observation that the Greek prepositional phrase "in the midst" / ἐν μέσῳ (5:6) "can refer to an interval between two things . . . [in terms of] the position of the Lamb . . . in close proximity to the throne."[34] Or, to put it another way, the one on the throne is the Lamb; he is indeed one with God who cannot be seen in his holiness by sinful people except for his self-giving atonement. The inseparability of God and the Lamb is essential to John's atonement theology.

As Beale says,

> the present victorious effect of the Lamb's overcoming resides not only
> in the fact that the Lamb continues to "stand" but also in the fact that
> it continues to exist as a *slaughtered* Lamb; . . . That is, Christ as a Lion
> overcame by being slaughtered as a Lamb, which is the critical event in
> Ch. 5 . . . . The notion of Christ's death by itself as a victory is highlighted
> also by 5:10, which directly links Christ's making his people "a kingdom
> and priests," not to his resurrection, but to his death for them (5:9).[35]

To make this same point, Boring states rather forcefully, "The relationship between them [the Conquering Lion and the Slain Lamb] is *crucial*
to understanding all of Revelation's theology."[36] He provides four different
paths along which interpreters have traveled. One he calls "pop-eschatology"
in which "The Lamb becomes a Lion (Lindsey). The author presents Jesus
as having 'two roles': his 'first coming' as a lamb and his 'second coming'
as a lion. Those who do not respond to the love offered by Jesus in his first
coming get the apocalyptic violence of the second."[37] A second he identifies
as "Lamb to some, lion to others." By that he means that Christ shows his
lamb attributes to believers but he shows his lion attributes to unbelievers,
making Christ a "part-lion, part-lamb."[38] A third option is that "The lamb
is really a lion," in which case the lamb is the "violent Messiah expected in
Jewish apocalyptic."[39] Finally, a fourth option is that "The 'lion' is really the
lamb, representing the ultimate power of God."[40]

This latter understanding Boring stresses with the qualified meaning
associated with the word "conquer" / νῖκάω (found twenty-three times in
Revelation). As he notes, following in part A. Y. Collins,

> "Conquering" in both cases, that of the Christ and that of Christians,
> means no more or less than dying. It never in Revelation designates any
> destructive judgment on the enemies of Christ or Christians. Jesus stood
> before the Roman court, was faithful unto death, and this was his victory
> and his reign . . . . "Conquer" (*nikao*) has in John's situation not only the
> military, violent connotation which he likewise redefines: "In the context
> of the Apocalypse as a whole, 'conquering' means being acquitted in a
> court of law. The acquittal of the faithful is paradoxical . . . . But the testi-
> mony they give and their acceptance of death will win them the acquittal
> that counts—in the heavenly court, in the eyes of eternity" (A. Y. Collins,
> *The Apocalypse*, p. 14). For Christians what it means to "win" has been
> redefined by the cross of Jesus.[41]

14:4

Tying together previous themes that relate to the Lamb, Revelation 14:1-4 pictures the Lamb once again "standing" / ἐστός (cp. 5:6; 7:9), this time on Mount Zion along with the 144,000 (cp. 7:7). Implied in "his [the Lamb's] and his father's name written on their foreheads" / τὸ ὄνομα αὐτοῦ καὶ τὸ ὄνομα τοῦ πατρός αὐτοῦ γεηραμμένον ἐπί τῶν μετώπων αὐτῶν (14:1) is new ownership and a new branding or marking on their persons[42] (cf. 7:3 for the first mention of "sealing" or "marking" in Revelation). There is music (cf. 14:2-3 cp. 7:10-12) as well as the four living creatures and the elders (cf. 14:3 cp. 5:8 and 7:11, 13) who are worshiping the Lamb. While there is no mention of "ransom" in 7:1-17, in 14:3 and 4 ("the ones ransomed from the earth" / οἱ ἠγορασμένοι ἀπὸ τῆς γῆς and "these were ransomed from mankind as firstfruits to God and the lamb" / οὗτοι ἠγοράσθησαν ἀπὸ τῶν ἀνθρώπων ἀπαρχη τῷ θεῷ καὶ τῷ ἀρνίῳ), John echoes 5:9 ("because you were slain and ransomed to God by your blood out of every tribe, and tongue and people and nation" / ὅτι ἐσφάγης καὶ ἠγόρασας τῷ θεῷ ἐν τῷ αἵματί σου ἐκ πάσης φυλῆς καὶ γλώσσης καὶ λαοῦ καὶ ἔθνους).

Moreover, since these believers have been redeemed (5:9; 14:4), they "follow the Lamb wherever he goes" / οὗτοι οἱ ἀκολουθοῦντες τῷ ἀρνιῷ ὅρου ἂν ὑπάγῃ. They likewise are led by the Lamb "because the Lamb in the midst of the throne will shepherd (or lead) them" / ὅτο τό ἀρνίον τὸ ἀνὰ μέσον τοῦ θρόνου ποιμανεῖ αὐτούς (7:17). That is, they are indeed "a kingdom, priests to his God and Father" / βασιλείαν, ἱερεῖς τῷ θεῷ καὶ πατρί αὐτοῦ (1:6) whose duty is to do that which the Lamb has done. Imagery of a sacrificial offering is also obvious in 14:4-5 where the followers of the Lamb are identified as both "firstfruits to God and the Lamb" / ἀπαρχή τῷ θεῷ καὶ τῷ ἀρνίῳ and "blameless" or "without blemish" / ἄμωμοί. Koester acknowledges that "[i]n Jewish tradition the first fruits included grain, grapes, and other crops (Exod 34:22; Num 13:20), which were to be brought to the temple before the rest of the harvest took place (Lev 23:10-14; Deut 26:1-11)."[43] Beale makes the astute connection to Jeremiah 2:2-3 in which firstfruits apply to "the whole nation of Israel redeemed from Egypt 'holy to the Lord, the first of his Harvest.'"[44]

This section also depicts a wedding song and anticipates the marriage supper of Revelation 19. "The new song," as Koester suggests, "speaks of being purchased by the Lamb, which the redeemed understand because they have received the benefits of Christ's death."[45] The notion of a wedding song is also implied, says Koester, because they were purchased from humankind:

> The word "purchase" could connote redemption from bondage (Note on 5:9). Young women could be purchased out of slavery for marriage, and Jewish marriage contracts included assurances that the husband would redeem the woman if she was taken captive (Mur XX, 6; m. Ket. 4:8; Zimmermann, "Nuptial"). In Revelation, Jesus the Lamb plays the part of the faithful husband, who redeems the people who constitute his bride (Rev 5:9; 14:3-4).[46]

While Revelation depicts the Lamb having purchased his followers by his own sacrifice, Koester acknowledges:,

> The cross was "the tree of shame," not honor (Cicero, Rab. Perd. 4.13). To say that the victim of crucifixion was the agent of God's power was foolishness (1 Cor 1:18). Yet the new song identified the Lamb as the one who purchased (*agorazein*) people by his blood (Rev 5:9). Here, the 144,000 are said to have been purchased (*agorazein*) by the Lamb, which means they have received the benefits of his sacrifice (14:3). They understand the song's praise of the Lamb because they have been redeemed by him.[47]

Having acknowledged their redemption, Johns suggests that "a closer look at how John deals with Christ's death in Revelation shows that his primary interest lies in Christ's death as the key turning point in divine warfare—a warfare in which the army of believers follow the Lamb wherever he goes (i.e., in his faithful witness all the way to martyrdom)."[48]

While it remains unstated in the Apocalypse precisely what the concept "slain Lamb" means, an emerging picture is developing. Beale identifies two different proposals. He says that either the Old Testament Passover lamb or the one "led as a sheep to the slaughter" mentioned in Isaiah 53:7 is possible. His conclusion is that "neither should be excluded, since both have in common with the metaphorical picture in Rev 5:6 the central function and significance of the sacrifice of a lamb, which accomplishes redemption and victory for God's people."[49] For this reason the followers of the Lamb are pictured as singing (14:2-3).

Even though the language of victory is not used in Revelation 14, the implications are surely there. The Lamb who is pictured as standing is simultaneously the slain Lamb. In fact, Aune concludes, "The slain Lamb thus represents the image of a conqueror who was mortally wounded while defeating the enemy. Christ's death, the end-time sacrifice of the messianic Lamb, becomes interpreted as a sacrifice that not only redeems but also conquers. The idea of conquering is evoked by Genesis 49, Isaiah 11, and the 'horns' of the lamb."[50]

"THE TREE OF LIFE": 2:7

John's reference to the "tree of life" / τοῦ ξύλου τῆς ζωῆς requires some attention. Because of its connection to "the paradise of God" / τῷ παραδείσῳ τοῦ θεοῦ, echoing Genesis 2:9 and 3:22-24, it anticipates "the tree of life [that] produces twelve kinds of fruit . . . and the leaves of the tree are for the healing of the nations / ξύλον ζωῆς ποιοῦν καρποὺς δώδεκα . . . , καὶ τὰ φύλλα τοῦ ξύλον εἰς θεραπείαν τῶν ἐθνῶν (Rev 22:2).

As Aune indicates, "A number of other Jewish texts use the eating of the fruit of the tree of life as a metaphor of salvation (1 Enoch 25:5; 3 Enoch 23:18; T. Levi 18:11; Apoc. Mos. 28:4; Apoc. Elijah 5:6) . . . ."[51] Certainly John is drawing upon the rich biblical tradition of Adam and Eve having been expelled from the garden, whereas when he mentions to the Ephesian believers (contrasting the Artemisian Temple) this "tree," Beale notes, he "refers to the redemptive effects of the cross, which bring about the restoration of God's presence . . . ."[52]

It is not that much of a stretch to conclude with Colin J. Hemer (who followed Sir W. M. Ramsay): "Ramsay has shown that there is a studied concentration of meaning into all the symbolism of these letters, and it is not impossible that here ξύλον may contain an allusion to the cross."[53] Since, indeed, the Temple of Artemis at Ephesus was a place of asylum, the parallel to the cross is not so far-fetched. Hemer recalls that "[t]he fame of the temple as a place of refuge persists throughout its history."[54] John may be alluding to the cross as true refuge in contrast to the temporary, pseudo-refuge of the Artemisian. Certainly nothing is said of the meaning of the atoning effect of the "tree of life," should it be an allusion to the cross.

"BLOOD OF THE LAMB," "SAINTS," "WITNESSES OF JESUS," AND "THE PROPHETS"

In both Revelation 7:14 and 12:11, John uses "blood of the lamb" language—"blood of the lamb" / αἵματι τοῦ ἀρνίου and "blood of the lamb" / αἷμα τοῦ ἀρνίου respectively. In these two texts the prominence of "blood" stands out. In 7:14 "they washed their robes and made them white in the blood of the lamb" / ἔπλυναν τὰς στολὰς αὐτῶν καὶ ἐλεύκαναν αὐτὰς ἐκ τῷ αἵματι τοῦ ἀρνίου. A similar phrase is found in 12:11 where the "blood of the lamb" is mentioned in relation to the defeat of the Dragon—"and they conquered him by the blood of the lamb" / καὶ αὐτοὶ ἐνίκησαν αὐτὸν διὰ τὸ αἷμα τοῦ ἀρνίου.

7:14

Aune suggests that John has a penchant for "paradoxical metaphor (see other such paradoxical metaphors in 5:5-6; 7:17 [in 5:5-6 the 'lion' is simultaneously 'lamb' and in 7:17 the 'lamb' in 'the midst of the throne will shepherd (or lead) them'])."[55] Using communication to which readers have grown accustomed, Boring states,

> John's mind-jarring rebirth of imagery continues in paradoxical juxtapositions and deformation of language. The robes of the martyrs are white because they are washed in the blood of the Lamb (7:14). Their own death is not an accomplishment of which they can boast. It is Christ's death, not their own courage and determination, which has given them their victor's garment. Their death becomes one with the Lamb's death; Christology and discipleship fade into each other (cf. 12:11).[56]

Aune points out a contrast, however, between 7:14 and 12:11, that in the latter "the notion of atonement is absent, though the idea of martyrdom is very much present [in 12:11] as it is here."[57] Having thus disclaimed atonement language in 12:11, he provides a compelling, extended treatment of the concepts "the blood of the Lamb," "blood of Christ," and "blood of Jesus" found across the New Testament (although not in Revelation), identifying each of these as "metonymy for the death of Christ or more particularly the atoning death of Christ."[58] His conclusion about Old Testament sacrifice, which he sees as background to John's thought in 7:14, is that in "the OT, blood derived from sacrificial animals both removes sin and consecrates only the persons or objects to which it is *physically* applied for purposes of purification (Exod 29:12, 16, 20-21)."[59] In this case John's mention of whitened robes means that "the sin of those who wear them has been atoned for by the sacrificial death of Christ."[60] Moreover, "The martyrs are able to stand before God only because of their purity, based on the atoning death of Christ."[61] Note that purity is in John's thinking.

Koester recalls that "[t]he messianic Lion of Judah was to wash his garments in 'the blood of grapes' (Gen 49:11; Rev 5:5),"[62] which must

be in John's mind when he states that believers have washed their robes
in the blood of the Lamb. He further suggests, "The imagery combines
connotations from crucifixion and sacrifice. Jesus' blood was shed through
scourging, the nailing of hands and feet, and other wounds (Matt
27:24-26; John 19:34; 20:25; cf. Josephus, *J. W.* 2.613)."[63] John, if he means
these things, is clearly being more inferential than explicit. He is, however,
quite direct in saying that these faithful believers are so only because they
"continue to trust in the Lamb, who bought them by his blood (5:9). Such
enduring faith to the end demonstrates that they have been 'released from
their sins by his blood' (1:5) so that their sins have been washed away and
they have been purified (cf. Heb. 9:14; 1 John 1:7)."[64]

To be sure, "[t]he blood that was shed through violent death was
usually understood to bring uncleanness (Num 35:33; Ps 106:38; Isa 59:3;
1QM XIV, 2–3), but Revelation reverses this understanding so that the
crucifixion is a sacrifice that brings cleansing (cf. Heb 9:14; 1 Pet 1:2;
1 John 1:7)."[65] As Koester further maintains,

> Thematically, those who are cleansed by the Lamb's blood bear witness to
> Christ's power to save (12:11), while his opponents shed innocent blood
> (6:10; 17:6; 18:24; 19:2). The threatening visions show the moon and
> water turning to blood as a sign that perpetrators of violence will one day
> succumb to it (6:12; 8:7-8; 11:6; 14:20; 16:3-4).[66]

Moreover, Beale suggests, "The reference in ch. 7 is a fulfillment of Daniel
11–12 preview of the latter-day tribulation, where the saints are 'made
white' through the 'refining,' 'purging,' and 'cleansing' fire or persecution,
so that they come out as undefiled and blameless (cf. 14:4-5)."[67]

Smalley concurs that the group described in "7:13-14 encompasses the
entire company of the redeemed, from all times and all places (as in verse
9), including those who have died for their faith, and not simply a select
group of martyrs . . . ."[68] Such a notion finds precedent in 4 Macc 6:10;
7:4b where martyrs are described as victorious over their persecutors.[69]

12:11

While in 7:14 the language of washing in blood is certainly evocative,

> [s]ome interpreters suggest that the imagery refers specifically to baptism,
> which early Christians construed as cleansing and putting on a garment
> (Acts 22:16; Gal 3:27) . . . . Other interpreters propose that washing in

the Lamb's blood entails martyrdom and link cleansing to purification through suffering (cf. Dan 11:35; 12:10 RSV). Nevertheless, martyrdom is unlikely [here] since redemption by Christ's blood benefits all Christians, not only martyrs (Rev 1:5-6; 5:9-10), and when the author has martyrs in mind, he makes it clear, as in 12:11.[70]

These comments notwithstanding, Aune, following the lead of a number of others,[71] sees Revelation 12:10-12 as a redactional interpolation due to its emphasis on martyrdom that he finds "otherwise touched on only in 12:17."[72] Beale comments precisely on the matter:

> The saints' status in heaven has been legitimized finally by Christ's suffering on the cross. All believers, past, present, and future, "have overcome him [the devil] because of the blood of the Lamb." The death of Jesus is the ultimate basis for their ability to "overcome." But the second affirmation, that they overcame also "because of the word of their testimony," indicates that the testimony of their faith in the word of the gospel is the second ground on which they obtain saving benefits of Jesus' death and "overcome" existentially.[73]

Ladd likewise confirms that the "background of martyrdom stands behind these words. They loved their Lord more than life itself and willingly suffered death rather than deny Christ . . . . Their martyrdom was their victory over Satan . . . . It is clear that victory over Satan is a spiritual victory which is often won even in the terrible experience of martyrdom."[74] Therefore, "the picture does not primarily connote the idea of a select group of martyrs, but encompasses the entire company of the redeemed."[75] Of course, "[i]n Revelation, the martyrs are emblematic of the faithful. The writer does not assume that every faithful Christian will die violently, but the martyrs show readers the kind of steadfast faith to which the whole community is called."[76]

Beale reaches his conclusion, in part, based on John's use of "διά with the accusative ["by the word" / διὰ τὸν λόγον] to indicate the basis of something [which] is very close to the idea of means, as in 13:14."[77] In other words, God uses both Jesus' death and that of the saints in his victory scheme. Both the Lamb's blood and the believers' own blood ("and they conquered him by the blood of the Lamb and by the word of their testimony ["witness" or "martyrdom"] and they did not love their life to the point of death" / καὶ αὐτοὶ ἐνίκησαν αὐτὸν διὰ τὸ αἷμα τοῦ ἀρνίου καὶ διὰ τὸν λόγον τῆς μαρτυρίας αὐτῶν, καὶ οὐκ ἠγάπησαν τὴν ψυχὴν αὐτῶν ἄχρι θανάτου) are the means of victory over the Dragon. Hill agrees that the "victory is attained because the Lamb has already shed his own blood, and as a result, also because the redeemed who confess him on earth follow his example in giving up their lives rather than their confession."[78]

While who or what the Lamb has conquered is not identified directly here, Bauckham concludes that it is "probable that we should see the defeat of Satan by Michael, depicted in 12:7-9, as a symbol of the Lamb's victory."[79] Moreover, "[t]he continuing and ultimate victory of God over evil which the rest of Revelation describes is no more than the working-out of the decisive victory of the Lamb on the cross."[80]

To Beale's credit, he anticipates the role of the Satan's defeat in the matter of redemption. He notes, "The actions described are the heavenly counterpart of earthly events recorded in vv 1–6 . . . . When there is conflict between the saints and the world on earth, there is corresponding conflict in the heavenly dimension."[81] Mark R. Bredin is correct as well: "Jesus conquers Satan by uncovering this deception; he shows that the way of God is that of nonviolent faithful witness."[82] Similarly, in an apt turn of phrase, Gerald L. Stevens reminds readers that "as we have seen, John's conquering language is subversive rhetoric against both Jewish and Roman storylines. His ideology of victory is antithetical to the themes of Jerusalem or Rome, because John's ideology is driven by the gospel story."[83]

Certainly, Bauckham, Beale, and Bredin are all correct to look ahead to Revelation 12 for further insights into the meaning of the atoning death of Christ. These atonement images all point in the direction that Revelation 12 (a piece of which was explored above) will address by contrasting self-surrender in one scene with victor-warrior imagery in the adjoining scene.

19:2

In the next-to-last mention of "blood" / αἷμα, ατος, τό in Revelation (see below Rev 19:13, "Dressed in a Garment Dipped in Blood," for the final reference to "blood"), the heavenly chorus sings, a portion of which includes "true and just are his judgments, because he judged the Great Harlot" / ἀληθιναι καὶ δίκαιαι αἱ κρίσεις αὐτοῦ· ὅτι ἔκρινεν τὴν πόρνην τὴν μεγάλην (19:2). At the news of the implosion of "The Great City / ἡ πόλις ἡ μεγάλη (17:18), which is "the judgment of the Great Harlot" / τὸ κρίμα τῆς πόρνης τῆς μεγάλης (17:1), John says, "Fallen, fallen is Babylon the great" / Ἔπεσεν, ἔπεσεν Βαβυλὼν ἡ μεγάλη (18:2). Why her fall occurs, and why she is judged, is because she has shed "the blood of his servants out of her hand" / τὸ αἷμα τῶν δούλων αὐτοῦ ἐκ χειρὸς αὐτῆς (Rev 19:2).

The meaning of the Greek construction "out of her hand" / ἐκ χειρὸς αὐτῆς has led to either of two conclusions: "on her" or "by her hand." If LXX 2 Kings 9:7 is background for this partial verse ("you will judge the blood of my servants the prophets and the blood of all the servants of the LORD at the hand of Jezebel" / ἐκδικήσεις τὰ αἵματα τῶν δούλων μου τῶν προφητῶν καὶ τὰ αἵματα τῶν πάντων δούλων κυρίου ἐκ χειρὸς Ιεζαβελ), then, as Aune states, it "does not mean that vengeance would be taken upon her."[84] In other words, the verse means that God "avenged the death of his servants caused by her."[85] Otherwise, as Koester observes, this Great Harlot, the "city that ruins the world through its alliance with the beast is finally ruined when the beast turns against it (Rev 17:3, 16). The whore who lured earth's kings into immoral relationships is stripped bare by kings (17:2, 16) . . . . Evil becomes evil's own undoing."[86]

God's plan of vengeance on the evil perpetrators is to allow evil to have its way, which leads to its self-defeat (cf. chapter 6, "The Revelation of Redemption," below) by turning inward upon itself.[87] This means of God's judgment for "the blood of his servants from her hand" / τὸ αἷμα τῶν δούλων αὐτοῦ ἐκ χειρὸς αὐτῆς (Rev 19:2) is consistent with God and the Lamb's wrath (cf. chapter 1, "Sacrifice and the Wrath of the Lamb") identified elsewhere in the Apocalypse. God allows evil to do as it wills to do, which results in its very self-destruction.

"WHITE GARMENTS"

Inasmuch as in 7:14 they "washed their robes and made them white in the blood of the Lamb" / ἔπλυναν τὰς στολὰς αὐτῶν καὶ ἐλεύκαναν αὐτὰς ἐν τῷ αἵματι τοῦ ἀρνίου, there are a few other occasions that John mentions "white robes" or their equivalent. Some "will walk with me in white" / περιπατήσουσιν μετ᾽ ἐμοῦ ἐν λευκοῖς (3:4), others "might be dressed in white garments" / ἱμάτια λευκὰ ἵνα περιβάλῃ (3:18), and other believers "are dressed in white garments" / περιβεβλημένους ἐν ἱμάτοις λευκοῖς (4:4).

3:4

Koester offers a reasonable summary of the "white garments" as denoting purity, holiness, and honor.[88] While in 3:4, there are "a few names in Sardis who have not soiled their garments" / ὀλίγα ὀνόματα ἐν Σάρδεσιν ἃ οὐκ ἐμόλυναν τὰ ἱμάτια αὐτῶν, "they will be dressed in white garments" / περιμαλεῖται ἐν ἱματίοις λευκοῖς. These faithful believers will not be blotted out of the book of life (a matter at which we will look below at "Revelation 3:5"). Koester mentions that "[s]ome interpreters suggest that the readers' 'clothing' refers to the identity they received in baptism, when they 'put on' Christ . . . . It is clear that the garment signifies Christian identity, but whether it connotes baptism is uncertain."[89]

Should it be that baptism is in the background of John's meaning here, the relation between baptismal washing and atonement is possible, especially if Paul's understanding of baptism from Romans 6:3-4 is in view: "we were buried therefore with him by baptism into his death" / συνετάφημεν οὖν αὐτῷ διὰ τοῦ βαπτισματος εἰς τὸν θάνατον. Paul's mention of death suggests that there is some relationship between Jesus' death, burial, and resurrection and that of a believer's symbolic death that relates to being "justified from sin" / δεδικαίωται ἀπὸ τῆς ἁμαρτίας. This intriguing Pauline phrase—"justified from sin"—speaks to that which God accomplished through Jesus and is not far removed from John's counsel to the Sardians to live faithfully in the reality of their forgiveness. Certainty, however, about the baptismal robe analogy in Revelation is not possible.

3:18

In John's counsel to the Laodicean believers, he directs that they "should put on white garments" / ἱμάτια λευκιὰ ἵνα περιβάλῃ (3:18). While some have suggested that "the white clothing is a direct contrast to the local black wool that provided revenue for the city (Ramsay, *Letters*, 429; Hemer, *Letters*, 208),"[90] one cannot be certain. Most likely there is a contrast with nakedness rather than (or at least as much as) with local inference.

Aune, moreover, says, "White garments are frequently referred to in Revelation (3:4-5; 4:4; 6:11; 7:9, 13, 14; 19:8, 14 . . .). Such garments have several kinds of association. They are the color used on festal or sacral occasions and can also symbolize purity (cf. Eccl 9:8; Ps 104:2)."[91] Aune mixes freely "white garments" / ἱμάτια λευκὰ and "white robes" / στολὴ λευκή (6:11) without differentiation.

The relation between the white robes here and atonement is certainly implied by means of a contrast that Rowland points out. He says that the "nakedness anticipates the fate of Babylon in 17:16, when it is stripped of wealth, a fate the reader is warned to avoid (16:15). The address to the angel (v. 18) repeats the importance of white robes to clothe nakedness."[92]

What is not obvious in Rowland's observation about 17:16, however, is the role that the color white plays. Of course, only those who have been washed in the blood of the Lamb have cleansed garments (see above "White Garments" and "Blood of the Lamb" and below "White/Washed Robes").

4:4

Revelation 4:4 pictures "twenty-four elders seated [on thrones] dressed in white garments" / εἴκοσι τέσσαρας περεοβυτέρους καθημένους περιβεβλημένους ἐν ἱματίοις λευκοῖς. Any connection between the atoning death of the Lamb and the elders depends in large part on the identity of these elders.

Elders appear occasionally in the Old Testament as present before Yahweh. Aune points out each of these places as well as the role that elders played in the Qumran Community, in the synagogue, and in early Christianity.[93] He likewise provides a lengthy excursus in which he says that "no solution has found universal acceptance"[94] as to the twenty-four elders' identity. Given the seven different options that he catalogs, most agree that the group "symbolizes both cosmic kingship and the sum of the twelve tribes of Israel plus the Twelve Apostles, together constituting the new people of God."[95]

This "heavenly entourage,"[96] as Beale calls them, wear white clothing applicable to "deceased saints" anticipating that believers "will receive a like reward."[97] Koester adds that "[w]hite was widely thought to be suitable for God or the gods and for those who worshiped them. White robes connote purity, holiness, and honor. They are worn by angelic beings and the people who come into God's presence through resurrection."[98]

While Smalley sees the main emphasis of white garments to be "spiritual purity, and therefore of victorious morality,"[99] Boring concludes that "triumphant authority" associated with "martyrdom" is tied to the "white garments" of those around the throne as well as those identified in other places in Revelation.[100] Should it be that these twenty-four are representatives of the twelve tribes and the twelve apostles, their presence in the heavenly scene is guaranteed only by the sacrificial death and presence of the Lamb. When the Lamb takes the book, they, "the twenty-four elders[,] fall before the lamb . . . and sing a new song saying: 'Worthy are you to take the book and to open the seals of it, because you were slain and you purchased to God by your blood from every tribe and tongue and people and nation, and you made them a kingdom and priests to our God, and they shall reign on earth'" / οἱ εἴκοσι τέσσαρες

περσβύτεροι ἔπεσαν ἐνώπον τοῦ ἀρνιου . . . καὶ ᾄδουσιν ᾠδὴν
καινὴν λέγονετες· Ἄξιος εἶ λαβεῖν τὸ βιβλίον καὶ ἀνοῖξαι τὰς
σφραγῖδας αὐτοῦ, ὅτι ἐσφάγης καὶ ἠγόσασας τῷ θεῷ ἐν τῷ αἵματι
σου ἐκ πάσης φυλῆς καὶ γλώσσης καὶ λαοῦ καὶ ἔθνους, καὶ ἐποίησας
αὐτοὺς τῷ θεῷ ἡμῶν βασιλείαν καὶ ἱερεῖς, καὶ Βασιλεύουσιν ἐπὶ τῆς
ψῆς (5:8-10).

Given that the Lamb is truly the centerpiece of the twenty-four elders'
attention, his sacrifice is undoubtedly of significance for the clothes that they
wear. The elders are in this place for the purpose of worship only because
of the "Lamb standing as having been slain" / τὰς ψυχὰς τῶν ἐσφαγμένων
(5:6) and because of his blood (see above "Blood of the Lamb").

"WHITE/WASHED ROBES"

In a slight change in terminology, John introduces the word "robe" / στολὴ
and uses it in four places instead of continuing with the more familiar
"garment" / ἱμάτοιν that he has previously used. There is, however, no
difference in meaning between these terms but rather only that "the two
alternate."[101] Only once in Revelation are white robes identified specifically as such because of the "blood of the Lamb" / τῷ αἵματι τοῦ ἀρνίου
(cf. 7:14).

6:11

With the Lamb's opening of the seven seals (Rev 6:1–8:2), at seal five
"there was given to each of them a white robe" / ἐδόθη αὐτοῖς ἑκάστῳ
στολὴ λευκή (6:11). The image of "souls of those who had been slain" /
τὰς ψυχὰς τῶν ἐσφαγμένων crying out and then receiving a white robe
conjures much speculation that fills commentaries. Namely, does this text
suggest something of the state of physically dead believers? Are they in a
state of "blessedness and rest, even though the state of final and perfect
blessedness awaits the return of Christ and the resurrection of the body?"[102]

Caird's language is beneficial here:

> When a slaughtered beast was laid on the altar of burnt offering in the
> Jerusalem temple, its blood was allowed to run around the foot of the
> altar. John presumably has some such analogy in mind . . . . They are
> now underneath the altar because at some time in the past they have been
> offered in sacrifice on it. The heavenly altar is counterpart to the earthly
> gibbet.[103]

In every way, given that life was associated with the blood, John is surely indicating "lives or selves"[104] as being tantamount to blood. Boring even suggests, "Without intending to speculate on the nature of an 'intermediate state' after death, but before the final resurrection, John uses this constellation of imagery to picture the 'selves' of the Christian martyrs as already present in heaven, having been taken there through their death at the hands of the Romans."[105] Beale, however, leans in a more theological direction, concluding that believers receive glorified bodies at the final resurrection so that the giving of white robes here is a "metaphor" that "connotes the idea of a purity resulting from persevering faith tested by the refining fire of tribulation."[106] At the very least, being invested with a white robe in Revelation symbolizes "victory, purity, and bliss,"[107] similar to Koester's nomenclature of purity, holiness, and honor.[108]

Aune admits that the "[t]iming of this investiture is puzzling, for garments are given to the souls of martyrs (separated from their earthly bodies) only when they complain that they have not been avenged. This seems to suppose an intermediate state of indeterminate duration between death and the assumption of the heavenly mode of existence symbolized by the white robe."[109]

The question about the timing of the investiture may find an answer in John's words that "they will rest yet a little time" / ἀναπαύσονται ἔτι χρόνον μικρόν (6:11). This intriguing phrase "yet a little time" / ἔτι χρόνον μικρόν resurfaces when

> [a]n angel reiterates the promise given to the martyrs by saying that the time (*chronos*) [χρόνον] of waiting is about to "end" (10:6) and God's mysterious purposes will be completed (*telein*, 10:7). Yet if one asks how long this will be, later visions simply repeat what was said to the martyrs: The time will continue until the faithful have finished (*telein*) [ἐτελέσθη] giving their witness (11:7). Only then will the last trumpet sound.[110]

Koester further notes,

> Revelation identifies the "short time" in which the martyrs rest and others bear witness (6:11) with the "short time" in which Satan persecutes the saints on earth (12:12). In the visionary world this short time is three and a half years (11:2–3; 12:6, 14; 13:5), yet . . . [t]he Apocalypse gives readers no way of knowing how long the time will last. Readers will see God's justice being worked out against the perpetrators of injustice in a way that allows for repentance. The people who have shed the blood

of the martyrs will eventually be given blood to drink, which seems just (16:6); yet this is not simple retribution, since those who have killed do not suffer death but are allowed to live so that repentance is still possible (16:8, 11).[111]

John realizes that during the "short time" / χρόνον μικρόν (related to the grand scheme of eternity), more violence will come against believers until the time "is fulfilled" / πληρωθῶσιν. This passive verb, which as Koester points out "appears in some Greek manuscripts (A C 2344) and early versions, works equally well . . . [as] [t]he aorist active subjunctive *plērōsōsin* [that] appears in some sources (ℵ 025 046; Oecumenius; Andreas) . . . . Finally, however, both the active and passive forms yield a similar sense: God's justice will take place when the faithful on earth have finished bearing witness."[112]

John's language of "they will rest" / ἀναπαύσονται (6:11) has a variety of uses across the literature: for the righteous dead, for burial, for the assembly of the dead, for those in heaven, for paradise, and for the repose of the soul.[113] Koester notes, "Rest is a sign of divine favor (14:13; cf. Heb 4:10); the followers of the beast experience torment, not rest (Rev 14:11). The idea that the faithful rest until the final resurrection is traditional (*L.A.B.* 3:10; 19:12; 28:10; 1 Thess 4:14) . . . , but visionary time does not correspond to ordinary time."[114]

The location of these martyrs that are under the altar and before God's heavenly throne (6:9) means that they have found favor with God.[115] The fact that they are given a white robe

> signifies the hope of resurrection. It was traditional to picture heavenly beings in radiant white attire, like that worn by the elders around God's throne (4:4; cf. Dan 7:9; 2 Macc 11:8; Mark 9:3; 16:5; Acts 1:10). Some writers also envisioned the dead being "clothed" with everlasting life and glory through resurrection (*1 En.* 62:15-16; 1 Cor 15:53-54; 2 Cor 5:1-4; *Mart. Asc. Isa.* 4:16; 9:9, 17), so giving the martyrs white robes assures them that they will share in these things (Rev 20:4-6, 11-15).[116]

7:9 (on 7:13–14, see above, "Blood of the Lamb")
In three related phrases, "having been dressed in white robes" / περιβεβκημένους στολὰς λευκάς, "these were dressed in white robes" / Οὗτοι οἱ περιβεβκημένοι τὰς στολὰς τὰς λευκάς, and "they washed their robes and made them white in the blood of the Lamb" / ἔπλυναν τὰς στολὰς

αὐτῶν καὶ ἐλεύκαναν αὐτὰς ἐν τῷ αἵματι τοῦ ἀρνίου, John sees in his vision the fulfilled relationship that believers will have with God.

The "white robes" / στολὰς λευκὰς differ very little from other of the references to "white garments" / ἱμάτια λευκὰ (3:18) found in Revelation. In fact, Aune links all of these sayings together including "pure white linen" / βύσσινον λαμπρὸν καθαρόν. He says, "White garments are frequently referred to in Revelation (3:4-5; 4:4; 6:11; 7:9, 13, 14; 19:8, 14 . . .)."[117] Sometimes, however, the phrase is "white robe" (6:11; 7:9, 14, 14), other times "white garments" (3:4-5; 4:4; and also "pure white linen" / βύσσινον λαμπρὸν καθαρόν (19:8, 14).

Koester is likely correct when he suggests, "The white robes signify purity, holiness, and honor. They are appropriate for people in worship as well as for heavenly beings."[118] These robe and garment references, being white, all tie together with John's atonement theme—namely that "the blood of the Lamb" / τὸ αἷμα τοῦ ἀρνίου has accomplished this whitening.

22:14

The final mention of "robes" / τὰς στολὰς is in Revelation 22:14. John says, "Blessed are those who wash their robes" / Μακάριοι οἱ πλύνοντες τὰς στολὰς αὐτῶν. He surely means that those robes are white, as is the case elsewhere in Revelation. At any rate, those whose robes are washed have the "right" / ἡ ἐκξουσία to eat "from the tree of life [that] means everlasting life in God's presence."[119] Koester also acknowledges that cleansed robes "assumes that access to the tree comes from the cleansing provided by Christ (7:14)."[120]

Tying together the robes with the atonement theme, Caird recalls,

We have already been told that Christ has "released us from our sins with his own life-blood" (i.5), and have been shown the white-robed throng of Conquerors safely installed in paradise, because "they have washed their robes and made them white in the life-blood of the Lamb" (vii.14; and now we can add the those who wash their robes, that is, those who face martyrdom in the confidence that the Cross is the sign of God's victory over evil with ant evil within, already see the city of God descending out of heaven with it gates open to receive them, giving them immediate access to the tree of life).[121]

"Fine Linen, Pure and Bright": 19:7-8; 19:14 (21:2, 9)

In yet another turn of phrase, John introduces "pure fine linen" / βύσσινον λαμπρὸν καθαρόν when describing the bride of the Lamb: "and it was given to her that she should be dressed in bright pure linen" / καὶ ἐδόθη αὐτῇ ἵνα περιβάληται βύσσινον λαμπρὸν καθαρόν (19:7). He continues to qualify the meaning of this expression, indicating "for the linen is the righteous deeds of the saints" / τὸ γὰρ βύσσινον τὰ δικαιώματα τῶν ἁγίων ἐστίν (19:8).

The connection between "pure fine linen" as given to her [the bride] / ἐδόθη αὐτῇ and "righteous deeds of the saints" / τὰ δικαιώματα τῶν ἁγίων is intriguing. In fact, the translation of τὰ δικαιώματα as "righteous deeds" is questionable if not properly qualified. Ladd points out that the "basic meaning of the word is 'statute' or 'ordinance,'"[122] as the word is used in 15:4 for God's "righteous judgments" forthcoming in the bowls of wrath. What is as stake is the well-known "tension in biblical theology, between faith (membership of the bridal community) and good works (the need for righteous behaviour)."[123] The phrase "righteous deeds [or "righteous judgments"] of the saints" / τὰ δικαιώματα τῶν ἁγίων prompted Beale to note one of the classical Greek grammatical questions addressed by Moulton, Howard, and Turner (*A Grammar of New Testament Greek III*) with which interpreters have wrestled:

> There is much ambiguity [with regard to genitives] in NT interpretation. Often a Gen might equally well be subjective or objective: it is moreover important not to sacrifice fullness of interpretation to an over precise analysis of syntax. There is no reason why a Gen in the author's mind may not have been both subjective and objective.[124]

In other words, does John intend the linen to be "for" the saints as a gift from God or "as a result" of the works of the saints?

Beale pours over this matter with precision and thoroughness before concluding with "the dual notion of *righteous acts by the saints* and God's *righteous acts for the saints . . . .*"[125] His understanding is that

> readers can be encouraged to obey the exhortation by the knowledge that God has provided grace for them to clothe themselves now by the power of the Spirit (note "it was given to her" in 19:8a and see on 1:4, 12 for the relation of 1:4, 4:5; and 5:6 to 1:20) and also be recalling that they will

receive "pure garments" from God at the end of their pilgrimage individually and corporately (3:5; 6:11; 7:13-14; 19:7-8), all of this representing escalated levels of redemptive blessing. 19:8 is vague temporally, so that it includes saints being clothed both throughout the age and at the end of the age. From the human side, the good works focus on the saints' witness to their faith in Christ, which is supported by the focus on witness in v 10 and by the direct linkage in 3:4-5 of white clothing with the notion of witness (cf. likewise 3:14 with 3:18).[126]

Aune makes the perceptive observation of the "list of luxury goods in 18:12 and by the depiction of Babylon-Rome as clothed in 'fine linen and purple and scarlet [garments]' in 18:16. There is an intentional contrast here between the 'fine linen' of Babylon-Rome (a symbol of decadence and opulence) and the 'fine linen, shining and pure' of the bride of the Lamb."[127]

John takes up the bridal theme once more in 21:2, 9 when he compares the new Jerusalem to "a bride adorned for her husband" / νύμφην κεκοσμηένην τῷ ἀνδρι αὐτῆς. While there is no mention of the clothing, the connection to the "pure fine linen" of 19:7-8 is certainly in view. Since Revelation 21 pictures the new heaven and new earth, and its particular emphasis on "the dwelling of God is with men" / σκμνηνὴ τοῦ θεοῦ μετὰ τῶν ἀνθρώπων, only the purity accomplished by the Lamb on behalf of the bride makes such a relationship possible.

What remains unambiguous for John is that the blood of the Lamb, as counterintuitive as that image seems, is the means by which garments of believers are washed clean. The blood makes the garments white.

"DRESSED IN A GARMENT DIPPED IN BLOOD" AND "THE WINEPRESS OF THE FURY OF THE WRATH OF GOD" 19:13

With a final image, of a "garment dipped in blood" / ἱμάτιον βεβαμμένον αἵματι (19:13), John describes how "the heavenly army follows him on white horses, dressed in pure white linen" / τὰ στρατεύματα τὰ ἐν τῷ οὐρανῷ ἠκολούθει αὐτῷ ἐφ᾽ ἵποις λευκοῖς, ἐνδεδυμένοι βύσσινον λευκὸν καθαρόν (19:14). Before John introduces the heavenly army, however, he describes the "white horse, and the one seated upon it called Faithful and True, and with righteousness he judges and makes war . . . and his name is called The Word of God" / ἵππος λευκός, καὶ ὁ καθήμενος ἐπ᾽ αὐτὸν πιστὸς καλούμενος καὶ ἀληθιός, καὶ ἐν δικαιοσύνῃ κρίνει καὶ πολεμεῖ . . . , καὶ κέκληται τὸ ὄνομα αὐτοῦ ὁ Λόγος τοῦ Θεοῦ (19:13). Reddish rightly points out, "This entire scene has been shaped by Isaiah 63:1-6, which portrays God as a warrior returning victoriously from his battle against the Edomites. One of the most obvious borrowings is the statement that he wears 'a robe dipped in blood' (19:13)."[128]

Certainly the heavenly army's dress as "pure white linen" / βύσσινον λευκὸν καθαρόν (19:14) echoes that of the bride of the Lamb of "pure bright linen" / βύσσινον λαμπρόν καθαρόν (19:8). These nearly identical phrases reflect the atoning work of the Lamb as described in the texts previously evaluated. What to make of the garment of the "Faithful and True" being dipped in blood is a source of concern. Some commentators suggest that this blood is that of those who oppose the Lamb, while others say that it is Jesus' own blood. For instance, Ladd says, "We must agree with the majority of modern commentators [of his day] that the robe dipped in blood refers to garments bloodied from conflict and battle, not from Christ's blood on the cross."[129] Beale concurs with Ladd, but not before presenting his investigation including those arguing on either side.[130] Boring (agreeing with Caird[131] and Rowland[132]), however, parts company with Beale:

They are thus identical with the martyr church previously pictured as already triumphant in heaven (7:9-17; 14:4; 17:14), and wear the same white linen garment that signals the faithful martyr church (19:14; cf. 6:11; 7:14; 19:8; 22:14). In John's paradoxical imagery their garments are white because they have washed them in the blood of the Lamb, and his are red because he has died for all, even those he "conquers" in the eschatological "battle." Unlike some portrayals of the eschatological battle (e.g. the War Scroll of the Qumran community), in Revelation the saints do not participate in the final battle. The victory belongs to God/ Christ alone, and was already achieved in the Christ event that spans incarnation and crucifixion.[133]

Koester concurs with Boring's assessment and suggests, "The most probable is that this is Christ's own blood."[134] Reddish's conclusion adds clarity to the debate:

In the Apocalypse, Jesus is indeed the mighty conqueror, the warrior on the white horse (19:11-21). He conquers not by violence, however, but by his own death, for John sees Christ's robe dipped in blood. The blood is likely Christ's own blood, a visual reminder that he conquered by his own death. His weapon was not a sword, but a cross. John's interplay of lion-lamb imagery in chapter 5 is also a reminder that Christ's conquering is martyrological. Through this imagery, John declares that the only "conquering" that is consistent with the values of God is conquering that occurs through self-sacrifice and love, not through violence.[135]

Judith Kovacs and Christopher Rowland concur that 19:11 in patristic exegesis was viewed as a "symbolic depiction of the incarnation and sacrifice of Christ, thus rendering the violent imagery harmless."[136] The white robe is pictured as bloody before the final battle takes place, which surely means that the triumph of the conquering messiah "comes through suffering and death."[137] In most cases, those who argue for the rider's blood-sprinkled garment being blood of his enemies do so only if they conclude similarly about the winepress of 14:18-20 (see above, "Temple," 14:15, 17) being unbelievers' blood.

Bauckham speaks in summary fashion to this question at the conclusion of his chapter "The Apocalypse as a Christian War Scroll":

As we have seen, human participation in the eschatological war is not rejected in Revelation, but emphasized and, again, *depicted* in terms drawn from traditions of holy war, which are then carefully reinterpreted in terms of faithful witness to the point of death. The distinctive feature of Revelation seems to be, not its repudiation of apocalyptic militarism, but its lavish use of militaristic *language* in a non-militaristic *sense*. In the eschatological destruction of evil in Revelation there is no place for real armed violence, but there is ample space for the imagery of armed violence . . . .

He aims to show that the decisive battle in God's eschatological holy war against all evil has been won—by the faithful witness and sacrificial death of Jesus.[138]

Kovacs and Rowland reach deeply into the historical well and cite both Cyprian and Origen who identify this scene as the incarnation "which brings judgment on Israel and salvation to the gentiles," with Origen instructing that "the robe dipped in blood (19:13) is a symbol of Christ's incarnation and sacrifice (*On Martyrdom*, 50)."[139]

19:15, 21 (1:16; 2:12, 16; 2:27; 12:5)

An additional comment is necessary about the scene with the rider on the white horse in 19:11-21. He is described as having "a sharp sword coming out of his mouth with which to strike the nations, and he will shepherd (or rule) them with a rod of iron; and he will tread the wine press of the fury of the wrath of God the Almighty" / ἐκ τοῦ στόματος αὐτοῦ ἐκπορευ-ʹεται ῥομφαία ὀξεῖα, ἵνα ἐν αὐτῇ πατάξῃ τὰ ἔθνη, καὶ αὐτὸς ποιμανεῖ αὐτοὺς ἐν ῥάβδῳ σιδηρᾷ καὶ αὐτὸς πατεῖ τὴν ληνὸν τοῦ οἴνου τοῦ θυμοῦ τῆς ὀργῆς τοῦ θεοῦ τοῦ παντοκράτορος (19:15). The "sharp sword," "rod of iron," and the "shepherd/rule" / ποιμανεῖ language that John uses is relevant to the atonement discussion.

John's first mention of the "sharp two-edged sword coming out of his mouth" / ἐκ τοῦ στόματος αὐτοῦ ῥουφαία δίοτομος ὀξεῖα ἐκπορευομ-ένη refers to the son of man in 1:16. The description of the sword in 1:16 is virtually duplicated in 19:15 with the exception of the word "double-edged" / δίοτομος that is absent in 19:15. The function of sword in 2:16 is to fight those in Sardis who do not repent. Its function in 19:15 is against "the nations" / τὰ ἔθνη and in 19:19-21 is against "the armies" / τα στρα-τεύματα. Uniquely, the sword is always described as coming "out of the mouth" / ἐκ τοῦ στόματος of both the Son of Man (1:16; 2:12; 2:16; 19:21) and the rider on the white horse (19:15). Aune, therefore, rightly concludes, "That the sword issues from the mouth of Christ suggests that the sword is a metaphor for the tongue, i.e., the word he speaks."[140] John, undoubtedly, is using inverted imagery again since nowhere in "the liter-ature of Judaism"[141] is such language found of Messiah or of any other warrior.

When John adds "shepherding" (or "ruling") with a rod of iron" / ποιμανεῖ αὐτοὺς ἐν ῥάβδῳ σιδῃᾷ (19:15) (calling on language from Isa 11:4, which in the LXX says "he will strike the earth with the word of his mouth" / πατάξει γῆν τῷ λόγῳ τοῦ οτόματος αὐτοῦ, while the Hebrew text uses in place of the word "word" the word "rod" / בְּשֵׁבֶט), he is acknowl-edging the means of victory to be that of the spoken word, yet a word of unbreakable power. He has already pointed in this direction in Revelation 2:27 when the Son of Man declares to the church at Thyatira that "he will shepherd/rule them with a rod of iron, as when earthen vessels are broken" / ποιμανεῖ αὐτοὺς ἐν ῥάβδῳ σιδηρᾷ ὡς τὰ σκεύη τὰ κεραμικὰ συντρι-βεται. Once that image is combined with the same of Revelation 12:5 when the "male child is about to shepherd/ rule all the nations with a rod of iron" / υἱόν, ἄροεν, ὃς μέλλει ποιμαίειν πάντα τὰ ἔθνη ἐν ῥάβδῳ σιδηρᾷ, John's meaning becomes even clearer. By understanding the inversion of imagery that he uses so frequently, translating the word ποιμανεῖ as "shepherd" rather than "rule" makes the best sense. After all, shepherds used wooden rods, not iron ones. So the phrase "rod of iron" that John chooses should not turn the rider on the white horse into an earthly warrior or ruler who pummels people into submission. This rider is likewise the Lamb who was slain. His "shepherding," nevertheless, is unbreakable like the "rod of iron" / ῥάβδῳ σιδηρᾷ indicates. He leads by his own self-giving sacrifice.

These images are preliminary and anticipatory of John's concluding comment about the rider on the white horse. What he sees and says in summary is, "he treads the winepress of the fury of the wrath of God the almighty" / αὐτὸς πατεῖ τὴν ληνὸν τοῦ οἴνου τοῦ θυμοῦ τῆς ὀργῆς τοῦ θεοῦ τοῦ πάτοκράτορος (19:15). By remaining consistent with the inversion of images, that which John sees does not permit a shift in perspective of the slain Lamb becoming a violent warrior, something that John has taken care to avoid as indicated above in each text thus far. Caird's consistent reading of John is quite compelling. He observes,

> If we study the present passage without prejudice, we shall certainly conclude that the wine of the fury of the wrath of God is John's symbol for judgment, and that the winepress represents something quite different, namely the means by which the wine of judgment is prepared. When we remember that the cup of wrath is the cup which Babylon herself mixed (xviii.6), it becomes reasonable to suppose that the winepress, like the Cross, is a place where God has turned the murderous acts of men into the means of their own judgment. The third point confirms this view; for having mentioned the winepress, John at once reverts to the garment, which we have seen to be already soaked in blood before ever the judgment of God's enemies has begun.[142]

In all thus far, John "envisions an end to the injustice that has plagued the world"[143] based on the sacrificial death of the Lamb and his followers. Moreover, reference to the "white robes," "white garments," and "fine linen, pure and bright," all suggest victory, purity, and bliss, which Beale mentions[144] and which Koester in his summary of purity, holiness, and honor[145] suggests. How believers come to receive these white robes and pure linen garments, and equally how the rider on the white horse has a "garment dipped in blood" with a metaphorical double-edged sword for a tongue, while holding an iron rod in hand, are all tied to the atoning death of Jesus—the blood of the Lamb—his self-sacrificial death. All of these

images contribute to yet another theme: how names come to be written in
the Book of Life.

"THE BOOK OF LIFE (OF THE LAMB)"

Revelation 3:5; 13:8b; 17:8b; 20:12b; 20:15; and 21:27 include a distinct
phrase: "the book of life" / τῆς βίβλιον τῆς ζωῆς (3:5), τῷ βίβλιον τῆς
ζωῆς τοῦ ἀρνίου (13:8), τὸ βίβλιον τῆς ζωῆς (17:8), βιβλίον . . . τῆς
ζωῆς (20:12), τῇ βιβλῳ τῆς ζωῆς (20:15), and ἐν τῷ βιβλῳ τῆς ζωῆς τοῦ
ἀρνίου (21:27) respectively. Only in 13:8 and 21:27 are "the book of life"
and "of the Lamb" combined. Moreover, only in 13:8 is the most complete
picture shown. There the reader finds "the book of life" / τῷ βιβλῳ τῆς
ζωῆς, "of the Lamb" / τοῦ ἀρνίου, and "having been slain" / ἐσφαγμένου.
Altogether 13:8 reads, "in the book of life of the Lamb having been slain
from the foundation of the world" / ἐν τῷ βιβλῳ τῆς ζωῆς τοῦ ἀρνίου
τοῦ ἐσφαγμένου ἀπὸ καταβολῆς κόσμου. In each of these descriptions
the connection to atonement is evident.

3:5

The message to the Sardians is that "thus the one who conquers will be
robed in white garments, and his name will not be blotted out of the book
of life" / ὁ νικῶν οὕτως περιβαλεῖται ἐν ἱματίοις λευκοῖς, καὶ οὐ μὴ
ἐξαλείψω τὸ ὄνομα αὐτοῦ ἐκ τῆς βίβλου τῆς ζωῆς (3:5). In this text
John introduces the "book of life" for the first of six times and combines
two atonement-related themes: the book and blotting out of names.

John is likely relating the book of life to Psalm 69:28 and "the scroll of
the living" and "the scroll" God has written in Exodus 32:32 that contains
the living. Koester suggests,

> Those passages warn of sinners being blotted out of God's scroll, meaning
> that they are threatened with death. Other sources expect those recorded
> in the scroll to have a glorious future in God's city (Isa 4:3), which came
> to be understood as resurrection to deathless life (Dan 12:1) . . . .
>   Some thought people were listed in the scroll as a reward for righteous
> living (Herm. Sim. 2.9; Apoc. Zeph. 3:6-9), but others said they were
> included in the scroll through divine grace, which gave them citizenship
> in heaven and hope of everlasting life (Luke 10:20; Phil 3:20–4:3). This
> is the perspective of Revelation, in which the Creator inscribes people
> in the scroll from the time the world was made (Rev 13:8; 17:8). To
> have one's name in the scroll of life gives assurance of divine preservation

(4Q504 1–2 VI, 14), and to have one's name blotted out connotes death (4Q381 31 8). When extended to the future, having one's name removed from the scroll signifies final condemnation (Jub. 30:22; 36:10; 1 En. 108:3; Shem. Es. 12), whereas those whose names are not blotted out receive everlasting life (Jos. As. 15:4). In Revelation, those inscribed in the scroll find endless life in New Jerusalem (Rev 20:15; 21:27).[146]

Besides the Jewish traditions, Greco-Romans also kept lists of their citizens to ensure benefits of citizenship the same way that criminals once executed would have their names removed from citizenship records.[147]

The theological question implied in the language of "his name will not be blotted out of the book of life" / οὐ μὴ ἐξαλείψω τὸ ὄνομα αὐτοῦ ἐκ τῆς βιβλου τῆς ζωῆς (3:5) is an important one. Some see this whole matter as a veiled threat with divine grace prevailing over human account-ability. By virtue of names being in the Lamb's book of life before the world was created (13:8; 17:8), they are there by God's plan the same way that those who worship the beast are not in the book of life. In particular, those concluding a positive predestination maintain that "those whom God has placed in the scroll never fall away, whereas those who engage in false worship were never in the scroll at all. If people who appear to be believers fall away, this is taken to mean that they were never truly in the scroll . . . ."[148]

To be sure, "Revelation leaves readers with a tension. There is no sugges-tion that God determined to exclude some people from his scroll at the dawn of time, thereby consigning them to the beast."[149] While this theolog-ical matter will likely continue to be debated, John's atonement inferences point to the significance of the blood of the Lamb as his priority. Of course, only a full reading of the Apocalypse makes this emphasis clear (see the references above and below—especially 7:14).[150] Those who are included in the book of life are so only because of the blood of the Lamb. What that blood accomplished is precisely the goal that this project is pursuing.

13:8

Reference to the "book of life" appears a second time in 13:8—"the one whose name was not written in the book of life of the Lamb who was slain from the foundation of the world" / οὗ οὐ γέγραπται τὸ ὄνομα αὐτοῦ ἐν τῷ βιβλίῳ τῆς ζωῆς τοῦ ἀρνίου τοῦ ἐσφαγμένου ἀπὸ καταβολῆς κόσμου (13:8).

This verse has translation challenges to be sure. Were the names written in the book of life before the world was created, or was the Lamb slain before the world was made?[151] Certainly, the close proximity of the words "slain Lamb" to the "foundation of the world" leads many to connect these two rather than to connect "foundation of the world" with the "book of life." Koester says what most translators admit: "The Greek word order is confusing."[152] Some interpreters, having looked ahead to 17:8, may arrive at a conclusion based on what is found there that informs John's meaning here (see "17:8b" below). However, knowing or not knowing what John says in 17:8, he may very well mean both things. Lupieri says that "both the sacrifice of the Lamb and the salvation that this sacrifice brings have existed from the foundation of the world. Faced with the discontinuous presence of Satan, John affirms the unchangeable stability of the 'scroll of life' that is the Lamb's book and that existed before the world itself."[153] Caird suggests as much in his confirmation that John should "be allowed here to say something complementary. For the elect are those who have been predestined by God to be ransomed out of all the nations by the lifeblood of the sacrificial Lamb . . . . If the cross is indeed the full revelation of God's love and purpose, then must it not belong to the eternal order?"[154]

While this theological predestinarian matter may not be settled definitively to many readers' satisfaction, the relationship between those who are named in the book of life and the slain Lamb is indisputable. Any person whose name is found there is so because of the atoning death of the Lamb. John could hardly have been clearer on this point.

17:8b

John revisits the matter of the one "whose name is not written in the book of life from the foundation of the world" / ὧν οὐ γέγραπται τὸ ὄνομα ἐπὶ τὸ βιβλίον τῆς ζωῆς ἀπὸ καταβολῆς κόσμου (17:8b) in the context of the judgment and fall of the great harlot. In this scene there is amazement on the part of those whose names are not written in the book of life that "the great city Babylon the Great" / ἡ πόλις ἡ μεγάλη, Βαβυλὼν ἡ πόλις ἡ ἰσχυρά (18:10) is about to collapse. From every indication she seems indestructible, but not so according to John's vision.

While the phrase in question echoes 13:8, it connects "the name written in the book of life" / γέγραπται τὸ ὄνομα ἐπὶ τὸ βιβλίον τῆς ζωῆς (17:8) exclusively with "from the foundation of the world" / ἀπὸ καταβολῆς κόσηου and does not include reference to "the Lamb having been slain" / τοῦ ἀρνίου τοῦ ἐσφαγμένου (13:8). John's point is simply that believers are not so enamored with this beastly city that is destined to collapse in contrast to "the ones who dwell upon the earth" / οἱ κατοικοῦντες ἐπὶ τῆς γῆς (17:2). The reason for their disbelief is that the "beast that you saw was and is not, and is about to rise out of the bottomless pit and go into destruction" / τὸ θηρίον ὃ εἶδες ἦν καὶ οὐκ ἔστιν, καὶ μέλλει ἀναβαίνειν ἐκ τῆς ἀβύσσου, καὶ εἰς ἀπώλειαν ὑπάγει (17:8a). In other words, the seemingly relentless beast will come to an end, all present appearances to the contrary. While the beast will make a final appearance, it will be only to "go to destruction" / εἰς ἀπώλειαν ὑπάγει (17:9).

The connection of this reference and mention of the book of life to other references to it elsewhere in Revelation, along with the immediate context, confirms its association with atonement. In fact, in this same passage in which John mentions the book of life he likewise mentions that "he saw the woman drunk on the blood of the saints and the blood of the witnesses of Jesus" / εἶδον τὴν γυναῖκα μεθύουσαν ἐκ τοῦ αἵματος τῶν ἁγίων καὶ ἐκ τοῦ αἵματος τῶν μαρτύρων Ἰησοῦ (cf. 17:6 in the section above, "Temple," 16:1; 16:17).

Of course, only a full reading of the Apocalypse makes this point clear (see the references above and below—especially 7:14). [155] Again, those who are included in the book of life are so only because of the blood of the Lamb. In terms of being added to the book of life, John says that this is only on the basis the Lamb's blood. He never says specifically in these texts what this blood accomplishes. Only in other places where John mentions ransom language and purification language does he give any indication of what the Lamb's atoning work accomplishes (cf. 5:6, 9 in particular). John does, of course, suggest something additional in Revelation 12 that clarifies his atonement thinking.

20:11-15 (20:12b); 22:1-3

As for the "great white throne" / θρόνον μέγαν λκευκὸν (20:11), John pictures in it the power of redemption at its zenith. With the opening of the books of judgment and of life, the Lamb of God, although unnamed in the scene, is present by inference in unmistakable ways. When John reports that he "saw the dead, great and small, standing before the throne, and the books opened" / εἶδον τοὺς νεκρούς, τοὺς μεγάλους καὶ τοὺς μικρούς, ἑστῶτας ἐνώπον τοῦ θρόνου, καὶ βιβλία ἠνοίχθησαν (20:12a), there would be no standing in the presence of God without the redeeming, purifying power of the Lamb. While these opened books recall a tradition in which good and bad actions were recorded in an appropriate ledger [indicating] . . . that God's judgment is not arbitrary but is based on written evidence . . . [h]ere, no arguments are presented. Satan formerly acted as the accuser (Rev 12:10-12), but he no longer has that role. The vision mentions only the judge, the people, and the record.[156]

The reason the former accuser has no role in this judgment scene is because "another book was opened, which is [the book] of life" / ἄλλο βιβλίον ἠνοίχθη, ὅ ἐστιν τῆς ζωῆς (20:12b). This book of life has a direct relationship with the Lamb. He or she whose "name is [found] in the book of life" [has been so] "from the foundation of the world" / τὸ ὄνομα ἐπὶ τὸ βιβλίον τῆς ζωῆς ἀπὸ καταβολῆς κόσμου (17:8), the same way that "the Lamb was slain from the foundation of the world" / τοῦ ἀρνίου τοῦ ἐσφαγμένου ἀπὸ καταβολῆς κόσμου (13:8). Koester suggests, "The implication is that being named in the scroll is a gift of God rather than the result of one's good deeds. It is a form of grace, which should be encouraging to readers."[157] John conveys that "[t]he scroll of life gives assurance that salvation is ultimately God's doing."[158]

Koester concurs as well that "[s]ince Christ shares God's throne (Rev 3:21; 12:5), some interpreters think that here he shares the role of judge . . . , but Christ's role is implicit at best."[159] Certainly in the throne room scenes of Revelation 4–5 and 22:1-3 the Lamb is present. In the former scene, "he came and took out of the right hand of the one seated on the throne. And when he took the book, the four living creatures and the twenty-four elders fell before the Lamb" / ἦλθεν καὶ εἴληφεν ἐκ τῆς δεξιᾶς τοῦ καθημένου ἐπι τοῦ θρόνου. καὶ ὅτε ἔλαβεν τὸ βιβλίον, τὰ τέσσαρα ζῷα καὶ οἱ εἴκοσι τέσσαρες πρεσβύτεροι ἔπεσαν ἐνώπιον τοῦ ἀρνίου (5:7-8).

Similarly, as John is nearing the close of the Apocalypse, and his "theology" is coming to full expression, there is another throne room scene in Revelation 22. Strikingly, there is a great river "flowing out of the throne of God and the Lamb" / ἐκπορευόμενον ἐκ τοῦ θρόνου τοῦ θεοῦ καὶ τοῦ ἀρνίου (22:1, 3). In something of a grand theological finale, God and the Lamb are presented as the co-equals that they have always been. In fact, there is no inference in this scene; rather the Lamb and God are unambiguously one. The redemptive Lamb and the One on the throne are strictly unified. By all accounts, John's comments at the climax of the Apocalypse sound remarkably like his introductory ones: "Grace to you and peace from the One who is, and the One who was, and the One who is coming, and from the seven spirits which are the ones before his throne, even from Jesus Christ, the faithful witness/martyr, the firstborn from the dead and the leader of the kings of the earth" / χάρις ὑμῖν καὶ εἰρήνη ἀπὸ ὁ ὢν καὶ ὁ ἦν καὶ ὁ ἐρχόμενος, καὶ ἀπὸ τῶν ἑπτὰ πνευμάτων ἃ ἐνώπιον τοῦ θρόνου ἀτοῦ, καὶ ἀπὸ Ἰησοῦ Χριστοῦ, ὁ μάρτυς ὁ πιστός, ὁ πρωτότοκος τῶν νεκρῶν καὶ ὁ ἄρχων τῶν βασιλέων τῆς γῆς (1:4-5). Moreover, because of the redemptive work of the Lamb, "they [believers] will see his [God's] face" / ὄψονται τὸ πρόσωπον αὐτοῦ (22:4) echoing Matthew 5:8—"Blessed are the pure in heart, for they shall see God" / μακάροι οἱ καθαροὶ τῇ καρδίᾳ, ὅτι αὐτοὶ τὸν θεὸν ὄψονται. Only "if someone was not found having been written in the book of life, was he thrown into the lake of fire" / εἴ τις οὐχ εὑρέθη ἐν τῇ βίβλῳ τῆς ζωῆς γεγραμμένος, ἐβλήθη εἰς τὴν λίμνην τοῦ πυεός. (20:15). Koester concludes,

> At the last judgment, people are judged according to their works, but salvation ultimately depends on divine favor, as shown by their names being inscribed in the scroll of life (20:12-15; 21:27). Logically, the tension is awkward, but it shapes the readers' perspectives in a twofold way: On the one hand, people are accountable for what they do, so they are to resist sin and evil. On the other hand, if the world seems so dominated by evil that resistance appears futile (13:4), the scroll of life gives assurance that salvation is ultimately God's doing. The tension encourages people to resist compromise with evil without making them despair of the future.[160]

21:27

John's final mention of "only the ones having been written in the Lamb's book of life" / εἰ μὴ οἱ γεγραμμένοι ἐν τῷ βιβλίῳ τῆς ζωῆς τοῦ ἀρνίου occurs at 21:27. At this point in his vision "God Almighty and the Lamb are the temple" / ὁ θεός, ὁ παντοκράτωρ, ναός αὐτῆς ἐστιν, καὶ τὸ ἀρνίου (21:22). Of special note is that "nothing unclean enters into it and no one who does abomination or falsehood" / οὐ μὴ εἰσέλθῃ εἰς αὐτὴν πᾶν κοινὸν καὶ ποιῶν βδέλυγμα καὶ ψεῦδος (21:27) is present there either. Moreover, nothing "alien to the character of God"[161] will ever be in God's presence. The Lamb's atonement, in other words, has purified all who are present, that is, all whose names are written in the Lamb's book of life.

"Nowhere," Caird concludes, "in the New Testament do we find a more eloquent statement than this of the all-embracing scope of Christ's redemptive work."[162] The power of the sacrificial Lamb secures the names of all who are in God's presence. Aune, interestingly, suggests, "It is likely that the phrase 'except those inscribed in the Lamb's book of life' was added during a final stage of composition."[163] As the text stands, however, the atoning power of the Lamb rises yet again to prominence in John's Apocalypse. Beale says that for those whose names are in the book, "salvation has been determined: their names were entered into the census book of the eternal new Jerusalem before history began."[164] He further acknowledges that "they were identified at that time as ones who would benefit from the Lamb's redemptive death. Therefore, they have been given the protection of eternal *life*, which comes as a result of the Lamb's death."[165] Koester concurs with these insights himself: "People are written in the scroll from the foundation of the world, which makes it an act of divine favor . . . . At the last judgment, people are held accountable for what they do, yet access to God's city ultimately comes from inclusion in the scroll, which is an act of grace."[166]

CONCLUSION

This conglomerate of atonement metaphors and images that John uses is quite remarkable by all accounts. The richness in his choice of terms is a welcome contribution to the biblical tradition of sacrifice. Among the things that he emphasizes, the Lamb certainly takes priority with the sacrificial connotations and Passover blood that relate to it. Purchased (ransomed), cleansing, and purifying are the dominant themes found in connection with the Lamb.

John does make clear as well that the Lamb was slain and that believers who follow him may be slain themselves—either intentionally or as collateral damage in a war-torn world operating with the misguided notion that war brings lasting peace. Behind these slayings, John makes evident that there are evil powers at work in Four Horsemen, varieties of monster-like creatures, Beasts of Land and Sea, a Great Red Dragon, Evil Angels, a False Prophet, and a Great Harlot (metaphorically Babylon described as a blood-drunkened harlot), all related to and empowered by one whom John describes as "the great Dragon, the ancient serpent, called the Devil, and Satan, the deceiver of the ones who inhabit the earth—the one cast down into the earth, and his angels cast down with him" / ὁ δράκων ὁ μέγας, ὁ ὄφις ὁ ἀρχαῖος, ὁ καλούμενος, Διάβολος καὶ ὁ Σατανᾶς, ὁ πλανῶν τὴν οἰκουμένην ὅλην—ἐβλήθη εἰς τὴν γῆν, καὶ οἱ ἄγγελοι αὐτοῦ μετ᾽ αὐτοῦ ἐβλήθησαν (Rev 12:9). These iterations of evil are granted permission by God to do their worst, and this they do with great vitriol—shedding the blood of the Lamb, the blood of believers, and the blood of unbelievers throughout the ages.

John's atonement imagery is that of purchase and ransom, a temple, throne, altar, blood, fire, winepress and wine, bowls of incense, cup, grain and grape harvests, white garments and robes, fine linen, and God's wrath all pointing consistently to the redemption theme found at the heart of the Apocalypse. Those who are cleansed and ransomed by this blood have their names written in the Lamb's book of life. In all of these blood allusions, John's atonement language is prevalent. He characteristically inverts concepts and uses language that reflects God's capacity to convert negatives into positives. Blood that whitens, a slain lamb and martyrs who conquer and sit on thrones, an altar of sacrifice that speaks, and a slaughtered lamb who is ironically the author of the book of life are all counterintuitive images that John puts into service to speak the truth of God's redemptive plan. The slain yet victorious conqueror communicates this message of victory through a metaphorical double-edged sword that is his very tongue with which he speaks the message with an iron-like strength. All of these concepts are at one with the atoning death of Jesus—the blood of the Lamb—which is his self-sacrificial death after whom follow his faithful believers who are committed to a similar fate should that be their spiritual privilege and destiny.

Notes

1. Craig R. Koester, *Revelation: A New Translation with Introduction and Commentary*, The Anchor Yale Bible (New Haven: Yale University Press, 2014) 652.

2. G. K. Beale, *The Book of Revelation: A Commentary on the Greek Text*, The New International Greek Testament Commentary, ed. I. Howard Marshall and Donald A. Hagner (Grand Rapids MI: Eerdmans, 1999) 808–809.

3. Ibid., 190. See also Paul Ellingworth, "The *Marturia* Debate," *Bible Translator* 41 (1990): 138–39.

4. Koester, *Revelation*, 216.

5. George B. Caird, *The Revelation of St. John the Divine* (New York: Harper and Row, 1966) 154.

6. George E. Ladd, *A Commentary of the Revelation of John* (Grand Rapids MI: Eerdmans, 1972) 41.

7. Loren L. Johns, "Atonement and Sacrifice in the Book of Revelation," *The Work of Jesus Christ in Anabaptist Perspective: Essays in Honor of J. Denny Weaver*, ed. Alain Epp Weaver and Gerald J. Mast (Telford PA: Cascadia, 2008) 129.

8. Elisabeth Schüssler Fiorenza, *The Book of Revelation: Justice and Judgment* (Philadelphia: Fortress, 1985) 71. See also D. R. Carnegie, "Worthy Is the Lamb: The Hymns in Revelation," in *Christ the Lord: Studies in Christology Presented to Donald Guthrie*, ed. Harold H. Rowdon (Downers Grove IL: InterVarsity, 1982) 246–47.

9. Ladd, *Commentary of the Revelation of John*, 27.

10. Ibid.

11. Koester, *Revelation*, 217.

12. Charles E. Hill, "Atonement in the Apocalypse of John: A Lamb Standing as if Slain," in *The Glory of the Atonement: Biblical, Historical & Practical Perspectives, Essays in honor of Roger Nicole*, ed. Charles E. Hill and Frank A. James III (Downers Grove IL: InterVarsity, 2004) 192.

13. David Aune, *Revelation 1–5*, Word Biblical Commentary (Dallas: Word, 1997) 47.

14. Christopher C. Rowland, "The Book of Revelation," *The New Interpreter's Bible*, vol. 12, ed. Leander Keck (Nashville: Abingdon, 1998) 602.

15. Beale, *Book of Revelation*, 353.

16. Ibid., 193.

17. Caird, *Revelation of Saint John the Divine*, 73.

18. Johns, "Atonement and Sacrifice in the Book of Revelation," 132.

19. Beale, *Book of Revelation*, 354.

20. Richard J. Bauckham, *Theology of the Book of Revelation*, New Testament Theology, ed. James D.G. Dunn (Cambridge: Cambridge University Press, 1993) 66–67.

21. Aune, *Revelation 1–5*, 368.

22. Ibid., 373.

23. Rowland, "The Book of Revelation," 602–603.

24. Bauckham, *Theology of the Book of Revelation*, 74.

25. Ibid.

26. Ibid., 71.

27. Hill, "Atonement in the Apocalypse of John: A Lamb Standing as if Slain," 194.

28. John T. Carroll and Joel B. Green, "The Death of Jesus in Hebrews, 1 Peter, and Revelation," *The Death of Jesus in Early Christianity* (Peabody MA: Hendrickson, 1995) 144–45.

29. Ibid., 146.

30. Aune, *Revelation 1–5*, 361.

31. Bauckham, *Theology of the Book of Revelation*, 72.

32. Koester, *Revelation*, 377, notes the following:

1. Vulnerability. Revelation contrasts the lion, which was known for killing sheep, with the Lamb, who was killed (Rev 5:5-6). The LXX used *arnion* in metaphors connoting vulnerability: a gentle lamb led to the slaughter or dragged away by predators (Jer 11:19; 50:45 [27:45 LXX]). Other texts pictured the righteous as innocent lambs among the nations (Pss. Sol. 8:23) or lambs in the midst of wolves (2 Clem. 5:2-4). The word *amnos* was also used for vulnerable lambs, which could not live safely with predators—at least not in the current age (Mic 5:7; Sir 13:16-17; Isa 11:6; 65:25; cf. Babrius, the word *arēn* was used similarly, T. Gad 1:7). The suffering servant of Isa 53:7 was like a lamb led to the slaughter.

2. Sacrifice of deliverance. Like the lambs at Passover, Jesus was slain (*sphazein*, Rev 5:6; Exod 12:6). In the Passover tradition, lambs' blood was smeared around the doors of Israelite houses. The blood did not atone for sin but protected people from death and helped bring liberation from slavery so they could serve as God's kingdom of priests—as is accomplished by Jesus' blood (Exod 12:21-27; 19:6; Rev 5:9-10). Passover motifs appear in Revelation's plague visions (Rev 8–9; 16; Exod 7–12), the redeemed singing the song of Moses and the Lamb beside the sea (Rev 15:2-4; Exod 15), and the woman who represents God's people being carried on eagles' wings to safety in the desert (Rev 12:14; Exod 19:4). Therefore, the Lamb motif might also recall the exodus (cf. 1 Cor 5:7; John 1:29; 19:14, 37; 1 Pet 1:19; Justin Martyr, Dial. 111.3).

3. Sacrifice of atonement. The introduction to Revelation said that Jesus "released us *from our sins* by his blood, and made us a kingdom, priests to his God and Father" (Rev 1:5-6; emphasis added). Similar language is used in 5:9-10 without the reference to sins. But given the similarities, readers may have identified the Lamb as a sacrifice for purification and removal of guilt (Lev 14:12-13, 21; John 1:29; cf. Sib. Or. 3:625-26; Beckwith; Müller; Hofius, "Ἀρνίον"; Slater, Christ, 166) However, lambs were most commonly offered in the temple each morning and evening, and in other contexts they were not clearly linked to atonement (Exod 29:38-41; Num 28:3-4; Sib. Or. 3:578). So if atonement is suggested in Rev 5, it remains a subtheme (Johns, Lamb, 128–30).

33. Bauckham, *Theology of the Book of Revelation*, 64.

34. Aune, *Revelation 1–5*, 352

35. Beale, *Book of Revelation*, 352.

36. M. Eugene Boring, *Revelation*, Interpretation (Louisville KY: John Knox, 1989) 109.

37. Ibid. By "Lindsey," he means Hal Lindsey, *There Is a New World Coming* (Ventura CA: Vision House, 1973); Hal Lindsey with C. C. Carlson, *The Late Great Planet Earth* (Grand Rapids MI: Zondervan, 1970).

38. Boring, *Revelation*, 109.

39. Ibid., 110.

40. Ibid.

41. Ibid., 111.

42. David Aune, *Revelation 6–16*, Word Biblical Commentary (Dallas: Word, 1998) 455, says, "The combination of the notions of sealing or tattooing with the term δοῦλοι, "slaves, servants," indicates that this metaphor is derived from the Eastern practice of tattooing secular and religious slaves, (Dölger, *Sphragis*, 58)."

43. Koester, *Revelation*, 611. He also points out that "a few manuscripts say that the redeemed are *ap' archēs* (from the beginning; 𝔓47 א), perhaps recalling that the redeemed are in the scroll of life from the foundation of the world (Rev 13:8)."

44. Beale, *Book of Revelation*, 743.

45. Koester, *Revelation*, 609.

46. Ibid., 611.

47. Ibid., 617–18.

48. Johns, "Atonement and Sacrifice in the Book of Revelation," 126.

49. Beale, *Book of Revelation*, 351.

50. Ibid.

51. Ibid., 152.

52. Ibid., 235.

53. Colin J. Hemer, *The Letters to the Seven Churches of Asia in Their Local Contexts* (Grand Rapids MI: Eerdmans, 1986) 43. He provides expanded detail of the usage of ξύλον and δένδρον to buttress his conclusion. Also Edmondo, F. Lupieri, *A Commentary on the Apocalypse of John*, trans. Marian Poggi Johnson and Adam Kamesar (Grand Rapids MI: Eerdmans, 1999) 117; 354; 360, arrives at a similar conclusion.

54. Ibid., 48.

55. Aune, *Revelation 6–16*, 474.

56. Boring, *Revelation*, 131.

57. Aune, *Revelation 6–16*, 474–75.

58. Ibid., 475.

59. Ibid.

60. Ibid.

61. Ibid.

62. Koester, *Revelation*, 422.

63. Ibid.

64. Beale, *Book of Revelation*, 436.

65. Koester, *Revelation*, 422.

66. Ibid.

67. Beale, *Book of Revelation*, 437.

68. Stephen S. Smalley, *The Revelation of John: A Commentary on the Greek Text of the Apocalypse* (Downers Grove IL: InterVarsity, 2005) 198.

69. Aune, *Revelation 6–16*, 702.

70. Koester, *Revelation*, 429–30.

71. Aune, *Revelation 6–16*, 702.

72. Ibid.

73. Beale, *Book of Revelation*, 663.

74. Ladd, *Commentary of the Revelation of John*, 172–73.

75. Beale, *Book of Revelation*, 438.

76. Koester, *Revelation*, 552.

77. Beale, *Book of Revelation*, 664.

78. Hill, "Atonement in the Apocalypse of John: A Lamb Standing as if Slain," 205.

79. Bauckham, *Theology of the Book of Revelation*, 74.

80. Ibid., 75.

81. Beale, *Book of Revelation*, 651. What Beale does not say in his comments on 12:7 is that there is a connection between what is described here and what 12:5 mentions. We shall, however, be making that connection ourselves below (see chapter 6).

82. Mark R. Bredin, "Hate Never Dispelled Hate: No Place for the *Pharmakos*," *Biblical Theology Bulletin* (Fall 2004): 112.

83. Gerald L. Stevens, *Revelation: The Past and Future of John's Apocalypse* (Eugene OR: Pickwick, 2014) 391.

84. David Aune, *Revelation 17–22*, Word Biblical Commentary (Dallas: Word, 1998) 1023.

85. Ibid.

86. Koester, *Revelation*, 735.

87. Beale, *Book of Revelation*, 928–29, suggests that God is pictured here as actively punishing those who reject the truth and preserving his "just reputation by punishing those who deny him."

88. Koester, *Revelation*, 314:

> 1. Purity. White clothes are the opposite of those that are stained, which here means tainted by sin (Rev 3:4). The multitude in 7:13-14 wears robes that have been made white in the blood of the Lamb. Those who enter New Jerusalem wash their robes, whereas those outside are unclean (21:27; 22:14-15). The heavenly armies that come with Christ wear pure white linen (19:14). Greco-Roman religious practice also associated white with purification (Aelius Aristides, *Orations* 48.31).
>
> 2. Holiness. Holiness means setting what is clean apart for service to God. Those who wear pure white are said to walk with Christ. Since Christ is holy, those who are with him must be holy (Rev 3:7). This meaning is evident in visions in which worshipers wear white as

they stand before the throne of God, who is holy (4:4; 7:9). Heavenly beings were described wearing white (Dan 7:9; Matt 17:2; John 20:12; Acts 1:10; *1 En.* 14:20). Participants in Greco-Roman religious rites in Asian cities commonly wore white, since that was the color most appropriate to the gods (Plato, *Leg.* 956A; Aelius Aristides, *Orations* 48.30; Plutarch, *Mor.* 771D; P.Oxy. 471.101).

3. Honor. Honor is the positive value that people receive from others. Here, those in white are called worthy and are acclaimed as conquerors, both of which connote honor (Rev 3:4-5; 4:11; 5:12). The white robes that people receive from Christ cover their shame and give them dignity (3:18; 16:15). The martyrs who cry out for justice are given white robes to show divine approval (6:11). In apocalyptic writings, bright garments point to the glory of those who are raised (*1 En.* 62:15-16). Culturally, white garments could connote death and grief (Plutarch, *Mor.* 270F), but Revelation relates them to life and celebration (cf. Eccl 9:8).

89. Ibid.

90. Ibid., 338.

91. Aune, *Revelation 1–5*, 259.

92. Rowland, "The Book of Revelation," 587.

93. Aune, *Revelation 1–5*, 287.

94. Ibid., 288.

95. Ibid., 314.

96. Beale, *Book of Revelation*, 322.

97. Ibid.

98. Koester, *Revelation*, 363.

99. Smalley, *Revelation of John*, 84.

100. Boring, *Revelation*, 106.

101. Ulrich Wilckens, "στολή," TDNT VII:690.

102. Ladd, *Commentary of the Revelation of John*, 106.

103. Caird, *Revelation of Saint John the Divine*, 84.

104. Boring, *Revelation*, 125.

105. Ibid.

106. Beale, *Book of Revelation*, 394.

107. Ibid.

108. Koester, *Revelation*, 314.

109. Aune, *Revelation 6–16*, 410.

110. Ibid.

111. Koester, *Revelation*, 411.

112. Ibid., 401.

113. Ibid., 411.

114. Ibid., 400.

115. Ibid.

116. Ibid.

117. Aune, *Revelation 1–5*, 259.

118. Koester, *Revelation*, 419–20.

119. Ibid., 842.

120. Ibid.

121. Caird, *Revelation of Saint John the Divine*, 285.

122. Ladd, *Commentary of the Revelation of John*, 249.

123. Smalley, *Revelation of John*, 483.

124. Beale, *Book of Revelation*, 936, quotes J. H. Moulton, W. F. Howard, and M. Turner, *A Grammar of New Testament Greek III* (Edinburgh: T & T Clark, 1906–76) 210.

125. Beale, *Book of Revelation*, 941–42, with a full discussion on pages 933–44.

126. Ibid.

127. Aune, *Revelation 17–21*, 1030.

128. Mitchell G. Reddish, *Revelation*, Smyth & Helwys Commentaries (Macon GA: Smyth & Helwys, 2001) 367.

129. Ladd, *Commentary of the Revelation of John*, 254. Aune, *Revelation 17–22*, 1057; Smalley, *Revelation of John*, 491; Beale, *Book of Revelation*, 958–59, agree with Ladd's assessment on this point.

130. Beale, *Book of Revelation*, 957–64.

131. Caird, *Revelation of Saint John the Divine*, 243–44.

132. Rowland, "The Book of Revelation," 699.

133. Boring, *Revelation*, 197.

134. Koester, *Revelation*, 755.

135. Reddish, *Revelation*, 25.

136. Judith Kovacs and Christopher Rowland, *Revelation*, Blackwell Bible Commentaries (Victoria, Australia: Blackwell, 2004) 197.

137. Ibid.

138. Richard Bauckham, *The Climax of Prophecy: Studies on the Book of Revelation* (Edinburgh: T&T Clark International, 1993) 233–34.

139. Kovacs and Rowland, *Revelation*, 196.

140. Aune, *Revelation 1–5*, 98.

141. Smalley, *Revelation of John*, 494.

142. Caird, *Revelation of Saint John the Divine*, 246.

143. Koester, *Revelation*, 630.

144. Beale, *Book of Revelation*, 394.

145. Koester, *Revelation*, 314.

146. Ibid.

147. Aune, *Revelation 1–6*, 225, 227.

148. Koester, *Revelation*, 319.

149. Ibid.

150. Rowland, "The Book of Revelation," 583.

151. Aune, *Revelation 6–16*, 746–47, provides a summary of scholarly opinion as does Koester, *Revelation*, 575.

152. Koester, *Revelation*, 575.

153. Lupieri, *Apocalypse of John*, 208.

154. Caird, *Revelation of Saint John the Divine*, 168.

155. Rowland, "The Book of Revelation," 583.

156. Ibid., 791.

157. Ibid.

158. Ibid., 792.

159. Koester, *Revelation*, 779.

160. Ibid., 319.

161. Caird, *Revelation of Saint John the Divine*, 280.

162. Ibid.

163. Aune, *Revelation 16–22*, 1175.

164. Beale, Ibid., 1102.

165. Ibid.

166. Koester, *Revelation*, 833.

CHAPTER 4

Time and Space, Satan (Devil, Ancient Serpent, Deceiver, and Accuser), and Michael

In John's ongoing articulation of atonement in Revelation, the biblical characters Satan and Michael enter the scene at Revelation 12. While the "woman clothed with the sun" / γυνὴ περιβεβλημένη τὸν ἥλιον (12:1), "a great red Dragon" / δράκων μέγας πυρρός (12:3), and a "male child" / υἱόν, ἄεσεν (12:5) all narratively precede mention of Michael and the Dragon's battle, they are of equal importance to John (and will be addressed more fully in chapter 5). But first, "Michael" / ὁ Μιχαὴλ (who appears only twice in the New Testament—once in Jude 9 and once in Rev 12:7), while perhaps nothing of a surprise in the story of Satan's defeat, and "Satan" / ὁ Satan (who appears frequently in the New Testament particularly in Rev 2:9; 2:13, 2:24; 3:9; 12:9; 20:2; and 20:7) must be addressed because of their signal importance to John's emerging atonement theology.

TIME AND SPACE
To understand Satan and Michael's role in the Apocalypse, a summary investigation of their function and purpose in the broader biblical story is helpful. Before commencing with that exploration, however, another question of equal importance must be asked: What respective roles do "time" and "space" play in John's visions and signs? While in some ways that question has been raised and answered indirectly in the explorations above of the heavenly throne, temple, and altar, we turn to it directly now.

For millennia, spatial-temporal matters have been of interest to philosophers, theologians, and physicists,[1] and they are likewise of interest to non-specialists who are curious about how the world's time and space work and how they should be understood. John communicates in his own way how to comprehend these realities in the world in which he lives. In the various scenes of Revelation, particularly Revelation 12, he articulates the interaction of the heavenly and earthly realms. When he addresses Satan's defeat in a heavenly battle (12:7-9), he correlates that scene with an earthly event (12:5). In so doing, the space and time relationship between these scenes is consistent with space and time scenes found elsewhere in Revelation. In fact, given John's frequent narrative movement from earth to heaven (Rev 4:1-2a being the first example[2]) and heaven to earth, the correspondence between "heavenly time" and "earthly time" partially informs the meaning and importance of events associated with the death of Jesus.

Since John uses spatial language of heaven and earth in the Apocalypse, identifying which space and what time is in his thoughts as he writes is relevant for understanding his meaning. Jorunn Økland notes that

> [t]he author jumps from heaven to earth and back again, and we do not always know whether the phenomena he describes are here or there. This paradox leaves artists, preachers, scholars and other readers alike with the exciting and challenging task of putting together the pieces of this spatial-visual jigsaw-puzzle . . . .[3]

Steve Gregg, in *Revelation: Four Views. A Parallel Commentary*,[4] has summarized what Økland calls four main trajectories of interpretation that have time as their axis: preterist, historicist, futurist, and spiritual.[5] Økland also calls to attention a "related spatial-temporal taxonomy where notions both of time and space are made more explicit and brought into interaction [involving] millennialist, pre-millennialist, dispensationalist, postmillennialist, and amillennialist readings of Revelation."[6] These so-called millennial views, while of interest, have implications for Revelation 12 only if, and to the unlikely degree, that what John has envisioned is related to the time of "millennium" or "millennial reign" of Christ (the phrase "1,000 years" / τὰ χίλια ἔτη is mentioned only in Rev 20:2, 3, 4, 5, 6, 7). In particular, the millennial views have implications for understanding Revelation 12 if what John is describing in that chapter happens with specific reference to a time prior to, following, or without any reference to the so-called second coming of Christ, amillennialism being an exception that Økland identifies below.

His summary is useful:

> These distinctions concern the exact temporal sequence of a set of events, usually including the coming of the Antichrist, the great tribulation, Christ's return, the millennium, the (possible) rapture and Christ's final victory, and various answers to certain spatial questions, including the location of the millennium and the whereabouts of the saints during the millennium. Millennialism is the older and more general term, often used generally for a range of end-time expectation including the return of Christ, and the rule of the saints for a thousand years (i.e. a millennium). In premillennialism, the great tribulation is followed by the second coming of Christ who then reigns for a millennium on Earth. In Dispensationalism, one particular form of pre-millennialism, the saints will be raptured to a better place before the tribulation. Post-millennialism sees the term "millennium" as indicating a long period of peace and intensive mission, at the end of which Christ will return. Amillennialism sees the millennium as merely symbolizing the time of the Church.[7]

Jonathan Roberts makes an additional contribution to this discussion in "Decoding, Reception History, Poetry: Three Hermeneutical Approaches to the Apocalypse."[8] As he says, "In answer to this question [about time] I wish to consider the operation of time in a very different type of writing: poetry."[9] After engaging Hans-Georg Gadamer's understanding of time and how a written text relates to history, Roberts is not satisfied that "the work of effective history (*Wirkungsgeschichte*)"[10] removes the subject/object divide by 'fusing the horizons,' as Gadamer thought." He suggests instead, as Økland points out, "that one way of dealing with the 'chronological demands' of Revelation is to use a poetic form, where time is not constructed chronologically."[11]

One need not see

> Revelation . . . [as] a text ticking away until it explodes in Armageddon, but it is a mode of understanding, a way of seeing. He engages with it not as a list of events that have taken or will take place, but as a space in which present experience comes into dialogic relationship with the biblical text. As poetry, it is demanding of the reader, but it is simultaneously theologically un-coercive. Revelation provides a framework of understanding, and that understanding is personal, and inseparable from the art through which it is discussed . . . . The poetry offers us, as readers, a form of affective or aesthetic experience, formed, in part, from the text of Revelation,

and this offers new perspectives on both the Apocalypse, and—from a hermeneutical perspective—on our allegiances to time and history.[12]

Ladd indirectly acknowledges as much with his observation that John "parts the curtain that separates earth from heaven to depict a great warfare in the spiritual world" and that "Chapter 12 describes in mythological terms this heavenly warfare."[13] Moreover, he says, "We misunderstand the character of John's thought if we try to place this heavenly battle somewhere in the stream of time."[14] Lupieri, with more detail, notes that the scenes of Revelation 12 are

> "in heaven," that intermediate site outside the categories of space and time where visions can exist . . . . That heaven is not subject to temporal or spatial laws accounts for one of the most disconcerting features in apocalyptic texts: ch. 12 moves back and forth continually between past, present, and future, with only one clear linear movement—the movement of the scenes from heaven to earth.[15]

En route to understanding what, if any, correlation exists between these scenes, Aune is right to point out "that 11:19 is intended to introduce 12:1-17."[16] He makes this observation based in large part on the "term ὤφθη, 'appeared,' [that] is an aorist passive verb that occurs in this form just three times in Revelation (11:19; 12:1, 3)."[17] Such close proximity of these verbs certainly favors the heavenly scene described in 11:19 serving as the introduction to these scenes. Revelation 11:19 connects thematically to what precedes it (the seventh trumpet—11:15-18) such that the summary of the seventh trumpet has close ties to what follows it. Without interruption of thought between the "opened temple and the ark of his covenant [that] appeared in his temple" / ἠνοίγη ὁ ναὸς, καὶ ὤφθη ἡ κιβωτὸς τῆς διαθήκης αὐτοῦ ἐν τῷ ναῷ αὐτοῦ of 11:19 and 12:1, John describes that "a great sign appeared in heaven . . ." / σημεῖον μέγα ὤφθη ἐν τῷ οὐρανῷ . . . (12:1). His point is that the scenes of Revelation 12 are certainly of a part with what precedes the transitional verse 11:19, namely that the events about to be described in Revelation 12 have much to do with why and how "the temple of God *in heaven* [emphasis added] was opened" / ἠνοίγη ὁ ναὸς τοῦ θεοῦ ὁ ἐν τῷ οὐρανῷ (11:19) and access granted to it by someone other than the high priest on the Day of Atonement (see above chapter 2, "Temple," 11:19). In particular, Satan being cast down from heaven allows for open access to the inner sanctuary of the temple—to

God. Why that is so becomes increasingly clearer as the collective parts of Revelation 12:1-12 coalesce, not the least of which is the central figure of the Child being snatched up to God (Rev 12:5—see chapter 5 below).

In terms of the spatial-temporal, Revelation 12:9 describes Satan as "cast down into the earth" / ἐβλήθη εἰς τὴν γὴν (12:9) as the outcome of "the war in heaven [with] Michael" / πόλεμος ἐν τῷ οὐρανῷ, ὁ Μιχαήλ (12:7), since there was "no longer a place found for them in heaven" / οὐδὲ τόπος εὑρέθη αὐτῶν ἔτι ἐν τῷ οὐρανῷ (12:8). This heavenly happening and earthly reality are interconnected with the outcome of the events described in one affecting and corresponding to the other. Furthermore, John strategically locates the two scenes of Revelation 12:3-5 and 12:7-9 to form a literary inclusion[18] between which "the child was snatched up to God and to his throne" / ἡρπάσθη τὸ τέκνον αὐτῆς πρὸς τὸν θεὸν καὶ πρὸς τὸν θρόνον αὐτοῦ (12:5) and "the woman fled into the wilderness" / ἡ γυνὴ ἔφυγεν εἰς τὴν ἔρημον (12:6). In these scenes the Dragon of 12:3-5, which is antagonistic toward the woman and the Child, is the same Dragon of 12:7-9 with whom Michael wars and defeats.

How these scenes play out, and how the characters within them relate to each other, is a matter of first importance. In particular, what, if any, is the relationship in time between the events described in these scenes? Do the central scenes of "the child being snatched up to God and his throne" / ἡρπάσθη τὸ τέκνον αὐτῆς πρὸς τὸν θεόν καὶ πρὸς τὸν θρόνον αὐτοῦ (12:5) and "the Dragon standing before the woman who is about to give birth so that when she should give birth he might devour her child" / ὁ δράκων ἔστηκεν ἐνώπον τῆς γυναικὸς τῆς μελλούσης τεκεῖν, ἵνα ὅταν τέκῃ τὸ τέκνον αὐτῆς καταφάγῃ (12:6) inform "Michael . . . warring with the Dragon" / ὁ Μιχαήλ . . . τοῦ πολεμῆσαι μετὰ τοῦ δράκοντος (12:7) and "the great Dragon [being] thrown down . . . thrown down to the earth" / ἐβλήθη ὁ δράκων ὁ μέγας . . . ἐβλήθη εἰς τὴν γῆν (12:9)? What is the correlation in time among these scenes? In other words, should the child being snatched up to God and the Dragon being defeated be viewed as synchronous?

While scholarship is somewhat ambiguous (if not for the most part silent) on this question, there are a few representatives who have determined that the battle scene in heaven between Michael and the Dragon (12:7-9) should be considered concurrent with "her child being snatched up to God" / ἡρπάσθη τὸ τέκνον αὐτῆς πρὸς τὸν θεὸν (12:5). To be sure, Aune is correct: "The reason Satan was cast out of heaven, i.e., the basis of the conflict between the Dragon and his angels and Michael and his angels, is not specifically mentioned."[19] Of course, few things are explicit in the Apocalypse, yet many images that John employs throughout do have recognizable implications for that to which John is pointing.

Gordon Campbell astutely identified the "narrative sandwiching technique of *two intercalated stories*: in Rev 12 two attacks mounted by the satan, first on Messiah (12.1-6) and then on the woman and her offspring (12.13-17), are tellingly separated by its own heavenly defeat in 12.7-12."[20] John's point is clear: "for the satan, attack is defeat . . . , [being] sealed in the blood of the Lamb—the victory of the cross . . . in Revelation, precedes everything else (1.5)."[21]

In fact, Boring says that the Dragon's defeat and "the expulsion of Satan from heaven is the result of the victory of Christ on earth (12:10-11)."[22] Moreover, "the 'time' of the fall of Satan from heaven is 'now' (12:10): in the story line of the vision, the time of the Christ event."[23] Even so, "It is Michael, commander of God's armies, who takes the initiative, as the visionary counterpart to God's saving act on earth in the event of Christ and his cross."[24] Smalley prefers to use the language of a "play within a play" to capture John's meaning. He says, "This is a controlling vision, which in one sense undergirds the theological significance of the drama of the Apocalypse in its totality. For it reminds the audience . . . that there is a perpetual battle in progress, both supernaturally and on earth, between evil and God . . . ."[25] He further adds that the "victory must be understood as a heavenly and symbolic counterpart of the historical achievement of the cross; since the real conquest of evil has by now been achieved in the death and exaltation of Jesus the Christ."[26]

Beale offers a "telescoping" analogy in which he sees these scenes as "a snapshot of Christ's entire life—his birth, his destiny of kingship, and his incipient fulfillment of that destiny in his ascent to God's heavenly throne after his postresurrection ministry."[27] He sees the locus of Satan's defeat both in "Christ's resurrection and the beginning of his rule [since they] are immediately reflected in heaven by Michael's and his angels' defeat of the devil and his hosts"[28] and the "victory won through Christ's blood [that] must be the basis, not only for the saints' earthly victory, but also for Michael's triumph in heaven."[29] He certainly sees a relationship between Jesus' death and Michael's defeat of the Dragon, but he does not suggest that John's vision reflects the simultaneity of these events. Rather than Satan's expulsion being because of the death of the child, Beale says, "The picture of the devil being thrown down indicates that in some way he is being punished by means of his own sin, since he unjustly 'threw down

the stars onto the earth' (v. 4)."[30] While that action on the Dragon's part
may have proven to be sinful, why John would single it out as the reason for
Satan's removal, seems to miss the Christological point that John is otherwise making. Another reason is more evident, and John has strategically
embedded it within these scenes.

Boring ultimately concludes, "The action which takes place in heaven
is a reflection of events in this world: the life and death of Jesus, the witness
of Christians who are 'faithful unto death' (2:10)."[31] Aune says that "it is
implicit that the heavenly battle was caused by the Dragon's futile attempt
to devour the male child."[32] The implication of the narrative, however,
suggests that the Dragon did devour the child, not that he merely attempted
to do so. Certainly the Woman of the narrative understood it that way
since she "fled into the wilderness" / ἔφυγεν εἰς τὴν ἔρημον (12:6) to
escape with her life, unlike the Child who forfeited his life. Aune does not
identify these events as simultaneous, but he certainly could have done so.
He clearly sees the "specific temporal occurrence of Satan's expulsion from
heaven narrated in v 9 and cited as the specific cause for this song of victory
in v 10."[33] That there is a simultaneity of Satan's expulsion and the victory
song of the saints, one heavenly event and one earthly, suggests that the
snatching up of the child (see chapter 5 below) and the throwing down of
Satan are likewise temporally interrelated.

After a summary exploration of Satan and Michael, some conclusions
and preliminary observations can be reached about John's understanding of
time and space, about Satan as the Devil, Ancient Serpent, Deceiver, and
Accuser, and how Michael's role informs John's atonement theology.

"THE SATAN" / ὁ Σατανᾶς[34]

The biblical character Satan has a rich and fascinating history that spans
not only the Bible and intertestamental period but also two well-known
Christian literary classics: one by Dante (*The Divine Comedy*) and one by
Milton (*Paradise Lost*). At its foundation, the Greek word ὁ Σατανᾶς ("The
Satan") translates the Hebrew noun שָׂטָן (*satan*), which is derived from the
verb שָׂטַן (*satan*) that means to be or act as an "adversary."[35] Peggy L. Day
has addressed in detail "the four passages in the Hebrew Bible (Num 22:22-
35; Zech 3:1-7; Job 1–2; 1 Chr 21:1–22:1) in which the noun *satan* is used
to describe a heavenly being" who is associated with "Yahweh . . . presiding
over a council of heavenly beings."[36] John undoubtedly has this very character in mind in Revelation 12, even if his depiction of him is significantly
advanced beyond what is found in these four Old Testament texts.

In fact, John's appropriation of "The Satan" / ὁ Σατανᾶς becomes even clearer based on the qualifiers that he uses to describe him in Revelation 12. He says of Satan that he is "the great Dragon, the ancient serpent, the one called Devil and The Satan, the one who deceives the whole inhabited world" / ὁ δράκων ὁ μέγας, ὁ ὄφις ὁ ἀρχαῖος, ὁ καλούμενους Διάμολος καὶ ὁ Σατανᾶς, ὁ πλανῶν τὴν οἰκουνένην ὅλην (12:9). Aune says of John's nomenclature for Satan, "The piling up of four aliases for Satan in this verse is reduplicated in 20:2 and has general parallel in the reptilian trinity mentioned in Isa 27:1, 'In that day the Lord with his hard and great and strong sword will punish Leviathan the fleeing serpent, Leviathan the twisting serpent, and he will slay the dragon that is in the sea.'"[37] Certainly something of a transition has occurred in this biblical character between the First Testament's description of the Satan and the way John writes about him in Revelation. Surely this is so since "nowhere in the Old Testament is there a devil as we understand him today."[38]

Indeed the word "Satan" in the Old Testament may be used as a verb meaning "to oppose as an adversary" as is the case in Psalms 38:20; 71:13; 109:4, 20, 29; Zechariah 3:1.[39] Marvin E. Tate explains that "the basic meaning of the word *satan* as adversary/accuser/opponent" is generally accepted.[40] The word can also mean a human adversary as it does in 1 Samuel 29:4; 2 Samuel 19:22; 1 Kings 5:4; 11:14, 23, 25.[41] Satan is also used in association with a supernatural being in Numbers 22:22, 32; Job 1:6, 7, 8; Zechariah 3:1; 1 Chronicles 21:1.[42] Only in two instances (Job and Zechariah) is the definite article attached to the word *satan* declaring the function of the noun in terms of its title. The only definitive place in the Old Testament where Satan is meant to be a name is in 1 Chronicles 12:1.[43] Of these occasions when Satan is mentioned, in Numbers 22 the divinely designated figure *satan*, while an adversary, is not an enemy of God but an obedient servant whom God sent to correct the misguided Balaam. Certainly Job provides the most detailed description of the Satan in the Old Testament.[44] And, as Tate points out, "The *satan* carries out his mission; adversative but clearly subordinate to divine authority. The narrative of Job leaves the *satan* figure with considerable ambiguity, but he is clearly not the inveterate foe of all humanity and a rebel against God."[45]

When Zechariah 3:1-10 introduces the Satan, he is located similarly as he was in Job in the heavenly court conversing with God. While echoing in some ways the Job story, Zechariah describes "the high priest Joshua standing before the angel of the LORD, and Satan standing at his right hand to accuse him" (Zech 3:1). Here the technical verb עֹמֵד לִפְנֵי, translated "standing before," suggests that the situation is paralleled to that of a court room setting for the purpose of legal prosecution.[46] The accuser's (*ha satan* — הַשָּׂטָן) role is to do his job, to accuse ("to accuse him" / לְשִׂטְנוֹ). *Ha satan* is in no way an intruder in this heavenly court room. He has a designated position "standing at his right hand."[47] The high priest, Joshua in this case, is being prosecuted for his alleged sinful behavior and *ha satan* is the designated prosecutor. His task is to "prove and test and accuse . . . this candidate for high priest."[48]

That John has these characteristics of Satan in mind as he shares his vision in Revelation 12 is without question. He certainly describes Satan as "being in the heavenly court, one whose specialized function was to seek out and accuse persons disloyal to God."[49] In the same way that Job and Joshua are both on trial in the heavenly court room, even at the distance between heaven and earth, John likewise pictures Satan, by implication, as a leading figure in the heavenly courtroom scene from which he is thrown down. This facet of the great Dragon as "the Satan, the one who deceives those who dwell on the earth" / ὁ Σατανᾶς, ὁ πλανῶν τὴν οἰκουμένην ὅλην is made clear in his capacity in Revelation as "the one who accuses our brothers, the one who accuses them before our God day and night" / ὁ κατήγωρ τῶν ἀδελφῶν ἡμῶν, ὁ κατηγορῶν αὐτοὺς ἐνώπιον τοῦ θεοῦ ἡμῶν ἡμέρας καὶ νυκτός (12:10). In other words, his deceptive powers are put in service of his prosecutorial role. By deceptively persuading wrongdoing in people, the Satan successfully builds an indefensible case against every defendant.

"The one called Devil" / ὁ καλούμενους Διάβολος

That John connects the Devil with Satan as one and the same figure is also at once apparent. Koester notes that in the LXX the Hebrew word *sāṭān* was

> translated *diabolos*, or devil, which means slanderer (1 Chr 21:1; Job 1:6; Zech 3:1; cf. Wis 2:24; Matt 4:1; *T. Naph.* 8:4). In Jewish and Christian tradition both names were given to the principal angelic opponent of God. This figure was also known as Belial (1QS I, 18; 1QM I, 1) or Beliar, the worthless one (2 Cor 6:15; *T. Sim.* 5:3; *Mart. Asc. Isa.* 4:4); Mastemah, the hostile one (*Jub.* 10:7); Beelzebul, the prince of demons (Matt 12:24; Mark 3:22); and "the evil one" (Matt 13:19; John 17:15).[50]

Aune qualifies the name a bit more stating that in 1 Chronicles, Job, and Zechariah the Hebrew word *satan* means "'one who separates,' 'the seducer,' 'the enemy.' The devil is called Sotona because his original name was Satanail, and he is the one who seduced Eve in the Garden (2 Enoch [Rec.J] 31:6)."[51] He also points out that in the New Testament "devil" occurs thirty-six times and "Satan" occurs thirty-four times.[52]

The word διάβολος in classical Greek could be used for one who slanders or makes a false accusation, although, as Werner Foerster identifies,

> The LXX also used διάβολος for שָׂטָן "devil," in the sense of "the one who separates," "the enemy," "the calumniator," "the seducer." Since this is an innovation in the LXX, we can only deduce the meaning from the rendering and from the context. The latter seldom suggests "calumniator," but rather "accuser" or "adversary." This is so in 1 Ch. 21:1 and Job 1 and 2, unless we prefer "seducer." Even in Zech. 3:1 ff., where he is in fact the accuser, the verb שׂטן is rendered ἀντικεῖσθαι: καὶ ὁ διάβολος ἱστήκει ἐκ δεξιῶν αὐτοῦ τοῦ ἀντικεῖσθαι αὐτῷ = וְהַשָּׂטָן עֹמֵד עַל־יְמִינוֹ לְשִׂטְנוֹ. This seems to force us to the conclusion that "accuser" is not the primary meaning. Since the rendering "seducer" does not fit all the contexts, "adversary" is the required translation. The work of the adversary implies always an attempt on the part of the διάβολος to separate God and man. It is an open question whether the verb διαβάλλειν influenced the usage.[53]

From every indication the Devil is synonymous with Satan. Certainly the adversary Satan seems to take on a role as seducer of people in the broader biblical tradition. John's language of "The Ancient Serpent" / ὁ ὄφις ὁ ἀρχαῖος, Deceiver" / ὁ πλανῶν and "Accuser" / ὁ κατήγωρ suggests that this is likewise his understanding.

"The Ancient Serpent" / ὁ ὄφις ὁ ἀρχαῖος, "Deceiver" / ὁ πλανῶν, and "Accuser" / ὁ κατήγωρ

John's association of Satan with the "ancient serpent" / ὁ ὄφις ὁ ἀρχαῖος is not original to him but reaches back to the intertestamental period. As far as Genesis 3:1 is concerned, the first time the serpent is mentioned in Scripture, "The Yahwist retains this mythological character of the snake, but affirms that it was a mere creature under the sovereignty of God."[54] Koester, furthermore, points out, "The serpent is not identified with Satan in Genesis, but that link had been made before Revelation was composed (1 En. 69:6; Wis 2:24; Apoc. Mos. 16 [OTP 2:277]; Apoc. Ab. 23:1-11; cf. 3 Bar. 9:7)."[55]

Of course, the Serpent's capacity to deceive is fully acknowledged by John. Rutledge concludes that "the serpent is uncanny, and its mysterious capacity for insinuation seems to suggest a nihilistic presence within creation that eludes explanation and can only be resisted . . . . Derek Kidner in his commentary of Genesis . . . writes that the New Testament 'unmasks' the figure of Satan standing behind the serpent."[56] Beale recognizes that Genesis 3 attributes to the serpent "two functions of *slanderer* and *deceiver*: his claims that God's command to Adam and Eve in Gen 2:16-17 is not true (Gen 3:1, 4) and that God has deceptive motives in forbidding them to eat of the tree (Gen 3:4-5) slander the character of God . . . ."[57] "Here," as Koester states, "the 'ancient serpent' identifies Satan with the snake that tempted Eve in Gen 3:1."[58]

In Satan's role as accuser in the Old Testament, he "presses God's case or does God's work of probing the integrity of human beings,"[59] that is until in the intertestamental period when "under the influence of Iranian dualistic religion and its evil god Ahriman, counterpart to the supreme god of light Ahura-mazda, . . . the figure of Satan emerged in Jewish tradition as the personification of evil and the transcendent opponent of God."[60] This background "affirms that the devil was originally created by God and therefore can never be entirely independent, let alone coequal."[61]

Surely Boring is correct in his conclusion that

> Revelation's talk of Satan and the Devil is thus not peculiar but belongs to the mainstream of Jewish and early Christian apocalyptic thought . . . . Echoing the sinister overtones of "Satan's" origin as accuser in court, John refers to him as "the accuser" (12:10), a designation powerfully appropriate in the situation of the Asian Christians who found themselves accused before the Roman courts.[62]

Paul Ricoeur perceptively points out,

> The serpent represents the following situation: in the historical experience of man, every individual finds evil already there; nobody begins it absolutely . . . . The serpent . . . represents the aspect of evil that could not be absorbed into the responsible freedom of man . . . . The Jews themselves, though they were well armed against demonology by their intransigent monotheism, were constrained by truth . . . to concede something . . . to the great dualisms which they were to discover after the Exile . . . . Of course, Satan will never be another God; the Jews will always remember that the serpent is part of the creation; but at least the symbol of Satan

allowed them to balance the movement toward the concentration of evil in man by a second movement which attributed its origin to a prehuman, demonic reality.[63]

In a manner of speaking, "The narrator [of Genesis] wants to say that it is not possible to come to terms with the origin of evil."[64] Rutledge concludes, "[W]e have an enemy whose wickedness, while neither created nor intended by the Creator, is nevertheless under his ultimate, sovereign authority."[65] Gregory of Nyssa, however, comes close to an explanation of the origin of evil:

> Now that angelic power who begot envy in himself by turning from the good developed an inclination toward evil. When this had once happened, he was like a rock breaking off from a mountain ridge and hurled headlong by its own weight. Divorced from his natural affinity with good, he became prone to evil; and as if by a weight he was spontaneously impelled and carried to the final limit of iniquity . . . . Cunningly he cheats and deceives man by persuading him to become his own murderer and assassin.[66]

While there is no satisfactory explanation for the origin of an evil Satan, John certainly intends to provide an explanation for the defeat of humankind's age-old enemy and nemesis. In John's explanation, the angel Michael plays a prominent role in Satan's overthrow.

"MICHAEL" / ὁ Μιχαήλ

Michael, although mentioned only in Jude 9 and Revelation 12:7 in the New Testament, is identified three times in the Old Testament by Daniel as both a prince (Dan 10:13, 21) and a protector of Israel (Dan 12:1). Koester acknowledges two primary roles for Michael: eschatological and primordial.[67] Of course, Michael also plays a role as advocate for God's people.

In a similar way that Michael defeats the prince of the Persians (Dan 10:13-21), and as Koester reports[68] that the Qumran War Scroll (1QM 17:5-9) tells of his victory over Belial, John depicts him as victorious eschatologically over Satan (Rev 12:7-12). Michael's primordial role as advocate is described in the intertestamental writings of the Life of Adam and Eve, in 1 Enoch, and also when he contended with Satan for the body of Moses (L.A.E. 48; Jude 9). In the former (L.A.E 12-16), he commands the devil to bow to Adam, and in 1 Enoch 10:11-13; 54:6 he binds the sinful angels until they face the last judgment. Michael's command to Satan to bow to Adam serves as an explanation for what provoked the animosity of Satan toward humankind, not to mention their respective opposing roles in the battle described in Revelation 12.

The nearest connection in the literature to Michael's defeat of a Dragon, Aune points out, is "an amulet of uncertain date discovered at Amorgos . . . which reads 'I adjure you, malign tumor, by the name of him who . . . killed the twelve-headed Dragon by the hand of Michael and Gabriel, his holy archangels' . . . ."[69] Michael also joins the eschatological battle against the sons of darkness as 1QM 17:7 reports. Aune provides a thorough excursus on Michael including how as "the Angel of Light (Michael) . . . [has] angelic armies at [his] disposal (1QM 13:10–12)."[70]

The diabolical figure identified by familiar Old Testament, intertestamental period, and New Testament writings is confronted by Michael in the heavenly scene in Revelation 12. It is Michael, as John envisions him, who is tasked and privileged to banish Satan once and for all from his heavenly place (see more below in chapter 5).

CONCLUSION

Time and space (heaven and earth), Satan (the Dragon who is the Ancient Serpent, Devil, Deceiver, and Accuser), and Michael (God's angelic champion) are anything but disparate, incongruent parts in John's thinking as he reveals the signs and visions of Revelation 12. He sees the happenings of heaven and earth as inseparably linked with each having bearing on the other. The interchange that John sees between heaven and earth is missed only when a narrow, chronological reading of Revelation is forced onto the text or when a reader is bound to a particular eschatological perspective sometimes associated with the word "millennium."

The way in which John communicates the relationship between time and space allows him to speak of the simultaneity of events in both the heavenly and earthly realms. Because the characters Satan and Michael are freely associated in the biblical and intertestamental periods as heavenly beings that have earthly interactions and connections, John identifies them as significant players in the visions that he shares. The solution to the problem of Satan to which John points includes his defeat and ouster (as the Ancient Serpent, Devil, Deceiver, and Accuser) from his prosecutorial role without which any and everyone whom he accuses is otherwise justly found guilty.

In other words, those whom Satan has successfully deceived (and that is everyone) will be found guilty as long as Satan is allowed to prosecute. How John settles that concern is found in the vision that he receives: "the accuser of our brothers [and sisters] has been thrown down" / ἐβλήθη ὁ κατήγωρ τῶν ἀδελφῶν ἡμῶν (Rev 12:10).

These visions all point to John's atonement theology, full disclosure of which is found in the complement of characters and scenes to be addressed in the forthcoming chapter. There is meanwhile a "woman clothed with the sun" / γυνὴ περιβεβλημένη τὸν ἥλιον (12:1), "a great red Dragon" / δράκων μέγας πυρρός (12:3), and a "male child" / υἱόν, ἄρσεν (12:5), all who figure into the redemptive drama. Satan finally meets his match in the atoning death of "the Lamb" which is "her child snatched up to God" / ἡρπάσθη τὸ τέκνον αὐτῆς πρὸς τὸν θεὸν of 12:5. In forthcoming chapter 5, the theological implications of the simultaneity of "her child snatched up to God" / ἡρπάσθη τὸ τέκνον αὐτῆς πρὸς τὸν θεὸν (12:5) and "the great Dragon, the ancient serpent, the one called the Devil and Satan thrown down" / ἐβλήθη ὁ δράκων ὁ μέγας, ὁ ὄφις ὁ ἀρχαῖος, ὁ κακούμενους Διάβολος καὶ ὁ Σατανᾶς (12:9) will be addressed.

Notes

1. Time and space have been investigated throughout history ranging in meaning from them being a simple measurement, how long it takes to get from point "A" to point "B," to something that is unreal. Following his Loeb Lectures in 1982, physicist Stephen W. Hawking chose to write a popular book decoding his more technical work of 1973, *The Large Scale Structure of Spacetime*. In *A Brief History of Time: From Big Bang to Black Holes* (Toronto: Bantam Books, 1988), he includes the contributions of Augustine, Kant, and earlier Greek philosophers. In *God & Time: Four View* (Downers Grove IL: InterVarsity, 2001), editor Gregory E. Ganssle approached the subject theologically and philosophically, calling upon William Lane Craig, Paul Helm, and Nicholas Wolsterhorff to provide chapters and critique. Their work engages Christian thinkers Augustine, Anselm, Aquinas, and Calvin as well as taking up subjects of timelessness, eternity, and omnitemporality. See also the earlier works of H. W. Schmidt, *Zeit und Ewigkeit Die letzen Voraussetzungen der dialektishcen Theologie* (1927), Martin Heidegger, *Being and Time*, trans. Joan Stambaugh (Tübingen: Max Niemeyer Verlag, 1953), and, more recently, Wolfgang Achtner, Stefan Kunz, and Thomas Walter, *Dimensions of Time: The Structures of the Time of Humans, of the World, and of God*, trans. Arthur H. Williams (Grand Rapids MI: Eerdmans, 1998).

2. Stephen S. Smalley, *The Revelation of John: A Commentary on the Greek Text of the Apocalypse* (Downers Grove IL: InterVarsity, 2005) 110.

3. Jorunn Økland, "Setting the Scene: The End of the Bible, the End of the World" in *The Way the World Ends? The Apocalypse of John in Culture and Ideology* (Sheffield: Sheffield Phoenix, 2009) 7.

4. Steve Gregg, ed., *Revelation: Four Views. A Parallel Commentary* (Nashville: Nelson, 2002).

5. Økland, "Setting the Scene," 8.

6. Ibid.

7. Ibid., 8–9.

8. Jonathon Roberts, "Decoding, Reception History, Poetry: Three Hermeneutical Approaches to the Apocalypse," *The Way the World Ends? The Apocalypse of John in Culture and Ideology* (Sheffield: Sheffield Phoenix, 2009) 31–42.

9. Ibid., 37.

10. Ibid., 11. See Hans-Georg Gadamer, *Truth and Method* (New York: Crossroad, 1985).

11. Roberts, "Decoding, Reception History, Poetry," 11.

12. Ibid.

13. George E. Ladd, *A Commentary of the Revelation of John* (Grand Rapids MI: Eerdmans, 1972) 166. Ladd makes this observation from his perspective as a Historic Premillennialist. See George E. Ladd, "Historic Premillennialism," in *The Meaning of the Millennium: Four Views*, ed. Robert G Clouse (Downers Grove IL: InterVarsity, 1977) 17–40.

14. Ladd, *Commentary of Revelation of John*, 170.

15. Edmondo, F. Lupieri, *A Commentary on the Apocalypse of John*, trans. Marian Poggi Johnson and Adam Kamesar (Grand Rapids MI: Eerdmans, 1999) 189.

16. David Aune, *Revelation 6–16*, Word Biblical Commentary (Dallas: Word, 1998) 679.

17. Ibid.

18. Smalley, *Revelation of John*, 317.

19. Aune, *Revelation 6–16*, 700.

20. Gordon Campbell, "Facing Fire and Fury: Reading Revelation's Violence," *The Book of Revelation: Currents in British Research on the Apocalypse*, ed. Garrick V. Allen, Ian Paul, and Simon P. Woodman, in *Wissenschaftliche Untersuchungen zum Neuen Testament* (Tübingen: Mohr Siebeck, 2015) 164.

21. Ibid., 165.

22. M. Eugene Boring, *Revelation*, Interpretation (Louisville KY: John Knox, 1989) 158.

23. Ibid.

24. Ibid., 159.

25. Smalley, *Revelation of John*, 322.

26. Ibid., 323.

27. G. K. Beale, *The Book of Revelation: A Commentary on the Greek Text*, The New International Greek Testament Commentary, ed. I. Howard Marshall and Donald A. Hagner (Grand Rapids MI: Eerdmans, 1999) 639.

28. Ibid., 652.

29. Ibid., 662.

30. Ibid., 655.

31. Boring, *Revelation*, 159.

32. Aune, *Revelation 6–16*, 691.

33. Ibid., 699.

34. See Jeffrey Burton Russell's five volumes: *The Devil: Perceptions of Evil from Antiquity to the Middle Ages* (Ithaca NY: Cornell University Press, 1977); *Satan: The Early Christian Tradition* (Ithaca NY: Cornell University Press, 1981); *Lucifer: The Devil in Middle Ages* (Ithaca NY: Cornell University Press, 1984); *Mephistopheles: The Devil in the Modern World* (Ithaca NY: Cornell University Press, 1986); *The Prince of Darkness: Radical Evil and the Power of Good in History* (Ithaca NY: Cornell University Press, 1988). Also see Elaine Pagels, *The Origin of Satan* (New York: Random House, 1995).

35. F. Brown, S. R. Driver, and C. A. Briggs, *Enhanced Brown-Driver-Briggs Hebrew and English Lexicon* (Oxford: Clarendon, 1977) 966.

36. Peggy L. Day, *An Adversary in Heaven: śāṭān in the Hebrew Bible* (Atlanta: Scholars Press, 1988) 1.

37. Aune, *Revelation 6–16*, 698.

38. Joseph F. Kelly, *Who Is Satan? According to the Scriptures* (Collegeville MN: Liturgical Press, 2013) 17.

39. D. Seal, "Satan," *The Lexham Bible Dictionary*, ed. J. D. Barry, D. Bomar, D. R. Brown, R. Klippenstein, D. Mangum, C. Sinclair Wolcott, W. Widder (Bellingham WA: Lexham, 2012, 2013, 2014, 2015).

40. Marvin E. Tate, "Satan in the Old Testament," *Review & Expositor* 89/4 (1992): 461.

41. Ibid.

42. Ibid.

43. James L. Crenshaw, *Defending God: Biblical Response to the Problem of Evil* (New York: Oxford University Press, 2005) 56.

44. T. J. Wray and Gregory Mobley, *The Birth of Satan: Tracing the Devil's Biblical Roots* (New York: Palgrave MacMillan, 2005) 59.

45. Tate, "Satan in the Old Testament," 463.

46. Ibid.

47. Ibid.

48. Wray and Mobley, *The Birth of Satan*, 65.

49. Carol A. Newsom, "The Book of Job: Introduction, Commentary, and Reflections," *The New Interpreter's Bible*, vol. 4, ed. Leander E. Keck (Nashville: Abingdon, 1996) 347.

50. Craig R. Koester, *Revelation: A New Translation with Introduction and Commentary*, The Anchor Yale Bible (New Haven: Yale University Press, 2014) 549.

51. Aune, *Revelation 6–16*, 697.

52. Ibid., 698.

53. Werner Foerster, "διαμάλλω, διάβολος →Σατανᾶς," *TDNT*, 2:72–73.

54. Brevard Childs, *Myth and Reality in the Old Testament*, 2nd ed., Studies in Biblical Theology 27 (London: SCM, 1962) 49

55. Koester, *Revelation*, 550.

56. Fleming Rutledge, *The Crucifixion: Understanding the Death of Jesus Christ* (Grand Rapids MI: Eerdmans, 2015) 420; Derek Kinder, *Genesis: An Introduction and Commentary*, Tyndale Old Testament Commentaries, vol. 1 (Downers Grove IL: InterVarsity, 1967) 71.

57. Beale, *Book of Revelation*, 656.

58. Koester, *Revelation*, 549.

59. Boring, *Revelation*, 164.

60. Ibid.

61. Rutledge, *The Crucifixion*, 421.

62. Boring, *Revelation*, 165.

63. Paul Ricoeur, *The Symbolism of Evil* (New York: Harper and Row, 1967) 235–36.

64. Claus Westermann, *Creation* (Philadelphia: Fortress, 1974) 92.

65. Rutledge, *The Crucifixion*, 422.

66. Gregory of Nyssa, "An Address on Religious Instruction," in *Christology of the Later Fathers*, ed. Edward Rochie Hardy and Cyril C. Richardson, Library of Christian Classics, vol. 3 (Philadelphia: Westminster, 1954) 280.

67. Koester, *Revelation*, 548.

68. Ibid.

69. Aune, *Revelation 6–16*, 692.

70. Ibid., 693–95.

CHAPTER 5

The Woman Clothed with the Sun, a Great Red Dragon, and a Male Child: Revelation's Atonement Theology as an Exposé of the Defeat of Evil

That the Apocalypse is a book filled with signs is obvious to the reader from its very first verse and throughout John's entire presentation. In fact, Revelation 1:1 declares this "apocalypse of Jesus Christ" / Ἀποκάλυψις Ἰησοῦ Χριστοῦ to be a revelation "*signified* [emphasis added] by sending his angel/messenger to his servant John" / ἐσήμανεν ἀποστείας διὰ τοῦ ἀγγέλου αὐτοῦ τῷ δούλῳ αὐροῦ Ἰωάννῃ. In other words, John's use of the verb σημαίνω ("signify," "make known") is an important reminder that a number of "signifiers" await the reader throughout this text.

To be sure, by the time John arrives at Revelation 12 he has expressed himself symbolically many times over and in a variety of symbolic ways. Revelation's preferred medium actually is signs—things that point beyond themselves to an intended meaning.[1] Indeed, signs direct the recipient of them to look beyond the common, surface-level meaning to a deeper reality that is being signified. As such, John's intention seems rather clear: he is preparing the reader to embrace the meaning implied or projected by his use of familiar (or perhaps unfamiliar) terms and images. As Bauckham notes,

> It should be clear that the images of Revelation are symbols with evocative power inviting imaginative participation in the book's symbolic world. But they do not work merely by painting verbal pictures. Their precise literary composition is always essential to their meaning. In the

first place, the astonishingly meticulous composition of the book creates
a complex network of literary cross-references, parallels, contrasts, which
inform the meaning of the parts and the whole. Naturally, not all of these
will be noticed on first or seventh or seventieth reading.[2]

Similarly, in his reference to Revelation 12 Bauckham says, "As well as their
pervasive allusion to the Old Testament, the images of Revelation also echo
mythological images from its contemporary world."[3]

Revelation 12, Aune states, "has been a matter of considerable scholarly
debate,"[4] particularly as it relates to the combinations of images, the structure of the entire narrative, and the various combat myths that possibly are
in the background of this chapter. Of these scenes Reddish acknowledges,
"Nowhere else in the work does John draw so heavily from Jewish and
pagan myths and from the contemporary political situation as he does in
this section. The heavy use of strange, even bizarre, images and numbers
demands a careful reading (or hearing) by those who want to comprehend
John's message to the churches."[5] To be sure, the complexity of Revelation
12 can be daunting, if not nearly overwhelming. Our purpose, however,
is not to attempt to sort out all the complexities but rather to follow the
general story line as likely the first hearers would have heard it en route to
John's contribution to atonement theology.

Initially, 12:1 identifies a sign appearing in heaven following a symbolic
path that John has traveled before. The mention of heaven directs the
reader to acknowledge that what he is about to describe is something of
signal importance. John established this pattern early in Revelation 1:20,
particularly with his mention of the seven golden lampstands among which
the Son of Man walks. The earthly lampstands, John indicates, have heavenly counterparts about which he says "the seven stars are angels of the
seven churches" / οἱ ἑπτὰ ἀστέρες ἄγγελοι τῶν ἑπτὰ ἐκκλησιῶν εἰσίν
(1:16, 20). This earthly/heavenly connection affirms that what happens on
earth has a heavenly correspondence and that what happens in heaven has
earthly consequences and correspondences as well. In other words, things
in heaven and on earth interconnect; each affects the other.

Moreover, that John declares in 12:1 that it is a "great sign" / σημεῖον
μέγα suggests it must be one of importance.[6] Aune addresses the word
"sign" / σημεῖον, tracing its usage across the Septuagint and finding at
least five variations. He notes that when John uses the plural σημεῖα, he
always refers to false miracles.[7] In 12:1 the use of the singular is noteworthy.
Aune makes the important observation that the "term σημεῖον [in biblical

and intertestamental literature] is used of heavenly phenomena that presage impending events upon the earth," and he thinks that the symbol John uses here "has deeper significance."[8] He is most likely correct as will be demonstrated below.

THE "WOMAN CLOTHED WITH THE SUN" / γυνὴ περιβεβλημένη τὸν ἥλιον: 12:1

Accordingly, the first sign of Revelation 12 is a "woman[9] clothed with the sun" / γυμὴ περιβεβλημένη τὸν ἥλιον (12:1a). The image of the sun, Beale points out, has Old Testament precedent in Joseph's dream where Genesis 37:9 reports that the sun, moon, and stars (representing Jacob, his wife, and the tribes of Israel) all bow down to Joseph. Clearly the intention of that dream was to communicate authority and subservience. Similarly, two themes concerning the patriarchs that emerged in Jewish Midrash are also relevant: Abraham, Sarah, and their offspring are referred to as sun, moon, and stars.[10] In addition to this biblical image, there is an immediate connection to the "moon that is beneath her feet" / σελήνη ὑποκάτω τῶν ποδῶν αὐτῆς (12:1b), suggesting that John likely has in mind the familiar solar myth and the battle between light and darkness well known to the first-century world. To make his point, John blends together images from his broader cultural context including the great patriarchal family out of which the male Child (Rev 12:4-5) was ultimately born.

Even so, Abraham is identified with the sun, Isaac with the moon, and Jacob and his sons with stars. Midrashim on Exodus 15:6; Numbers 2:4; and Psalms 22:11-12 describe faithful Israel with similarly radiant imagery. Isaiah 60:19-20 pictures restored Israel with sun and moon symbols without mention of stars. These dual emphases suggest that the woman has both an earthly and a heavenly identity. Both Philo and Josephus's Midrash on Exodus 28 identify a crown, sun, moon, and stars and include the vestments of the Israelite high priests.[11]

Aune sees more astrology present in Revelation 12 than he sees the biblical imagery mentioned above. His conclusions are based in part on a "tessera from Palmyrene [that] depicts an unidentified goddess standing on a crescent moon, with three stars, one over her head and the other two next to her right and left arms."[12] The twelve constellations of the Zodiac, Bruce Malina suggests, are likely in the background as well.[13] Surely there is a free mixing of images from the Old Testament (twelve tribes of Israel) and mythology (the solar myth—see below—of which the Zodiac is a part) to present an emerging picture further clarified by additional forthcoming symbols. Because in Revelation 1:16, 20 John describes the seven churches as seven stars, his allusion to stars on the woman's head in Revelation 12 may be an incorporation in his thinking of the church along with Israel.

Hanna Stenström notes that "the Woman Clothed With the Sun (Rev 12.1–2) . . . , alone of all biblical women, resembles the great ancient goddesses and is still, in spite of that, a positive figure."[14] Undoubtedly, this metaphorical woman is contrasted with the harlot of Revelation 17–18 and is viewed admirably here just as she is in chapter 19 when identified as the "woman/bride" / ἡ γυνὴ (Rev 19:7) and in chapter 21 as the "bride" / νύμφην (Rev 21:2). Mathilda Joslyn Gage comments that Revelation 12 speaks of importance about the woman in this strategic chapter. She says,

> Clothed with the sun, woman here represents the Divinity of the feminine, its spirituality as opposed to the materiality of the masculine; for in Egypt the sun, as giver of life, was regarded as feminine, while the moon, shining by reflected light, was looked upon as masculine. With her feet upon the moon, woman, corresponding to and representing the soul, portrays the ultimate triumph of spiritual things over material things— over the body, which man, or the male principle, corresponds to and represents.[15]

Gage is probably nearer to John's meaning than Ladd, who merely says that "the moon under her feet again is designed to represent no particular feature other than that of enhancing the heavenly glory of the woman."[16] Smalley sees that the "woman uses the moon as a footstool as indicative of the victory of the faithful, . . . over the powers of evil."[17] Koester is of a similar persuasion. He says, "The imagery conveys a sense of majesty. In Jewish tradition, God was robed with light, had the earth under his feet, and was surrounded by stars (Ps 104:2; Sib. Or. 1:137–40)."[18]

Because the moon is located beneath the feet of the sun-clothed woman, John is likely pointing the reader in a direction to notice the position of authority that the light/sun has relative to the darkness/moon. That this is the case is borne out by biblical language of "enemies as my footstool" (cf. Ps. 110:1; Acts 2:35). An extra-biblical source also qualifies this meaning. Egyptian pharaohs' thrones had a notably distinct feature that included a footstool on which were inscribed the images of those who were subservient to them. Pharaoh Amenhotep II (1448–1420 BCE), for example, placed his feet upon his enemies. The "footstool" mentioned in Scripture is a part of the throne of the king that symbolizes God's throne. Such imagery suggests the relationship between sun and moon, night and day, darkness and light, with light reigning over the darkness. An allusion to Genesis 1:4 and John 1:4-9 may be equally in place as well. Since the woman has "on her head a crown of twelve stars" / ἐπὶ τῆς κεφαλῆς αὐτῆς στέφανους ἀστέρων δώδεκα (12:1c), Beale, looking ahead to the bride of 21:12-14, sees her as the "female emblem of the true city of God . . . juxtaposed to the female and sun-moon emblems of the city of man (Rome) . . . ."[19]

In addition to these allusions, there is also a probable inference to the ancient solar myth.[20] As the Egyptian battle myth of Re and Apep identifies, the sun's rising in the east and setting in the west reflects the ongoing struggle between night and day. The prevailing question for the ancients was, which will win, daylight or darkness? Since at night the sun traveled beneath the world, ancient observers pondered whether or not the sun would rise victorious from the underworld. As the myth is developed, the sun is pictured as traveling through the dark underworld and locked in battle. Since at night the sun no longer gives its light and its warmth, the darkness was perceived to be in conflict with the light and, hence, viewed as something evil that may or may not prevail over light.

In Egyptian mythology each day Apep (Ἄποφις), the serpent-like Dragon, attempted to disrupt the passage of the solar barge that carried the sun-god Re as he traveled from east to west across the sky. Storms, darkness, rain, and eclipse all were weapons that Apep used against Re in the heavens. As each day ended, the dying god Re would continue his travels into the underworld, only to be reborn next morning at sunrise. This battle between Re and Apep was played out daily as a symbol of the natural cycle of life depicting the constant conflict between darkness and light, goodness and evil, and life and death.[21]

Of course, in Scripture light and darkness are often contrasted (cf. Gen 1:4; John 1:5). That John would borrow from the language of mythology to communicate his Christology via non-biblical as well as biblical media does not indicate that he embraced a mythological world. The world in which he believed is clearly identified throughout Revelation—a world in which heaven and earth's events affect and interact with each other. John has, however, used mythology for illustration purposes, just as he has used monsters and beasts elsewhere for illustrative purposes in a similar manner. Readers, frankly, are prepared for such language since early in the Apocalypse, when John first introduces the Lamb (who is clearly a "beast" of sorts himself). About this "beast" there is never any question of its intended identity. This familiar symbol is easily recognizable.

The collage of images draws contemporary readers into the world of John's original audience, a world that was filled with biblical and mythological language by means of which John skillfully weaves together his atonement theology. His revelation is anything but haphazard. The first sign of Revelation 12 indicates that the light prevails over darkness, that goodness is superior to evil, and that this symbolic woman is a strategic part of the story of the triumph about to be expressed in a most impressive way.

"SHE WAS PREGNANT" / ἐν γαστρὶ ἔχουσα: 12:2

The crowned and sun-clothed woman, with moon beneath her feet, is likewise described as being pregnant. With that added detail, John takes the reader into yet another mythological image—that of expectant Leto, who was herself once under great duress before giving birth to her twins Apollo and Artemis. As a "pregnant" (literally "having in the womb") / ἐν γαστρὶ ἔχουσα (Rev 12:2) woman, she represents something more than herself. While she is certainly a part of that which she carries, she is not identical with it.

The combat myth[22] with which John's vision has affinity is that of Leto, consort of Zeus, who in Greek mythology gave birth to Apollo[23] only after encountering great distress brought upon her by the Python. The myth reports that Hera, Zeus's wife and sister, as well as the goddess of marriage and birth, commissioned Python with clear instructions to attack Leto. While there are variations on the myth, Homer's *Hymn to Apollo* (sixth century BCE) speaks about Apollo's defeat of the serpent Drakaina in the following manner.

As variations on the story go, Zeus and the goddess Leto were lovers when she became pregnant with twins Artemis and Apollo. When Hera discovered their tryst, she flew into a jealous rage, prompting her to send the Python to pursue Leto in order to prevent her from delivering the children. Her instructions to the Python were that Leto was not to be allowed to give birth wherever the sun shone on land or sea. This command left pregnant Leto roaming the world exhaustedly until she, with the help of Poseidon, eventually found the island of Delos, which, according to the myth, was a floating island neither land nor sea. The Python's attempt to prevent the delivery of the twins was ultimately foiled, and Apollo and Artemis were born. To avenge his mother's prenatal agony, when Apollo was only four days old (yet already a strong boy), he took a silver bow and golden arrows and tracked the Python (a female Dragon—*Drakaina*—named Delphyne in Homer's *Hymn to Apollo*) to Delphi. During their battle, when the Python tried to devour the infant Apollo, the young warrior shot a golden arrow into her forehead. After thrashing about in agony for a bit, the Python eventually died and her decaying body parts sank deep into the rocky crevices at Delphi. As the myth further indicates, the decaying Python became the vapors that would rise up from the underground to inspire the virtuous Pythia of Delphi to speak her prophecies. All future Pythia would sit atop a tripod cauldron, receive their inspirations from the vapors, and then share their famed oracles with those who visited legendary Delphi.[24]

These mythic connections are hardly coincidental, and John surely meant for his listeners to understand that the "male child" / υἱόν, ἄρσεν (12:5)—Jesus—was in every way the true Son of God who like (but superior to) Apollo (the son of Zeus and known as the Greek god of light) would himself defeat both the darkness and the Dragon. Although John does not call him such in Revelation, the Gospel of John identifies Jesus as superior to darkness since he is "the light of the world" / τὸ φῶς τοῦ κόσμου (John 8:12). John of the Apocalypse reveals, instead, the male child who defeats the "great Dragon, ancient serpent, who is called the Devil and Satan" / δράκων ὁ μέγας, ὁ ὄφις ὁ ἀρχαῖος, ὁ καλούμενος Διάβολος καὶ ὁ Σατανᾶς (cf. 12:9) as a further indication of the triumph of light over darkness (recall the woman clothed with the sun with the moon beneath her feet). The means by which the "male child" Jesus defeats the Dragon, however, is a very different weapon than a silver bow and golden arrows. His weapon and way of victory, the cross, is at the heart of the Apocalypse's atonement theology.

While these background images are parsed variously by commentators, scholars are consistently agreed that the woman of Revelation 12 must not be taken literally. Those using an allegorical method of interpretation often identify her as Mary, Mother of Jesus.[25] Koester provides a reasonable summary of the assorted views about the woman[26] before concluding with the consensus that the woman is multifaceted. She is like Eve who faced the ancient serpent (cp., "the Dragon stood before the woman about to give birth" / ὁ δράκων ἔστηκεν ἐνώπιον τῆς γυναικὸς τῆς μελλούσης τεκεῖν) (12:4), who had pain in childbearing (cp. "she cries out in anguish" / κράζει ὠδίνουσα καὶ βασανιζομένη τεκεῖν, 12:2b); is like the people of Israel who escaped destruction in the wilderness with God's providential help (cp. "she flew into the wilderness to a place prepared for her where she was nourished" / πέτηται εἰς τὴν ἔρημον εἰς τὸν τόπον αὐτῆς, ὅπου τρέφεται, 12:14); is like Zion whom the prophets identified as a woman giving birth (Isa 66:7-9) while threatened by Babylon who like a Dragon filled its belly with victims (cp. "so that when she gave birth to the child he might consume it" / ἵνα ὅταν τέκῃ τὸ τέκνον αὐτῆς καταφάγῃ, 12:4); and is like Jesus' followers who keep the commandments of God and witness of Jesus (cp. "the word of their witness" / τὸν λόγον τῆς μαρτυρίας αὐτῶν, 12:11). Koester concludes, "The multiple layers of imagery allow John's readers to recognize the experiences of conflict and threat within their own social settings as part of the broader story of God's people."[27]

As such, the pregnant woman is best seen as "mother" of the people of God of both the Old Testament and the New Testament, and accordingly is representative of the people of God who have always been under assault by evil. Some prefer the language of "Messianic Community" to describe the woman, which includes all the faithful of God of the Old Testament and New Testament: the prophets, Jesus, and Jesus' followers yesterday, today, and tomorrow (and that means Mary too).[28] The male child is certainly both a product of and representative of all these images that John uses. The believing community and the male Child are the focus of John's attention since they are the ones who are in conflict with the Dragon.

John's point about the suffering community, personified in the agonizing woman (and later her offspring), is solidified by his choice of words in this scene. In fact, he uses a word to describe the woman's pain that is never associated with a woman's labor pains. John's word "being tormented" / βασανιζομένη (12:2) is found elsewhere in the literature only in connection with persecution.[29] Hence, this torment has to do with the suffering people of God of all time—including faithful Old Testament suffering, intertestamental suffering, Jesus' suffering, and the suffering of his followers—all personified in this representative woman whose role in John's understanding of atonement is of utmost importance.

"A GREAT RED DRAGON" / δράκων μέγας πυρρός: 12:3-4A

The "Dragon" / δράκων makes the first of its thirteen appearances in Revelation (a dragon is found only in Revelation in the New Testament) in 12:3. This "other sign" / ἄλλο σημεῖον likewise appears in "heaven" / ἐν τῷ οὐρανῷ (Rev 12:3). Boring suggests that "John knows that it 'takes two worlds to make sense out of one.' . . . The mythical story reflects and evokes images and events of his hearer-readers' experience, allowing them to see their struggles in a transcendent context."[30]

Like the woman above who is a "sign" that appears in heaven, but whose symbol includes the earth, the Dragon's appearance likewise affects the earth. In virtually every culture, dragons have been associated with evil in one way or another and are notorious for wreaking havoc wherever they are found. Beale provides an appropriate summary of this imagery from both the Old Testament and the non-biblical culture of the ancient world.[31] In many ways this Dragon is like the "chaos monster of ancient Near Eastern mythology that was defeated and held at bay at creation (Leviathan, Lotan, Tiamat). This Dragon has seven heads, as does the death monster in the Testament of Abraham 7:14."[32] As mentioned above, the Dragon also has affinity with the Python whom Apollo killed as well as Seth (whose Greek name was Typhon), the red Dragon and mythical enemy of Egypt's beloved Isis and Osiris.

John's Dragon differs in part, however, from other traditional dragons while having similarities to them as well. This "seven-headed and ten-horned [Dragon] has seven crowns upon its heads" / κεφαλὰς ἑπτὰ καὶ κέρατα δεκα καὶ ἐπὶ τὰς κεφαλὰς αὐτοῦ ἑπτὰ διαδήματα (Rev 12:3). These numerical symbols speak to the Dragon's seeming omnipotence and omnipresence[33] and use similar language to that echoed in the beasts of Revelation 13:1 and 17:3. The connection between the Dragon and Rome becomes clearer based on Daniel 7:7, 24.[34] The "ten horns" of the fourth beast of Daniel comes from the sea just as the beast does in Revelation 13:1. John, like Daniel before him, identifies yet another coming evil kingdom. The kingdom of his day was like those mentioned in Daniel. Both arise in opposition to God and God's people. While the evil of John's Revelation is Rome, his concern at this point is primarily to call attention to the source of this evil that he will describe momentarily as defeated and thrown down. As he says, the Dragon is synonymous with the Ancient Serpent, Devil, Satan, and Deceiver who is the power behind all the world's evil[35] (cf. Rev 12:9 and above, chapter 4, "Satan").

This Dragon, not uncharacteristically, has a "tail" / ἡ οὐρὰ (Rev 12:4) (perhaps with power like the tails of the monsters mentioned in Rev 9:3, 10) with which it "swept down a third of the stars of heaven, and threw them onto the earth" / σύρει τὸ τρίτον τῶν ἀστέρων τοῦ οὐρανοῦ, καὶ ἔβαλεν αὐτοὺς εἰς τὴν γῆν (Rev 12:4). This metaphorical action has a deliberate connection to Antiochus Epiphanes, who was mentioned in Daniel 8:10—"It grew as high as the host of heaven. It threw down to earth some of the host and some of the stars, and trampled on them." Aune suggests that this fractional destruction is like that "unleashed by the seven trumpets,"[36] while Beale adds that these are persecuted earthly saints who have heavenly counterparts (cp. Rev 1:20 where the seven stars are the "angels/messengers" / heavenly counterparts of the seven churches). The explanation of the swept-down stars, Beale continues, reaches back to Revelation 12:1 with the added detail of persecution. While the Daniel 8:10 reference related originally to Antiochus Epiphanes of 167–164 BCE, John applies it here to the real evil behind all earthly evil.[37]

John's mention of the Dragon's attack on the stars undoubtedly connects to the stars mentioned in the woman's crown in 12:1. The close proximity of the word "stars" influences this likely connection. Only Beale, however, entertains the possibility that "the falling stars of 12:4 do, after all, represent deceived Israel, who falls away and was never truly identified with the stars in 12:1."[38] It is surely possible that these fallen stars should be identified rather with a third of the churches that likewise are symbolized by stars in Revelation 1:20. If so, John's warning about the Dragon is also to the remaining churches to beware the potency of the Dragon's tail that is never hesitant to attack. John could hardly have made this point more clearly than in the forthcoming scenes that he describes in 12:13-18. Since only a third of the stars are identified as swept down by the dragon in the present scene, this detail points in the direction of other remaining stars that are subject to future assault. Certainly, as John develops this vision, the Dragon will "depart to make war against the rest of her offspring" / ἀπῆλθεν ποιῆσαι πόλεμον μετὰ τῶν λοιπῶν τοῦ σπέρματος αὐτῆς (Rev 12:17) with the implication that more stars (which are heavenly counterparts to the churches) may themselves fall.

"A MALE CHILD" / υἱόν, ἄρσεν: 12:4B-5

This same Dragon has its sights set on the woman and her unborn child "so that when she should deliver he might devour her child" / ἵνα ὅταν τέκῃ τὸ τέκνον αὐτῆς καταφάγῃ (Rev 12:4). This part of the verse sets the stage for what John envisions—ultimately the death of the child in Revelation 12:5. Beale references Qumran scroll 1QH 3:7-12 that tells a somewhat similar story of an anguishing pregnant woman who is about to give birth to a male child, a child who will deliver God's people that are in the "bonds of Sheol." A second story also appears in these verses that mentions another woman who is pregnant with an asp that in "the swelling waves of the Pit" uses the waves to work its terror against God's people.[39]

The point of connection between these Qumran images and Revelation is that a male Child is anticipated who will deliver the persecuted people of God from the evil persecutor who likewise is alive concurrently with the Child. Aune rightly identifies this male Child as "clearly designated as the Messiah through an allusion to Ps 2:9."[40] As John will make clear later, the means by which the Child achieves the deliverance is crucial. The Child will win the battle in a way that is certainly counterintuitive. At this point in the vision, however, Smalley is right that John

> illustrates the antagonism which will surround Jesus, throughout his earthly ministry: from the hostility of Herod in the infancy narratives (Matt. 2:1-12), to the temptations and dangers which were characteristic of his life (Mark 1.13; 3.6; John 5.18), up to the climax of his passion and crucifixion (John 18.1–19.42). Resurrection will follow, but that is not in view at the moment; rather, this vision concentrates on the suffering of the Messiah, and of his followers to the extent that they abide in him (John 15.18-25).[41]

John is not reticent to combine signs of authority (a star-crowned woman clothed with the sun who has the moon beneath her feet—12:1) with those of pain and suffering (a pregnant woman crying out in agony—12:2), both resident in the same character. Again, as counterintuitive as these combinations are, John repeats this pattern when he mentions the vulnerability associated with the "birth of a male Child who is [simultaneously] going to shepherd/rule all the nations with a rod of iron" / ἔτεκεν υἱόν, ἄρσεν, ὃς μέλλει ποιμαίνειν πάντα τὰ ἔθνη ἐν ῥάβδῳ σιδηρᾷ (Rev 12:5a).

Indeed, the Child is brought forth "to shepherd" or "to rule" / ποιμαίνειν (Rev 12:5a). Earlier in chapter 3 (cf. above "19:15, 21 [1:16; 2:12, 16; 2:27; 12:5]") we evaluated and concluded that John's expression "he will shepherd (or "rule") them with a rod of iron" / ποιμανεῖ αὐτοὺς ἐν ῥάβδῳ σιδηρᾷ (19:15) calls on the LXX language of Isaiah 11:4 that says "he will strike the earth with the word of his mouth" / πατάξει γῆν λόγῳ τῷ τοῦ στόματος αὐτοῦ, while the Hebrew text uses instead of the word "word" the word "rod" / בְּשֵׁבֶט. In other words, John acknowledges that the "iron rod" / ῥάβδῳ σιδηρᾷ of victory is none other than the spoken word of truth that comes from the mouth of the Son of Man in Revelation 2:27. This same Son of Man is the subject described as a "male child" / υἱόν, ἄρσεν (Rev 12:4b) born, about to die, and to ascend to this throne. The combination of these inverted images means that the "male Child is about to shepherd/rule all the nations with a rod of iron" /

υἱόν, ἄρσεν, ὃς μέλλει ποιμαίνειν πάντα τὰ ἔθνη ἐν ῥάβδῳ σιδηρᾷ. His "rod of iron" is the unbreakable truth that will soon be evident in the death of the "male Child." In every way this image parallels that of "the lamb standing as having been slain" / ἀρνίον ἑστηκὸς ὡς ἐσφαγμένον (Rev 5:6) who is likewise "the lion of the tribe of Judah" / ὁ λέων ὁ ἐκ τῆς φυλῆς Ἰούδα (Rev 5:5). John's capacity to turn seemingly contradictory notions into parallel analogies is truly remarkable.

Bauckham concurs with these connections. He says,

> By juxtaposing the two contrasting images, John has forged a new symbol of conquest by sacrificial death. The messianic hopes evoked in 5:5 are not repudiated: Jesus really is the expected Messiah of David (22:16). But insofar as the latter was associated with military violence and narrow nationalism, it is reinterpreted by the image of the Lamb. The Messiah has certainly won a victory, but he has done so by sacrifice and for the benefit of people from all nations (5:9) . . . . The continuing and ultimate victory of God over evil which the rest of Revelation describes is no more than the working-out of the decisive victory of the Lamb on the cross.[42]

Beale perceptively calls this verse a "snapshot" of Jesus' entire life.[43] While he mentions the Child's crucifixion, resurrection, and ascension as all being in mind here, an underemphasized part of this description is the Child's death. To be sure, these images tease the mind by redefining the words iron, power, and ruling. The conflicting images of a Child shepherding with a rod of iron prepares the reader as well for the unthinkable notion that the Child will prevail over the Dragon by, in fact, allowing the Dragon to devour him. Indeed, self-sacrifice is the essential feature by which the Child ascends to the throne.

Obviously, John's language, "and her Child was snatched up to God and to his throne" / καὶ ἡρπάσθη τὸ τέκνον αὐτῆς τὸν θεὸν καὶ πρὸς τὸν θρόνον αὐτοῦ (12:5c), is tantamount to the violent crucifixion of Jesus. Commentators routinely see this language as "temporal tele-scoping . . . of Christ's entire life—his birth, his destiny of kingship, and his . . . ascent to God's heavenly throne after his postresurrection ministry . . . given in one line."[44] While all of these life experiences of the Christ are implied, the immediate context, based on John's choice of words, seems to elevate one theme—the violent death of Jesus. While translations tend to soften the aggressive Greek word "was snatched" / ἡρπάσθη with the milder "caught up" (KJV, RSV, Moffatt, Goodspeed, NASB), this "snatching" is in reality a word used for taking away something forcefully.

Careful attention should be paid as well to the location of this part of the vision. Narratively speaking, John pictures the Dragon's assault on the woman and child as happening on earth. Since momentarily "her child is snatched up to God" / ἡρπάσθη τὸ τέκνον αὐτῆς πρὸς τὸν θεὸν, John clearly has in mind an earthly location at which this happens, just as Smalley observes.[45] With this conclusion in place, an exploration of the word ἁρπάζω / "I snatch up" proves suggestive of John's intentions.

András Dávid Pataki has noted,

> First, the use of the verb ἁρπάζω. If it refers to the ascension in itself, the usage of the more common ἀναλαμβάνω (Acts 1.2, 11, 22; 1 Tim 3.16) or ὑψόω (Acts 2.33; 5.31; cf. Phil 2.9 and perhaps John 12.32) would have been more comprehensible, even if the realization of Christian hope, i.e. the resurrection and the *catching up* of the believers at the *parousia* of Christ in relation of which ἁρπάζω is applied in 1 Thess 4.17, is some-times connected in the NT to the resurrected Lord's being taken up and reigning in glory (John 14.2-3; 17.24; 2 Tim 2.12; Heb 6.19-20).[46]

He further observes that "the force and violence inherent in ἁρπάζω, and with [it] the association of the cognate nouns ἁρπαγμός and ἁρπαγή with robbery"[47] is well known. While on the right track, Pataki stopped short, however, of arriving at the conclusion to which his analysis was taking him. He only suggests, "The dreadful enemy is definitively robbed of the possibility of devouring the Messiah. The irresistible force of the divine action is directed against his obvious intentions."[48] He would have been better served had he stayed on the course that he was traveling with the emphasis on the Dragon's force and violence. Ladd clearly did just this when he observed that

> all is symbolism portraying the hostility of Satan to God's anointed one. Many commentators see here an allusion to Herod's efforts to destroy the infant Jesus (Matt. 2:16). If this vision was intended to represent actual history, it ought to portray the crucifixion of Jesus, for the death of Jesus for a moment seemed to be the triumph of the powers of darkness (Luke 22:53) . . . .
>
> This can hardly be an allusion to the ascension of Christ, for his rapture did not have the purpose of escaping Satan's hostility. On the contrary, as the crucified and resurrected Christ he had already won his

triumph over satanic power (Heb. 2:14; Col. 2:15). This is John's vivid way of asserting the victory of God's anointed over every satanic effort to destroy him.[49]

Hence, "her child [being] snatched up to God and to his throne" / ἡρπάσθη τὸ τέκνον αὐτῆς πρὸς τὸν θεὸν καὶ πρὸς τὸν θρόνον αὐτοῦ (12:5c) is a brief description of the violent death that the Child suffered at the Dragon's hand. And, of course, the historical referent to which this death relates is Jesus' death on the cross.

The somewhat disconcerting statement introduced into the narrative at this point, that "the woman fled into the wilderness, where she has a place prepared from God, so that he might nourish her there 1260 days" / ἡ γυνὴ ἔφυγεν εἰς τὴν ἔρημον, ὅπου ἔχει ἐκεῖ τόπον ἡτοιμασμένον ἀπὸ τοῦ θεοῦ, ἵνα ἐκεῖ τρέφωσιν αὐτὴν ἡμέρας χιλίας διακοσίας ἑξήκοντα (Rev 12:6), actually prepares the reader to understand the present circumstance of the Messianic Community (see above "12:2")[50] in the aftermath of the Child's death and the Dragon being thrown down. The woman's fleeing is a likely allusion to the flight from Jerusalem by Christians to Pella in 66 CE among other allusions of testing and trials. Beale provides a careful summary in his excursus of "The Desert as a Place of Both Trial and Protection," articulating how John parallels the exodus theme in this image.[51] Revelation's point is to declare that the people of God have been and always will be targeted and subjected to attack. In other words, believers will experience a life similar to what the male Child has experienced—sometimes mortally and sometimes not—but their lives will be characterized as ones "in the wilderness" where trial, tribulation, and temptation mark their days, but likewise where their lives are also under the provision of God.

The mention of "wilderness" / ἔρημον brings to mind images of the Hebrew children's forty years of testing and trial, as well as Jesus' forty days of testing and satanic temptation (and, of course, his Gethsemane agony). Alongside these allusions is the three and a half years (the 1260 days of v. 6c) of Antiochus Epiphanes' control of Jerusalem (167–164 BCE) about which Daniel wrote in his "time, times, and half a time" reference in Daniel 7:25. This fraction of the number seven denotes the partial time of trial and testing that the people of God undergo even while they are likewise under God's spiritual care. The wilderness place is both one of "nourishment" / τρέφωσιν and τρέφεται (12:6 and 12:14) provided by God as well as one of testing like what the Hebrew children experienced in their wilderness sojourn. The biblical story reports that they were fed by manna just as Jesus was sustained not by "bread alone" but by "every word that proceeds from the mouth of God" (Matt 4:4). Knowledge of such a place of "nourishment" prompted the Qumran sect that was both prior to and contemporary with Jesus to locate in the wilderness themselves in preparation of the final battle that they believed they would fight for God.[52] This "prepared place" is certainly one of both testing and protection in which believers find themselves. John speaks to the physical persecution that comes on believers, but he also speaks of God's security that is available to all who endure, even those "who love not their lives even unto death" / οὐκ ἠγάπησαν τὴν ψυχὴν αὐτῶν ἄχρι θανάτου (cf. 12:11).

"A WAR IN HEAVEN" / πόλεμος ἐν τῷ οὐρανῷ: 12:7-9

In 12:7-9 John closes the "inclusio" that he opened in 12:3 when he first mentioned the Dragon. In chapter 4 (above), Gordon Campbell's identification of the "narrative sandwiching technique of two intercalated stories: in Rev 12 two attacks mounted by the satan, first on Messiah (12.1-6) and then on the woman and her offspring (12.13-17), are tellingly separated by its own heavenly defeat in 12.7-12."[53] John's point is clear: "for the satan, attack is defeat . . . , sealed in the blood of the Lamb—the victory of the cross . . . , [which] in Revelation, precedes everything else (1.5)."[54]

Boring likewise agrees that the Dragon's defeat and "the expulsion of Satan from heaven is the result of the victory of Christ on earth (12:10-11) . . . [and that] the 'time' of the fall of Satan from heaven is 'now' (12:10): in the story line of the vision, the time of the Christ event."[55] What John is conveying is that the intercalated war that is fought in heaven is the simultaneous assault and death of the Child with the angelic battle in heaven. The connection between the Dragon sign (12:3) and this event is made clear, in part, by the repetition of "in heaven" / ἐν τῷ οὐράῳ of 12:7.

The battle between Michael and the Dragon is in the spirit of an extended "Christian war scroll."[56] David Barr actually names Revelation 11:19–22:21 "The War Scroll"[57] just as Johns confirms: "There is a war going on in Revelation at several levels. The war in heaven symbolizes and gives new perspective for the war taking place on the earth."[58] As the narrative describes the war, Michael and his angels fight with the Dragon, and the Dragon and his angels fight / ὁ Μιχαὴλ καὶ οἱ ἄγγελοι αὐτοῦ τοῦ πολεμῆσαι μετὰ τοῦ δράκοντος. καὶ ὁ δράκων ἐπολέμησεν καὶ οἱ ἄγγελοι αὐτοῦ (12:7b). This war scene is clearly reminiscent of Daniel 10 where Michael is the close associate of the Son of Man who fights against the evil angels of Persia and Greece (Dan 10:13, 20-21; 12:1; cf. also 1 Enoch 54:6). Caird notes that in Revelation 12, "Michael, in fact, is not the field officer who does the actual fighting, but the staff officer in the heavenly control room, who is able to remove Satan's flag from the heavenly map because the real victory has been won on Calvary."[59]

The simultaneity of the heavenly and earthly visions emphasizes that the battle at the cross in which Jesus found himself on earth (and one that he lost by worldly standards of winning and losing) had a heavenly counterpart pictured in Michael's battle and victory over the Dragon. In the Daniel vision the "little horn" is too strong for the saints (Dan 7:21), but in John's vision things are reversed with Michael overpowering the Dragon and his evil angels. How the proverbial "table has turned" in Revelation is at the heart of John's atonement theology. The way in which the male Child wins the ultimate victory is the same as the means of the Child's ascendency to the throne. The Dragon's defeat in heavenly combat is one and the same with the Dragon's defeat in the earthly self-sacrifice of the Child. One of the Christian faith's great truths is clearly expressed by John in the Apocalypse—the power of suffering love modeled by the death of the Lamb. Moreover, John communicates that there are profound implications for the Dragon who has murdered this innocent Child, namely that he is thrown down as a consequence.

Bauckham says, "John portrayed the fall of Satan himself, the 'great red Dragon' (12:3) . . . ; but John, while sharing this hope for the future (Rev 20), placed the decisive encounter already in the past. The Dragon, then, must first appear in person and suffer defeat in heaven, before marshaling his forces to do battle on earth."[60] Reddish, from the vantage point of Rev 20, states:

> In 12:7-12, Satan and his evil angels have been thrown out of heaven and down to the earth where they waged war on God's people . . . . Now Satan's opposition to God will finally [as described in 20:1-3] be brought to an end as God acts to subdue the forces of evil. As in chapter 12, John is using the ancient combat myth here in depicting God's defeat of the dragon.[61]

More precisely, Bauckham says, "The defeat of the Dragon (12:7-9) is doubtless the same event as the victory of the Lamb (5:5-6), and both are to be historically located in the death and resurrection of Jesus Christ (continued in the witness and martyrdom of his followers: 12:11)."[62] The consequence of the Dragon's murder of the innocent Child means nothing less than the Dragon and his angels' loss to Michael and his angels. The unjust murder by the Dragon of the innocent Child means that "there was no longer a place found for them in heaven" / οὐδὲ τόπος εὑρέθη αὐτῶν ἔτι ἐν τῷ οὐρανῷ (Rev 12:8). John leaves room at this point for the reader to make a key connection. While some have likened this scene to Luke 10:17-18 when Jesus describes the beginning of Satan's defeat and that of evil in response to his disciples' ministry—"I saw Satan fall like lightning from heaven"—most, however, rightly distance themselves from such an interpretation. John simply is communicating that "the great Dragon was thrown down" / ἐβλήθη ὁ δράκων ὁ μέγας (12:9) as a result of his unjust attack and unlawful execution (murder!) of the Child.

Koester summarizes additional ways that some have associated Satan's fall with heavenly battles. Some see, he says, "a flashback to primeval history . . . to Satan's primeval fall"[63] based on two biblical texts and Jewish traditions. In Isaiah 14:12-15 Day Star (Lucifer) is cast down to Sheol for arrogantly assuming that he belonged above the stars like God (cf. also Ezek 28:16-17). The "Lucifer" name, of course, was associated originally with the Babylonian king that tradition turned into a supernatural being and that once was one of the archangels at the time of creation (2 En. 29:4-5). Koester continues, "The tradition was popular because it explained the origin of evil in the world that God created to be good, and it accounted for the fact that the garden of Eden included a malicious serpent that lured human beings into sin."[64] He concludes rightly against this connection because "[t]he literary flow makes this idea unlikely here, however, since the heavenly battle against the serpent is set after the exaltation of Christ,"[65] not before.

Aune likewise discredits the notion of Satan's fall being associated with the angels of primeval times that intermarried with human beings (cf. Gen 6:1-4; 1 En. 6–10; Jude 6). He concludes that this is unlikely since Genesis 6 says that the angels sinned by leaving heaven rather than being thrown down in defeat in a heavenly battle.[66] The final suggestion of Satan's expulsion referring to a later period at the end of the age wrongly requires an insertion of a thousand-year millennial reign, when, as Koester points out, "there are no literary signals to suggest that readers must discern a lengthy gap between 12:5 and 6."[67]

All in all, as Rutledge concludes with other theologians and philosophers, there is no satisfactory account for the origin of evil's arrival on earth.[68]
Rather, "Evil is a . . . monstrous contradiction that cannot be explained but
can only be denounced and resisted wherever it appears."[69] We are called
"to hold two seemingly contradictory concepts simultaneously," that "Satan
is an active intelligence who is striving for world domination yet does not
have ontological status of his own; he 'exists' only as the will to negate."[70]

In terms of Satan's ouster from heaven, John intends what he will say
directly in 12:11. But first there is a celebratory interlude in 12:10 that
signals the Apocalypse's summary expression of atonement theology.

REVELATION'S ATONEMENT THEOLOGY: VICTORY THROUGH SUFFERING AND DEATH 12:10

At the news of Satan's ouster, John writes, "And I heard a great voice in
heaven" / Καὶ ἤκουσα φωνὴν μεγάλην ἐν τῷ οὐρανῷ (Rev 12:10). What
the heavenly voice declares is that the "Devil" / Διάβολος, "Satan/Accuser"
/ ὁ Σατανᾶς, "Deceiver" / ὁ πλανῶν is "cast out" / ἐβλήθη of heaven. The
profundity of this celebratory message rings throughout the balance of the
verse with significant theological implications.

John reports that he heard a heavenly voice declaring, "Now has
happened the salvation, the power, and the kingdom of our God and the
authority of his Christ" /Ἄρτι ἐγένετο ἡ σωτηρία καὶ ἡ δύναμις καὶ ἡ
βασιλεία τοῦ θεοῦ ἡμῶν καὶ ἡ ἐξουσία τοῦ χριστοῦ αὐτοῦ (12:10b).
Commentators speculate among four options for the subject of the voice:
the twenty-four elders, angels, martyrs, or the redeemed in general.[71] This
detail, however, is secondary to John's main point: the salvation (and the
attending qualifiers of power, kingdom, and authority) brought by Christ
has happened in the simultaneous earthly/heavenly event of the Child's
death and the Dragon's defeat. Here is the Apocalypse's soteriology at its
zenith. God's alchemy, to use that expression, is on full display and is at its
theological height in this moment.[72]

Koester rightly understands John's meaning: "In Revelation God does
not simply disregard the accusations Satan brings but actually bars Satan
from the heavenly court."[73] To put it another way, "In legal terms, the devil
not only loses the case, but is barred from further appearances in court."[74]
This victory means that the accuser "has been thrown down" and has no
heavenly access any longer. The Satan may not bring further indictments

against the people of God. As 12:10 concludes, "the one who accuses them before our God night and day" / ὁ κατηγορῶν αὐτοὺς ἐνώπιον τοῦ θεοῦ ἡμῶν ἡμέρας καὶ νυκτός has now been officially banned from the court-room of God and is prohibited from bringing any more accusations. In a word, he has been fatally disbarred. The theological implications of the analogy of the prosecutorial accuser's ouster, of the Satan being thrown down and disbarred, are becoming increasingly more evident.

While pushing any analogy beyond its basic meaning is never wise, there are theological ramifications present in the Satan's banishment that should be carefully considered. In his role as an angel/messenger of God, the Satan's task (see above, chapter 4, "The Satan" / ὁ Σατανᾶς) was to bring accusations against God's people (cp. Job 1:6-12; Zech 3:1-2). The Satan's task as such was to serve the royal court of God in an adversarial role to test God's people. His identity, based on the Old Testament's under-standing of him, was not necessarily something malevolent. His role was simply to serve as an accuser and as one who tests people. Testing, after all, often proved useful for strengthening God's people. Of course, a test may also turn out to be a temptation to which a person yields, as often happened in the biblical story as well as in post-biblical human experience. As far as the Satan is concerned, his role as adversary is equally one as "the accuser" / ὁ κατηγορῶν and "the deceiver" / ὁ πλανῶν (12:9), as Revela-tion names him.

Certainly, in his capacity as the Satan, his success as a prosecutor is easily calculated. The Satan successfully prosecuted each and every defendant, including upright Job, who for all of his virtue eventually declared his own sinfulness in his confession to God: "I repent in dust and ashes" (Job 42:6). It is reasonable, therefore, to suggest that such success on the Satan's part stands in back of his ultimate fall. In other words, this tragic figure became consumed with a spirit of arrogance that is evident (as the Judaeo-Christian tradition and as Revelation concludes) in and since his first appearance in the serpent-related scene in which he successfully tempted the man and woman (uniquely created though they were in God's image—Gen 1:26). His ability to tempt with such subtlety and ultimate success, and to lure God's own image into sin, is without question, not to mention his flawless and extraordinary record as prosecutor.

The Satan's accusations against people, based on their sins, unani-mously resulted in airtight cases prosecuted beyond any possible defense. His ability to carry out his commission (which certainly is his role in the Old Testament and intertestamental period) seems to have led him to draw an erroneous conclusion about himself, namely that he was more successful in his role than God seems to have been in God's role. He, without fail, consistently persuaded people to fall to his schemes and temptations at some time (or many times) in their lives, while God, on the other hand, seems to have had very little (if any?) success in leading any person to a lifetime (or even short time) of faithful behavior and service. Even a man after God's own heart (1 Sam 13:14), David, failed and had to be restored. In short, the Satan's legal cases resulted in a guilty verdict every time for which only a requisite sacrifice proved to be an appropriate response (if temporary remedy) on people's part. Satan perfectly executed his task, demonstrating both his legal prowess and impeccable dedication to justice. Only John's recorded vision answers how the Satan's demand for justice at the bar of God was met; while it should mean the execution of all who stand before that bar and are found guilty, that in fact proves not to be the case.

As John points out, only on one occasion did the Satan fail. The Gospels point out that he was unable to test, tempt, or persuade Jesus to sin. This failure notwithstanding, the Satan neither admitted his own failure nor withheld making a false judgment against this lone innocent man. Yet despite his failure to build a successful case against Jesus, from every indication the Satan seems to have convinced himself that by eliminating (killing!) Jesus, he will finally have put an end to his rival and chief competitor. Success on this front, as his story seems to imply, would render him the sole remaining power in the world; that is, if power is to be defined by brute force, killing, and murder. Power is certainly the prominent theme that runs throughout the Apocalypse and its depiction of the human story. John's presentation of seals (and war horses), trumpets (and monster beasts), and the Dragon and the Great Harlot all represent the world's superpowers obsessed with acquiring more while exploiting people and abusing the planet. Once, however, the Satan overpowers the male Child with brute force, as Revelation 12 so precisely describes it, John's atonement theology begins to approach its analogical height. The Apocalypse makes clear that the Satan as Dragon (and the two beasts forthcoming in Rev 13) are the mocking trinity of evil behind the Harlot (Rome). They likewise are the political power responsible for Jesus' crucifixion and ultimately for the martyrdom of Jesus' followers who are the offspring of "the woman" identified in Revelation 12.

In fact, during the passion week of Jesus' life, as that week was nearing its end, the Satan wittingly and malevolently carried out the death sentence against this truly innocent person. He did so by means of his treachery and his deception of the religious system of Judaism's Sanhedrin and high priest, the deception of Jesus' close friend and associate Judas Iscariot, and the complicity of the Roman legal system. The timing of this grand conspiracy reached its worst in the events leading up to and finalized on the cross on Good Friday (another counterintuitive expression). The day of crucifixion was actually a culmination of the Satan's long history as adversary, deceiver, accuser, and devil all rolled into one. John of Revelation, frankly, had little interest in identifying the "time" of the Satan's original rebellion. His concern, rather, was simply to repeat what he heard coming from heaven: that the Satan has been legally disbarred as the result of his criminal activity in crucifying innocent Jesus. The word "legally" is a key interpretive term in the events that John reveals. The Satan, as a prosecutor in all other cases, achieved guilty verdicts only when he was successful in bringing compelling evidence against a defendant. This result, to be sure, he achieved successfully in each case that he brought before the bar of God, except the one that he failed to build against Jesus despite the trumped-up charges brought by the religious legal system, set in motion by Judas's betrayal of Jesus, and finally consummated in crucifixion by the Roman juggernaut.

The related scene of the Dragon devouring the Child depicts in compelling imagery the great miscarriage of justice in the execution of innocent Jesus, the "male child," at the hands of the Dragon himself—just as John describes it. As a consequence of this unjust action, John summarizes how the Satan was disbarred by Michael, advocate of God's people, so that the Satan is never allowed to bring another charge against anyone before the bar of God in the heavenly courtroom. As Caird says, "Thus, although John depicts the battle between Michael and Satan in military terms, it was essentially a legal battle between opposing counsel, which resulted in one of them being disbarred."[75] The unveiling of these details affirms that God need not and did not do anything that approaches the Satan's tactics of treachery, deception, or violence to defeat the ancient foe. The Satan, rather, became a victim of his own success and, consequently, the recipient of the justice that he so mercilessly demanded when he prosecuted others. That very justice, when applied to and turned on him, meant his ouster. In other words, what he ruthlessly and consistently meted out against humankind throughout the ages came back squarely to rest upon him, just as the seven bowls of wrath (see above, chapter 3, "16:1; 16:17 [8:3, 5"]) that John pictured in Revelation 16 came back upon the perpetrators who were drunk on the blood of the saints.

God's divine alchemy turned the great horror of the death of the Son of God into the world's greatest good. As John D. Crossan says, "How we think a deliverer should deliver and a savior save may not be exactly how God delivers and God saves."[76] Consistent with God's own character, God allowed the Satan to be responsible for his own undoing so that what he did was unquestionably disbar himself. God's wisdom in this entire scenario is consistently on full display. By allowing the Satan to do his worst, indeed to undo himself, God avoids any appearance whatsoever (true to God's character) that might remotely resemble the trickery or treachery of the Evil One.

There is a striking irony in this entire matter. As long as Jesus was alive, there remained the theoretical possibility (as unlikely as that might seem to some) that he could eventually sin and fall victim to a future temptation or deception of the Satan. A single misstep on Jesus' part would have rendered him subject to the Satan's legal prosecution and to death by the legal system of justice. The Satan's arrogance, however, once he set his plan in motion with his select cast of characters that carried out the passion drama, meant his very downfall. The moment (which seems to have been as long as the biblical story has included details about him) that the Satan became judge, jury, and executioner, he violated the law of justice under which he was commissioned to operate. In a manner of speaking, he became his own victim when he killed innocent Jesus. Consequently, he was summarily disbarred, cast forever out of the heavenly courtroom, and thus may never accuse anyone again.[77]

Assuredly, according to the Apocalypse, from the foundation of the world God envisioned this very event and its outcome. God used the free choices of the Satan and his emissaries to play out the drama of redemption. John pictures this day and the simultaneity of these events in his acknowledgment of "the Lamb slain from the foundation of the world" / τοῦ ἀρνίου τοῦ ἐσφαγμένου ἀπὸ καταβολῆς κόσμου (13:8). Could there be any other or better reason for John to report that he heard "a loud voice in heaven, saying: 'Now has happened the salvation, the power, and the kingdom of our God and the authority of his Christ'" / φωνὴν μεγάλην ἐν τῷ οὐρανῷ λεγουσαν· Ἄρτι ἐγένετο ἡ σωτηρία καὶ ἡ δύναμις καὶ ἡ βασιλεία τοῦ θεοῦ ἡμῶν καὶ ἡ ἐξουσία τοῦ χριστοῦ αὐτοῦ (12:10b)? Truly in this simultaneous moment redemption "happened" / ἐγένετο (12:10).

The Apocalypse has much to say about Satan's defeat and the implications for redemption that his defeat means since "the great Dragon was
thrown down" / ἐβλήθη ὁ δράκων ὁ μέγας (Rev 12:9). Charles E. Hill is
mostly correct:

> The key for understanding the idea of redemption in Revelation 12:7-12
> as well is to recognize that the serpent is defeated here explicitly in his role
> as accuser, reiterated in the listing of names, Devil and Satan (Rev 12:9),
> each of which has the connotation of accuser or adversary. Accusations
> have to do with guilt, and thus we are dealing with the idea of sin as a
> legal transgression . . . .
>
> Satan's violent removal from the heavenly courtroom, where he
> formerly had a place, is a distinctively Christian conception. This is
> because it is the direct result of the shedding of the Lamb's blood, the
> unique redemptive act of Jesus Christ that brought the entire sacrificial
> system of Judaism to a close.[78]

John's description, despite the military language he uses, need not be
understood as violent removal. God is much too wise for that. The description of these battle scenes certainly emphasizes that a parallel and equally
great conflict actually occurred alongside what happened on the earthly
cross, as gruesome and profound as the cross event was. In other words,
the death of Jesus on earth had a heavenly parallel. In the death scene that
John depicts using a male Child and a Dragon, he likewise uses the heavenly battle scene between Michael and the Dragon to portray the Dragon's
defeat. Jesus' death on the cross, and John's understanding of Jesus' atonement, require acknowledgment that the heavenly consequences described
are bound up inseparably with this earthly event; the two are not to be
separated and cannot be disconnected. The power of this image further
informs the meaning of the male Child who "shepherds/rules all with a
rod of iron" / ποιμαίνειν πάντα ἐν ῥάβδῳ σιδηρᾷ (Rev 12:5). This death
proves to be from John's perspective the most powerful, unbreakable force
that the world has ever known, more powerful than the warriors' weapons
in Rome's great army or the Dragon who is the force behind that army.
God's "rod of iron" / ῥάβδῳ σιδηρᾷ stands in stark contrast to the power of
the Dragon, whose only means of victory is to marshal brute force by coer-
cion like that depicted throughout Revelation (and manifest in history),
including the murderous crucifixion that the Dragon used to kill the male
Child.

Reddish acknowledges,

> The apocalyptic worldview conceived of earthly realities having heav-
> enly counterparts. Thus in Daniel, the struggles between the people of
> Israel and their enemies are told in terms of the battles between Michael,
> the patron angel of Israel, and the patron angels of the other nations
> (10:10-21). The defeat of the dragon by Michael is not a separate event
> from Christ's victory on the cross. Rather, the story of Michael and the
> dragon is the story of the cross, cast in mythological language.[79]

John's thinking is not too distant from the Gospel of Matthew where similar
language is found describing the cosmic disturbance that happened when
Jesus was crucified—"the earth shook, and the rocks were split; the tombs
were opened" / καὶ ἡ γῆ ἐσείσθη, καὶ αἱ πέτραι ἐσχίσθησαν; καὶ τὰ
μνημεῖα ἀνεῴχθησαν (Matt 27:51-52). This event happened simultaneously with Jesus' death on the cross, not at some time in the yet-to-happen
future. Truly this phenomenon was "the event" that marked the beginning
of the last days expressed in terms of the "many bodies of the saints that
had fallen asleep were raised" / πολλὰ σώματα τῶν κεκοιμημένων ἁγίων
ἠγέρθησαν (Matt 27:52). Similarly, Luke describes "the curtain of the
temple torn down the middle" / ἐσχίσθη δὲ τὸ καταπέτασμα τοῦ ναοῦ
μέσον (Luke 23:45) at the moment of Jesus' death so that the message
of God's redemption may spread freely throughout the world[80] (just as
Acts portrays). At this point, moreover, the Gospel of John's death and
enthronement language are also echoed at the cross with Jesus' lasts words:
"It is finished" / Τετέλεσται (John 19:30), meaning, of course, not just
Jesus' earthly life but also the very plan of God's redemption of humanity.

Rutledge affirms that "Christ conquered the devil as man had been
conquered by the devil," and as such acknowledged "God's irresistible inva-
sion of the orb of Sin from his own orb of greater power."[81] She does not,
however, recognize how Revelation 12 informs that perspective. Even in
her awareness that Anselm sees "our being liberated from forces too strong
for us" following the apocalyptic lead established by Ezekiel and Zechariah's
vision of vindicated Jerusalem and Daniel's depiction of the advent of the
Son of man,"[82] Revelation 12 is curiously absent. Nevertheless, she points
out correctly that the Christian tradition embraces "*a God who acts inde-
pendently of his people's response . . . [a]nd . . . God's salvation will encompass
the entire created order.*"[83]

The Apocalypse's portrayal of the Dragon and his angels being thrown down simultaneously with Jesus' death is borne out, moreover, in the coronation language of 1 Peter 3:18ff. The truth of Jesus harrowing the prisons, as Rutledge points out, is that the realm of reality of those "formerly disobedient" spirits—namely the perpetrators of evil—is routed by the power of the cross. Those inhabitants also are reached by "the death of the righteous Son of God 'for the unrighteous.'"[84] In every way, "The descent of Christ into hell meant that there is no realm anywhere in the universe, including the domain of Death and the devil, where anyone can go to be cut off from the saving power of God."[85]

From Revelation's perspective, when evil had done its worst to the Child, the result was the Child's ultimate enthronement. Near the end of the Apocalypse John pictures the slain Lamb seated on the throne (the "mercy seat" of judgment) with the river "coming out of the throne of God and the Lamb" / ἐκπορευόμενον ἐκ τοῦ θρόνου τοῦ θεοῦ καὶ τοῦ ἀρνίου (see chapter 2 above, "22:1-3"). Gordon Campbell summarizes the matter thus: "By symmetrically recapitulating Messiah's defeat of the Dragon in Rev 12, chapter 20 wraps up the story of an already defeated-and-banished dragon, irrevocably dispatching it to the abyss and then to the lake of fire."[86] Campbell cites Pierre de Martin de Viviés's compelling statement, "Christ's death and resurrection, metaphorically conveyed as the child's birth, toll the demise of the Dragon's revolt."[87]

12:11a and 12:12a

The ongoing effects of the Satan's defeat and ouster is played out in the additional commentary that John provides in the aftermath of the Accuser's self-destructive demise. The continuing means of victory, John reports, is taken up by believers who conquered "by the word of their testimony/witness/martyrdom, for they loved not their lives even unto death" / διὰ τὸν λόγον τῆς μαρτυρίας αὐτῶν, καὶ οὐκ ἠγάπησαν τὴν ψυχὴν αὐτῶν ἄχρι θανάτου (12:11b). The steadfast victory is spelled out as being "by the blood of the lamb" / διὰ τὸ αἷμα του ἀρνίου (12:11a) by which believers themselves participate in conquering Satan. As Ladd observes, "This shows clearly that the victory over Satan which John has described in mythological terms actually was accomplished in history at the cross. The shed blood of Christ is the real means of victory over Satan."[88] The only power necessary for Satan's defeat is "the blood of the Lamb" shed by the Dragon and his allies to which John consistently makes reference in the variety of images found throughout the Apocalypse. Reddish points out that "[o]ne should note that the martyrs conquer not by their testimony alone, but first of all 'by the blood of the Lamb' (12:11). Their witness, even their deaths, has no meaning apart from Christ."[89] Believers themselves rely on what Jesus did, and they declare the same themselves by their self-sacrificial actions that they are faithful to the Lamb and understand his unique and counterintuitive way of victory.

As John states, alongside the blood of the Lamb, it is "by the word of their witness/testimony/martyrdom" / διὰ τὸν λόγον τῆς μαρτυρίας αὐτῶν (12:11b) that "they conquered him" / αὐτοὶ ἐνίκησαν αὐτὸν (12:11a). While the interesting word μαρτυρίας may be translated with three options—witness, testimony, or martyrdom—likely all three are intended. As stated above in chapter 3 (cf. "12:11"), believers declare and demonstrate their trust in Jesus' blood by dying themselves. Their true belief is confirmed by the sacrifice of their very lives. In fact, John anticipates that believers will indeed lay down their lives like past martyrs did as a clear testimony of their trust in Jesus' nonviolent, anti-Satanic way. In so doing, they bear witness to God's way of victory in the world. The implication of their martyrdom is that they are truly one with their Lord, who allowed the Dragon to do its worst to him, even to take his life, something the Dragon may do to them since he has done this to others.

When he says, "and they loved not their lives even unto death" / καὶ οὐκ ἠγάπησαν τὴν ψυχὴν αὐτῶν ἄχρι θανάτου (12:11c), he means that by giving their lives, believers declare that their lives are not their own, but that they have been "ransomed for God by your blood" / ἠγόρασας τῷ θεῷ ἐν τῷ αἵματί σου (cf. 5:9). Moreover, by giving their lives for Christ, they demonstrate their solidarity with him and that their lives belong to Christ. By not loving their lives, even unto death, believers reclaim their designated place in God's created order; they are servants of the Lord whose goal is obedience, never simply self-preservation.

A.T. Hanson concludes, "This is the victory obtained by the blood of the Lamb, and both 'blood' and 'Lamb' retain this significance throughout the book . . . . In all 'victory' passages, Christ and the saints conquer by dying . . . ."[90] Johns echoes this conclusion himself:

Revelation's view regarding what Jesus did privileges the ethical and political. Whatever else Jesus' death is in this book, it is not exclusively, or even primarily, vicarious: it is unique and salvific, but it is also exemplary. In Revelation, Christ's death and resurrection are the keys to God's victory over evil in a battle whose outcome has already been settled, but the working out in history of which requires that believers maintain the same kind of faithful witness that eventuated in Jesus' own death. Revelation thus exhibits an understanding of Jesus' death and resurrection that directly supports a vision for discipleship. For those who wish to follow the Lamb wherever he goes must follow him in faithful witness . . . and perhaps even in death.[91]

John's celebratory message carries over into 12:12a with his exhortation: "because of this, 'Rejoice heavens[92] and the ones who dwell in them'" / διὰ τοῦτο εὐφραίνεσθε, οἱ οὐρανοι καὶ οἱ ἐν αὐτοῖς σκηνοῦντες. Since the victory has been won over the Satan "by the blood of the Lamb and by the word of their testimony" / διὰ τὸ αἷμα τοῦ ἀρνίου καὶ διὰ τὸν λόγον τῆς μαρτυρίας αὐτῶν (12:11), and the Satan has been thrown down as a result, heaven and its dwellers are called to celebrate. Beale suggests that the reason for rejoicing is that "Christ's kingdom has been established . . . ."[93] Boring is agreed that God is responsible for this event

> as the visionary counterpart to God's saving act on earth in the event of Christ and his cross. This too was a matter of God's initiative, not merely a reaction to human rebellion—the Lamb was slain "from the foundation of the world" (13:8). Christians are not passive spectators—they are involved in the defeat of Satan. Their blood flows together with the blood of the Lamb, as they make their own testimony/martyrdom as Jesus did his (12:10-11).[94]

Rutledge acknowledges the contribution that Käsemann makes to this matter. Being pronounced righteous is "an eschatological act of the Judge at the last day which takes place proleptically in the present."[95] That is, "The verdict of 'righteous' that God pronounces at the last day is already made a fact in the present. Thus, again, we may say, 'Become what you already are,' which is the only use of the imperative that carries the full force of the gospel."[96]

John, of course, was not naïve to the reality of the persecution that the churches to whom he wrote were facing. He proceeds in the balance of Revelation 12 to state why believers, never mind that Christ has won the victory because the Satan has been thrown down, still find themselves under constant duress. The Dragon is clearly enraged at his new situation, even though his anger originated within himself because of his own miscalculation in murdering the innocent male Child. His belief that he would finally be totally victorious proved to be his great blunder and own self-deception.

Consequently, he goes on the attack against believers in response to his own failure, despite being the one solely responsible for his own disbarment. Why and how he will come in great wrath against believers John clarifies in Revelation 12:12b–13:8. The self-inflicted death blow, meanwhile, from which he cannot recover, means "that he has only a little time left" / ὅτι ὀλίγον καιρὸν ἔχει (12:12b), and with his remaining time he becomes more violent than ever.

Notes

1. The words "sign," "signified," and "symbols" (above and below) take into account three branches of semiotics: syntactics, semantics, and pragmatics identified by Charles W. Morris, *Foundations of the Theory of Signs* (Chicago: University of Chicago Press, 1938).

2. Richard J. Bauckham, *Theology of the Book of Revelation*, New Testament Theology, ed. James D.G. Dunn (Cambridge: Cambridge University Press, 1993) 18.

3. Ibid., 19.

4. David Aune, *Revelation 6–16*, Word Biblical Commentary (Dallas: Word, 1998) 666–76.

5. Mitchell G. Reddish, *Revelation*, Smyth & Helwys Commentaries (Macon GA: Smyth & Helwys, 2001) 230.

6. John uses the word μέγας—"great"—8 times in Revelation but only twice when referring to a "sign"—here and in 15:1.

7. Aune, *Revelation 6–16*, 679.

8. Ibid.

9. See Hanna Stenström, "Feminists in Search for a Usable Future: Feminist Reception of the Book of Revelation," *The Way the World Ends? The Apocalypse of John in Culture and Ideology*, ed. William John Lyons and Jorunn Økland (Sheffield: Sheffield Phoenix, 2009) 240–66. That John envisions a woman in this scene, and does so positively, has not gone unnoticed by feminist interpreters of Revelation.

10. G. K. Beale, *The Book of Revelation: A Commentary on the Greek Text*, The New International Greek Testament Commentary, ed. I. Howard Marshall and Donald A. Hagner (Grand Rapids MI: Eerdmans, 1999) 626.

11. Ibid.

12. Aune, *Revelation 6–16*, 680. He provides a thorough summary of the many female figures that have been identified as possible referents for the woman. His conclusion, however, is that she is best understood as the church (712).

13. Bruce J. Malina, *On the Genre and Message of Revelation: Star Visions and Sky Journeys* (Peabody MA: Hendrickson, 1995) 155–60.

14. Stenström, "Feminists in Search for a Usable Future," 240–41. She directs readers to Inger Marie Lindboe, "Recent Literature: Development and Perspectives in New Testament Research on Women," ST 43 (1989): 153–63 (p. 155). She also points out that the "distinction between different kinds of feminist exegesis is present in the discussion between Tina Pippin and Elisabeth Schüssler Fiorenza." See also, e.g., Elizabeth A. Castelli, "Heteroglossia, Hermeneutics, and History: A Review Essay of Recent Feminist Studies of Early Christianity," *Journal of Feminist Studies in Religion* 10/2 (1994): 73–98; Pamela J. Milne, "Toward Feminist Companionship: The Future of Feminist Biblical Studies and Feminism," in Athalya Brenner and Carole Fontaine, eds., *A Feminist Companion to Reading the Bible: Approaches, Methods and Strategies* (Sheffield: Sheffield Academic, 1997) 39–60. Stenström writes, "In those articles, the differences I describe as between 'gender analysis' and 'liberation theological readings' are mentioned, although the actual wordings may differ."

Likewise, she approves of the importance of *The Woman's Bible*'s contribution in understanding the positive imagery of Revelation:

> Her [Mathilda Joslyn Gage's] interpretation of the Sun Woman goes beyond the esoteric into a splendid image of the (American) woman of the late nineteenth century, an image which may be considered the most magnificent feminist reclaiming of the female imagery of Revelation ever:
> "There was war in heaven." The wonderful progress and freedom of woman, as woman, within the last half century, despite the false interpretation of the Bible and by masculine power, is the result of this great battle; and all attempts to destroy her will be futile. Her day and hour has arrived; the Dragon of physical power over her, the supremacy of material things in the world, as depicted by the male principle, are yielding to the spiritual, represented by woman. The eagle, true bird of the sun and emblem of our own great country, gives his wings to her aid; and the whole earth comes to help her against her destroyer.

15. Mathilda Joslyn Gage, "Revelation 12," *The Woman's Bible*, ed. Elizabeth Cady Stanton (New York: European Publishing, 1898) 182–85.

16. George E. Ladd, *A Commentary of the Revelation of John* (Grand Rapids MI: Eerdmans, 1972) 168.

17. Stephen S. Smalley, *The Revelation of John: A Commentary on the Greek Text of the Apocalypse* (Downers Grove IL: InterVarsity, 2005) 315. See, as well, Judith Kovacs and Christopher Rowland, *Revelation*, Blackwell Bible Commentaries (Victoria, Australia: Blackwell, 2004) 137.

18. Craig R. Koester, *Revelation: A New Translation with Introduction and Commentary*, The Anchor Yale Bible (New Haven: Yale University Press, 2014) 543–44.

19. Beale, *Book of Revelation*, 628.

20. Geraldine Pinch, *Egyptian Mythology: A Guide to the Gods, Goddesses, and Traditions of Ancient Egypt* (Oxford: Oxford University Press, 2002) 91ff.

21. Jan Assmann, *Egyptian Solar Religion in the New Kingdom: Re, Amum and the Crisis of Monotheism*, trans. A. Alcock (London: Routledge, 1995) 49–57.

22. Adela Yarbro Collins, *The Combat Myth in the Book of Revelation* (Missoula MT: Scholars Press, 1976), demonstrated that the region of the seven churches of Revelation would have been well acquainted with the Python-Leto-Apollo myth.

23. Hesiod, "To Apollo," *Hesiod, The Homeric Hymns, and Homerica*, ed. Hugh G. Evelyn-White (Champaign IL: Project Gutenberg, n.d.) eBook Collection (EBSCOhost).

24. Koester, *Revelation*, 555, provides a summary of the Apollo myth but not the solar myth mentioned above in our comments at 12:1 (as more thoroughly does Aune, *Revelation 6–16*, 663–74, where he presents a number of combat myths alongside other mythical options).

25. Aune, *Revelation 6–16*, 680–81, provides a thorough summary of those who see the woman as Mary.

26. Koester, *Revelation*, 542–43.

27. Ibid., 556.

28. Beale, *Book of Revelation*, 625–32.

29. Ibid., 629.

30. M. Eugene Boring, *Revelation*, Interpretation (Louisville KY: John Knox, 1989) 152.

31. Beale, *Book of Revelation*, 632–33.

32. Boring, *Revelation*, 155.

33. Koester, *Revelation*, 545.

34. Beale, *Book of Revelation*, 633.

35. Richard Bauckham, *The Climax of Prophecy: Studies on the Book of Revelation* (Edinburgh: T&T Clark International, 1993) 185–98, concurs with the above descriptions and associations of the Dragon as well as additional connections with the serpent and Asklepios.

36. Aune, *Revelation 6–16*, 686.

37. Beale, *Book of Revelation*, 635–37.

38. Ibid., 637.

39. Ibid.

40. Aune, *Revelation 6–16*, 663.

41. Smalley, *Revelation of John*, 319.

42. Bauckham, *Theology of the Book of Revelation*, 74–75.

43. Beale, *Book of Revelation*, 639.

44. Ibid.

45. Smalley, *Revelation of John*, 318.

46. András Dávid Pataki, "A Non-Combat Myth in Revelation 12," *New Testament Studies* 57/2 (April 2011): 269.

47. Ibid.

48. Ibid.

49. Ladd, *Commentary of the Revelation of John*, 169–70.

50. This is only a summary of the general meaning of this verse. Our primary concern is with the preceding and proceeding verses, namely, what John portrays as accomplished in the child being snatched up to God (12:5) and the battle between Michael and the Dragon (12:7-9).

51. Beale, *Book of Revelation*, 645–46.

52. Ibid., 643.

53. Gordon Campbell, "Facing Fire and Fury: Reading Revelation's Violence," *The Book of Revelation: Currents in British Research on the Apocalypse*, ed. Garrick V. Allen, Ian Paul, and Simon P. Woodman, in *Wissenschaftliche Untersuchungen zum Neuen Testament* (Tübingen: Mohr Siebeck, 2015) 165.

54. Ibid.

55. Boring, *Revelation*, 159.

56. Bauckham, *Climax of Prophecy*, 210–237.

57. David L. Barr, *Tales of the End: A Narrative Commentary on the Book of Revelation* (Santa Rosa CA: Polebridge, 1998) 101.

58. Loren L. Johns, "Atonement and Sacrifice in the Book of Revelation," *The Work of Jesus Christ in Anabaptist Perspective: Essays in Honor of J. Denny Weaver*, ed. Alain Epp Weaver and Gerald J. Mast (Telford PA: Cascadia, 2008) 138. Johns seems to go too far in his footnote: "The 'battle' depicted between forces of God and forces of Satan [in Rev 12] was really the confrontation in history between the church, the earthly institution that represented the rule of God, and the Roman empire, the earthly structure used to symbolize the rule of Satan. The so-called cosmic battle was really imagery that gave . . . cosmic significance [to] the confrontation between the Roman empire and Jesus and his church."

59. George B. Caird, *The Revelation of St. John the Divine* (New York: Harper and Row, 1966) 154.

60. Bauckham, *Climax of Prophecy*, 185–86.

61. Reddish, *Revelation*, 379.

62. Bauckham, *Climax of Prophecy*, 186.

63. Koester, *Revelation*, 550.

64. Ibid.

65. Ibid.

66. Aune, *Revelation 6–16*, 698.

67. Koester, *Revelation*, 550.

68. Fleming Rutledge, *The Crucifixion: Understanding the Death of Jesus Christ* (Grand Rapids MI: Eerdmans, 2015) 439.

69. Ibid.

70. Ibid., 438.

71. Beale, *Book of Revelation*, 657.

72. My former colleague Professor R. Wayne Stacy was the first person I heard use this expression to articulate John's understanding of God's means of victory in The Apocalypse.

73. Koester, *Revelation*, 552.

74. Ibid., 564.

75. Caird, *Revelation of Saint John the Divine*, 155.

76. John D. Crossan, *The Greatest Prayer: Rediscovering the Revolutionary Message of the Lord's Prayer* (New York: HarperCollins, 2010) 55.

77. Rutledge, *The Crucifixion*, 351. While Rutledge's contribution to the apocalyptic war theme is commendable inasmuch as she identifies two kinds of apocalyptic: forensic and cosmic, she cautions unnecessarily against allowing the "courtroom image . . . to be made the controlling metaphor; it is too individualistic," she says, "and hence reductive; it deals too much in categories of guilt and innocence; it does not envision an Enemy against whom a war has to be fought." Had she included Rev 12 in her understanding, she would have found the enemy against whom a war has been fought—namely the Satan who is undone and thrown down by Michael and his angels (Rev 12:7-9).

78. Charles E. Hill, "Atonement in the Apocalypse of John: A Lamb Standing as if Slain," in *The Glory of the Atonement: Biblical, Historical & Practical Perspectives, Essays in honor of Roger Nicole*, ed. Charles E. Hill and Frank A. James III (Downers Grove IL: Inter-Varsity, 2004) 205–206.

79. Reddish, *Revelation*, 236.

80. Joel B. Green, *The Gospel of Luke*, The New International Commentary on the New Testament (Grand Rapids MI: Eerdmans, 1997) 825.

81. Rutledge, *The Crucifixion*, 350.

82. Ibid., 351.

83. Ibid.

84. Ibid.

85. Ibid., 466.

86. Campbell, "Facing Fire and Fury," 166.

87. Pierre de Martin de Viviés, *Apocalypses et cosmologie du salut* (Paris: Cerf, 2002) 167.

88. Ladd, *Commentary of the Revelation of John*, 172.

89. Reddish, *Revelation*, 237.

90. Anthony T. Hanson, *The Wrath of the Lamb* (London: SPCK, 1957) 165.

91. Johns, "Atonement and Sacrifice in the Book of Revelation," 139.

92. John uses the plural "heavens" / οἱ οὐρανοί only here in Revelation and "them" / αὐτοῖς to refer to "heaven" (translated "it").

93. Beale, *Book of Revelation*, 666.

94. Boring, *Revelation*, 159.

95. Rutledge, *The Crucifixion*, 336.

96. Ibid.

CHAPTER 6

Theological Conclusions: Implications for the Church and Christian Living

God's victory over Satan, John reveals, is certain from heaven's vantage point both *de jure* and *de facto*. Yet from every indication, Revelation was written to encourage believers who found themselves under some form of persecution, if not outright attack. The original hearers and readers of the Apocalypse faced the real possibility of their own martyrdom since some among them had already died (see Antipas of Rev 2:13). Their reality as persecuted people undoubtedly prompted them to question the veracity of Christ's victory over the Dragon-powers of the world that they were constantly facing. John answers that implied question with candor, offering no false assurances of an easy or prosperous life. He never suggests that they should expect to escape from life's troubles. Rather, he reinforces the likelihood that believers will be called upon to die for their faith. As such, Revelation's message continues to have implications for the church and for individual Christian living. Given the situation of today's conflicted world, the potential for mild, moderate, or more likely severe persecution is to be expected more so now than ever. John certainly saw this escalating tension in his own day, and he anticipates even worse conditions for the future.

"WOE TO THE EARTH AND SEA" / οὐαὶ τὴν γῆν καὶ τὴν θάλασσαν: 12:12B–13:8

As the Apocalypse's storyline continues to develop, the good news of the Satan's banishment from heaven has a negative component of seemingly bad news attached to it. Satan and his expelled allies are permitted to take their fight directly to earth. While heaven resounds with joy at the reality that there is no accuser found any longer before the throne of justice where the Child has taken his place (12:5), the bad news is that believers on earth now face the direct wrath of the expelled Dragon who has only a "little time" left in which to carry out his assaults. In fact, John says, "Woe earth and sea, because the devil has come down to you, having great wrath, knowing that he has a little time" / οὐαὶ τὴν γῆν καὶ τὴν θαλασσαν, ὅτι κατέβη διάβολος πρὸς ὑμᾶς, ἔχων θυμὸν μέγαν, εἰδὼς ὅτι ὀλίγον καιρὸν ἔχει (12:12b).

Koester is right that "Revelation likens Satan to a rogue animal that the angels have driven off the expansive plains of heaven into the fenced-in area of earth. The monster rampages within its newly limited circumstances, seeking to do as much damage as possible during the time that remains . . . ."[1] The expression "little time" / ὀλίγον καιρὸν (12:12b) that Satan has to carry out his tactics echoes Revelation 6:11 (after the Four Horsemen are described as released to do their horrors and killing) while the martyrs are told to wait a "little time" / χρόνον μικρόν "until should be completed also their fellow servants and their brethren who were about to be killed as they themselves had been" / ἕως πληρωθῶσιν καὶ οἱ σύνδουλοι αὐτῶν καὶ οἱ αδελφοὶ αὐτῶν οἱ μελλοντες ἀποκτέννεσθαι ὡς καὶ αὐτοί (Rev 6:11). In other words, during this "little time" other believers will themselves be called upon and will make the ultimate sacrifice just as Jesus made his sacrifice when Satan and his emissaries assaulted him.

The phrase "little time" has two additional parallels in Revelation as well, one of which refers to "him [for whom] it is necessary to remain a little while" / ὀλίγον αὐτὸν δεῖ μεῖναι (17:10). The character in question in this text refers to one of the Dragon's earthly allies whose reign of terror will last only a brief time. The final reference to "little time" / μικρὸν χρόνον (20:3) mentioned in Revelation contains John's account of Satan's demise following his imprisonment and the "little time" in which he is loosed to take out his wrath.

In particular, the "little time" of Revelation 12 includes the coming martyrdom of some of the saints (anticipated in 6:11). In other words, with the time that the Dragon has left to do his harm, God will indeed use the fallen Dragon's wrath to accomplish his purposes (once again as counterintuitive as that notion is) similarly as God used Jesus' death to accomplish the world's greatest good—its redemption. The martyrdom of the saints will continue, as John acknowledges, as testimony on earth that God continues to have followers and representatives who will remain faithful even unto death (cf. chapter 5, "12:11a," above). By implication, some believers of John's day, and believers throughout history, may be privileged to experience such a death. Christianity has certainly known its share of martyrs at many times and in many places during its two millennia. The scenes of Revelation 12:13–13:8 describe in relevant imagery the ongoing conflict that continues between the disbarred Satan (thrown down Dragon) and the offspring of the Woman who are on earth. John provides an overview of the animus exhibited by evil against believers in 12:13-17 where the Dragon is identified as in constant and relentless pursuit of the Woman and her offspring (v. 13). John describes the Dragon as not only toppled but also mortally wounded. With its last bit of strength, it becomes its most aggressive, much like a wounded wild animal that lashes out against its pursuers.

When John pictures the angry Dragon focused on believers in this scene, he does so because they are essentially the reason for the Satan's disbarment. In fact, had it not been for humankind being created in the first place, the Satan would have had no cause to bring a charge before the throne of God. Had human beings never existed, the Satan would have had no role to play as an accuser and prosecutor. As this line of thought suggests, he would have had no reason to attack the male Child when the Woman gave birth to him. Moreover, because of the Woman's association with the male Child, she and her offspring become the object of the fallen Dragon's full attention. Much like Pharaoh's pursuit with the intent to kill the liberated Hebrew children who had been set free by the deaths of the Passover lambs, the Dragon seeks to harm other of God's children who have been liberated by the death of the male Child, the slain Lamb (cf. Rev 5:6; 13:8). God's capacity to save life with death is repeated here just as in the exodus event to which John is alluding in this scene.

To make this connection more clearly, John depicts the Woman having been given two wings of the great eagle (12:14a), as Exodus 19:4 records God taking up the people on eagles' wings during their sojourn in the wilderness. Even so Deuteronomy 32:10-12 describes God taking up his people as on the back of an eagle that spreads its wings. Similarly, Isaiah 40:3 speaks as well of God's people mounting up "with wings like an eagle." In this scene in Revelation, the woman flies to the wilderness for nourishment for the familiar "time, times, and half a time = 3½ years" / καιρὸν καὶ καιροὺς καὶ ἥμισυ καιροῦ (12:14b) which parallels the "1260 days" / ἡμερας χιλίας διακοσίας ἐξήκοντα (cf. 11:3; 12:6) and "42 months" / μῆνας τεσσεράκοντα δύο (cf. 11:2; 13:5) found elsewhere in Revelation (see above, chapter 2 , "11:1-2").

The theme of "nourishment" that John mentions continues the exodus associations previously noted. Just as God sustained the people with manna, quail, and water (Exod 16) while they were en route to the promised land and experiencing wilderness duress, testing, and temptation, so too do the offspring of the woman experience trials, temptations, and tests by the fallen Dragon, yet they have eternal protection provided by God during their wilderness travail. John, by allusion and free association of the Serpent and the Dragon (cf. 12:9), suggests that God's people in the exodus account were themselves in tension with the Serpent once again. The situation that John described in his Revelation vision involves "the Serpent [that] spews water from his mouth after the woman like a river" / ἔβαλεν ὁ ὄφις ἐκ τοῦ στόματος αὐτοῦ ὀπίσω τῆς γυναικὸς ὕδωρ ὡς ποταμόν (12:15a), no doubt to drown her if possible just as Egypt's Pharaoh had hoped he might drown the former Hebrew slaves at the Red Sea. The figurative image of something coming "out of the mouth" / ἐκ τοῦ στόματος (12:15a) of the Serpent is either like that which comes out of the Dragon, Serpent, and the False Prophet found throughout Revelation that seeks to destroy, or it is like the Son of Man and Rider on the White Horse's mouth from which comes the truth that conquers all enemies (see chapter 3, "19:15, 21").[2] The Serpent's mouth, by contrast to the sword of truth coming from the Son of Man's mouth (1:16; 19:15, 21), spews only deception (cp. Gen 3:1–5; Rev 16:13) in his continuous attempt to destroy the people of God. God's people are not exempt from the Serpent's enhanced deceitfulness as he continues his treachery in the fleeting little time that he has remaining.

Beale describes the Serpent's deception as "Satanic agents—false teachers, compromisers, and demons—[that] infiltrate the church to deceive her and contribute to her demise."[3] The earth, God's good creation, however, comes to the Woman's rescue (v. 16), continuing something of the exodus imagery, where according to Exodus 15:12 "the earth swallowed" Pharaoh and his army. Similarly, in the wilderness "the earth opened its mouth and swallowed" the rebellious families of Korah, Dathan, and Abiram who were slandering Moses (Num 16:1-32). Thus the wilderness is a place where God's people are tested; but it also is a place where trust in God alone is all the provision necessary for ultimate, eternal survival.

This rebuff of evil by God's people (possible only with God's help) leaves the Dragon all the more enraged, so much so that he goes on an extended attack (12:17) against present and future believers, some of whom will one day find themselves fatally assaulted. The future attacks will certainly be in ways similar to the past but also in ways that some believers have not previously experienced. Revelation 12:13-16 provides a picture of believers that are and will continue to be under constant persecution. Yet despite this aggression, John declares that the believers' eternal protection is secure. That news granted, the Dragon relentlessly continues his pursuit. Nevertheless, as Reddish observes,

> But John can sing the song of victory because he knows that the decisive battle in the great war has already been fought. It occurred on Calvary. The skirmishes still continue, but the outcome of the eternal struggle between good and evil has already been decided. For John, the coming assault against the church is nothing more than the futile, desperate last gasps of a dying Satan.[4]

Revelation 12:18–13:18 describes the means by which the Dragon assails believers. He calls on his two beastly associates (of sea and land) to round out his trinity of evil to wreak as much earthly havoc as possible in the little time that he has remaining. In fact, the outcome of the continuing battle that occurs on earth that Revelation 12:18–15:4 describes results in the sum total of the blood that fills the seven bowls of wrath described in 16:1-21 (see above, chapter 2, "16:1, 17").

John's point in utilizing this violent, assault language, even given the defeat and ouster of the Satan, is that Christians must anticipate opposition. Stanley Hauerwas notes, "[Christians] had better be ready for a fierce counteroffensive as well as be prepared to take some casualties."[5] In other words, the Christian life will always be fraught with challenges, opposition, and pain. The seasons of joy and celebration that believers often have in life are also counter-balanced with the sober reality of the difficulties of life. There is a constant battle that rages even though the male Child has been victorious through giving up his life to the deadly Dragon.

Bauckham strikes the note sharply with his awareness that the life that believers live is still a battle:

> So the theme of messianic war has brought us back to the theme of witness to the truth. As usual, John's major themes serve to interpret one another. But the theme of the messianic war has its own importance. By using the military image for both assessments of what is happening when the martyrs die—the beast is victorious, the Lamb is victorious—John is able to pose most effectively the crucial issue of how one sees things. Is the world a place in which military and political might carries all before it or is it one in which suffering witness to the truth prevails in the end?

Thus Revelation offers its readers prophetic discernment guided by the core of Christian faith: that Jesus Christ won his comprehensive victory over all evil by suffering witness. It also calls for courageous adherence to that discernment in practice, as the calls "for the endurance and faithfulness of the saints" (13:10; cf. 14:12), inserted into the portrayal of the messianic war, indicate. Whereas modern terminology calls martyrdom "passive resistance," John's military imagery makes it just as active as any physical warfare. While rejecting the apocalyptic militancy that called for literal holy war against Rome, John's message is not, "Do not resist!" It is, "Resist—but by witness and martyrdom, not by violence."[6]

Johns says that "the references to 'the blood of the Lamb' in Rev 7:14 and 12:11 should not be understood as referring exclusively to Christ's death, but to the deaths of the Christian martyrs"[7] as well. Parts of Johns's observations are clearly correct. Christians participate "in the death of Christ through faithful witness to the point of martyrdom,"[8] as 12:11 implies and as 6:11 (see above chapter 2, "White/Washed Robes" 6:11; 7:9; 7:13-14; 22:14) says directly. "Once again," Boring acknowledges, "Christian existence is determined for John by sharing the ministry of Christ . . . . As a priestly community the church mediates to the world God's reconciliation of the world in Jesus, the Sacrificed Priest, and instead of sacrificing to the emperor on the Roman altar, the church sacrifices itself on the true altar of God (cf. 6:9-11)."[9]

The implications of this sacrifice are rooted in what happened in Jesus' atoning death. Rutledge, following J. Christian Beker and J. Louis Martyn, identifies that "a radical transformation of the present world order . . . ruled by Satan, death and the forces of evil"[10] has occurred. They are indebted to Ernst Käsemann, who declared that Jesus' Jewish apocalyptic emphasis meant that the "cross/resurrection event is a genuine *novum*, a first-order reversal of all previous arrangements—an altogether new creation *ex nihilo*, out of nothing."[11] Certainly, "[f]or those who have been baptized, there is an *apocalyptic transfer of aeons.*"[12]

In many ways this apocalyptic thinking reflects how God's righteousness is tied to God's justice, a familiar theme related to the Satan as prosecutor being disbarred for violating his own intractable commitment to justice. In Jesus' death God was actively "making right that which is wrong,"[13] even as God permitted the Dragon to kill the male Child. With the male Child's death and the Dragon's defeat, God was not merely overlooking the wrong as if it never happened.[14] Rather, as Karl Barth says in his commentary on the Heidelberg Confession, "Sinful man falls into the power of Satan, into the hands of a foreign power."[15] Thus, "Man cannot go forward. He stands under a historical power and he can do nothing about it."[16] Therefore, "[t]he passion of Jesus Christ . . . has at its heart and center the victory which has been won for us, in our place, in the battle against sin . . . it is the radical divine action which attacks and destroys at its very root the primary evil in the world."[17]

Victor Hugo's insight in *Les Misérables* speaks in part to this solution in a telling way: "If the soul is left in darkness, sins will be committed. The guilty one is not he who commits the sin, but the one who causes the darkness."[18] John's understanding of the atoning death of Christ offers God's remedy to the evil that is responsible for the darkness. Certainly all of this is "over our heads," Rutledge concludes, for the moment "we start trying to insert ourselves into the picture, we start to encroach once again upon God's righteousness . . . ."[19]

THE REVELATION OF REDEMPTION

Such is the wisdom and mystery of God's plan as revealed in the Apocalypse. God's redemptive solution is declared with theological intentionality in John's non-conventional articulation of atonement. In many ways, Revelation's redemptive message is similar to Paul's conclusion in Romans 11:11b—"But through their trespass salvation has come to the Gentiles / ἀλλὰ τῷ αὐτῶν παρατπώματι ἡ σωτηρία τοῖς ἔθνεσιν." In other words, just as God used the temporary infidelity of the Israelite people as the occasion for Gentiles to embrace and to be included in God's kingdom, John envisions God using universal human sinfulness, corruption, and failure (that God has permitted) to bring the world to the brink of disaster and its own self-destruction, something global and catastrophic that only divine intervention and renewal can overcome.

To right the self-inflicted and humanly imposed wrongs that have been perpetrated on the world and its peoples, God's solution to these satanically inspired travesties is foreseen from the foundation of the world and ultimately visualized as being overcome on the cross (the final outcome of which is realized in a renewed world called "New Jerusalem" / Ἰεερουσαλὴμ καινὴν—cf. Rev 21–22). John's vision reveals the basis of God's victory through the redemptive power of the slain Lamb. In fact, the means by which the world arrives at God's solution is the counterintuitive wrath of God and the Lamb. God's divine strategy is the absorption of the evil of Satan (Rev 12), who did his worst when he executed the innocent male Child. In this stunning turn of events and demonstration of divine power, God's permission for evil to do this deed brought about atoning redemption for humankind. Atonement in this case is neither propitiatory (appeasing God's wrath) nor expiatory (covering or removing sins) as such; rather it is God's absorption of sin in the slain but innocent Lamb that produces an anticipated yet unprecedented result. Only Revelation clarifies the implied meaning of this suffering and death.

God's wrath, indeed the wrath of the Lamb, is a strikingly counter-intuitive concept in which John foresees the sum total of Satan and his earthly allies' evil being revisited upon themselves. The particulars of this outworking are insightfully stated throughout the Apocalypse and most expressively in Revelation 12, where the Lamb absorbs Satan's fury and for doing so wins victory over evil. Similarly, in Revelation 16 the sum total of Satan's anger (which has meant the blood of believers and unbelievers throughout the ages) has not only filled the seven bowls of wrath but has also reached the tipping point and is spilled from those bowls back onto the perpetrators. In these scenes, God's alchemy is on full display and is at its theological height when God uses and turns this unthinkable evil into the world's greatest good. In Revelation 12 Satan is ousted as a result of his own actions, while in Revelation 16:12-16 evil turns self-destructively upon itself as is particularly expressed in the sixth bowl of Armageddon (see above, chapter 2, "16:1; 16:17 [8:3, 5]").

God and the Lamb's wrath are pictured as divinely permitted world horrors that are absorbed by God in Jesus' death, a wrongful death that was perpetrated against him (the male Child that died) on the cross in the Dragon's assault on him (see above, chapter 5, "Revelation's Atonement Theology: Victory through Suffering and Death"). This absorption that happened at the earthly level on the cross had a heavenly counterpart in Michael and his angels' fight against the Dragon and his angels. The intensity and profundity of this conflict was nothing less, and nothing more, than the omnipotence of self-sacrificial, suffering love. Evil's downfall and the disbarring of the satanic prosecutor, John reveals, did not require any violent or malevolent power to be returned in kind on Satan or to be perpetrated against Satan by God in order for God to be victorious. As Revelation 16 reveals, Satan's evil culminates in evil destroying evil. It is certainly a fight to the death as evil is pictured turning against evil.

In the horrid battle that John calls "the battle of the great day of God the Almighty" / τὸν πόλεμον τῆς ἡμέρας τῆς μεγάλης τοῦ θεοῦ τοῦ παντοκράτορος (16:14), evil does indeed die in what proves to be a nega-tion of negation. God has demonstrated the true might of divine power in defeating evil by allowing evil to defeat itself. God's victory is much like that which Gideon's army won in Judges 7. In that remarkable scene, after a dramatic reduction in military force down to only three hundred men, God delivered "the Midianites into their hand" (Jdg 7:2, NRSV). The victory was won even more dramatically without the people of God ever raising an implement of war. Their only weapons were trumpets, empty jars, and torches inside the jars (Jdg 7:16) in the hands of the three hundred stationed in the adjacent mountain passes overlooking the camp of the Midianites. When the three hundred blew their trumpets and smashed the empty jars, "the LORD set every man's sword against his fellow and against all the army; and the army fled as far as Beth-shittah toward Zererah, as far as the border of Abel-meholah, by Tabbath" (Jdg 7:22, NRSV). In other words, the enemy force turned on itself!

God's way of expelling the diabolical interloper is by a much more powerful means than anything the world has ever seen. All the cruelty and harm that Satan and his emissaries are pictured as inflicting on the world and its people through deceit, lies, seductions, and distortions of the truth, plotted and carried out by him and his devotees, meet their match in the all-powerful, counterintuitive death of Jesus on a Roman cross, which once accomplished results in the Dragon's warfare on earth that leads to evil's collision course with itself. Most tellingly, nothing in God required or allowed for more violence, cruelty, or hurt by God to be inflicted on Satan or his followers to achieve this victory. Should that have been the case God, arguably, would be reckoned violently worse and crueler than the Devil. God simply (but not simplistically) allows evil ultimately to burn itself out in its war against itself. Evil, as no less than the "absence of good" (*privatio boni*[20]), will never rest nor will it be satisfied until there is nothing good left for it to destroy. While God envisions and has ordered creation from the beginning to be oriented toward good, peace, and Sabbath, evil (as God's opponent) will not rest as long as any good or peace remains; and it will not cease its destruction until either it or the world on which it takes out its wrath comes to an end.

Indeed, God's "Lamb slain from the foundation of the world" / τοῦ ἀρνίου τοῦ ἐσφαγμένου ἀπὸ καταβολῆς κόσμου (Rev 13:8) is the summation of John's vision of atonement. The defeat of evil by means of the death of the male Child on the cross is one and the same as the very "Lamb standing as having been slain" / ἀρνίον ἑστηκὸς ὡς ἐσφαγμένον (Rev 5:6). Such a vision prompted praise to the Lamb since "you purchased [or ransomed] to God by your blood those from every tribe and tongue and people and nation" / ἠγόρασας τῷ θεῷ ἐν τῷ αἵματι σου ἐκ πάσης φυλῆς καὶ γλώσσης καὶ λαοῦ καὶ ἔθνους (Rev 5:9). By giving himself up to be slain, God demonstrated through the Lamb the true alternative to short-lived victories won through violence that the fallen world has known since the Serpent's initial deception of the first man and woman. As Genesis 3:1-5 records, it was serpent-inspired death that led to the end of innocence of Adam and Eve and, shortly thereafter, to the first murder, the fratricide of their own son Abel by his brother Cain (cf. Gen 4:8). Thus, for all its violent language, careful reading of the Apocalypse reveals John's understanding of counterintuitive redemption terminology through a careful redefinition and inversion in meaning of words like crown, rod of iron, sword, victory, lion, and wrath, as well as words associated with vulnerability and defeat like blood, lamb, pregnant woman, and death.

In theological terms, Karl Barth perceptively described the consistency of God's ways with telling clarity. Barth acknowledged "that God has ordained that in the place of the one acquitted He Himself should be perishing and abandoned and rejected—the Lamb slain from the foundation of the world."[21] In other words, God in Jesus took into himself the death that all men and women should deservedly die. God elected, moreover, to let himself be the one condemned by Satan and his earthly conspirators. Jesus submitted to crucifixion at the behest of the Dragon-powers of his day, and he used it as his means of winning victory over Satan, mastermind of those powers. "The suffering," Barth says, "borne on the cross of Golgotha by the son of man in unity with the Son of God, who is as such a sacrifice for the sins of the world, is a stage on the road, an unavoidable point of transition, to the glory of the resurrection, ascension, and session."[22] In every way, God in Jesus elects the cross of Golgotha to be his kingly throne for which reason John identified the throne on which God sits as the "throne of God and the Lamb" / θρόνου τοῦ θεοῦ καὶ τοῦ ἀρνίου (Rev 22:1).

Acknowledgment of Jesus' self-sacrifice as God's means of victory over evil produces confidence, joy, and hope in believers even in the gravest of circumstances. Even when the lives of God's children are required of them for their faith, or should they be accosted with catastrophe, trauma, mental and physical illness, or pain, they are not overcome by hopelessness, fatalism, or despair. They know that God will use their own sacrifice as affirmation of Satan's defeat in God's redemptive plan. In other words, their lives, pain, and deaths are not meaningless. Jesus' sacrifice has accomplished something for them that leads them to follow confidently in his footsteps. Barth states it clearly:

> Naturally we must know what it is that God wills to remove from us. But much more we must know what it is that He wills to give us. And we can know this only in terms of what God has put behind us because He willed to take it from us and has in fact done so. We can know it only in terms of the abyss on whose brink we are held. We cannot look at this abyss as though it were still the place to which we belong. We know that our place is in heaven where Christ sits as our Representative on the right hand of God. We cannot balance the fact that Adam fell, or David sinned, or Peter denied, or Judas betrayed, against the resurrection of Jesus Christ. The facts are true, but it is also true that they are far outweighed by the resurrection of Jesus Christ and that as the result of this resurrection they belong already to the vanished past.[23]

Of course, the path to Jesus' resurrection was the cross to which God in Christ submitted Himself "from the foundation of world" / ἀπὸ καταβολῆς κόσμου (Rev 13:8), as John impressively and undeniably describes it. Finally, this theological conclusion about John's predestination language is encouraging:

> The thought of God's predestination cannot, then, awaken in us the mixture of terror and joy which would be in order if we were confronted partly by promise and partly by threat. It can awaken only joy, pure joy. For this order is found in the divine predestination itself, and it cannot be revoked . . . . It is a way willed by God himself. At the end of this way God's glory is revealed in the fact that he Himself removed the threat and became our salvation. In the light of this end there is no place for anything but joy . . . . This is not a matter of optimism. It is a matter of being obedient and not disobedient, of being thankful and not self-willed. In obedience and thankfulness we can only rejoice at the double predestination of God.[24]

For these reasons the Apocalypse confirms that the perseverance of believers in times of persecution and martyrdom is the way that Christians bear witness to the rest of the world, not only of God's ways with the world but of the fact that God has elected them as his representatives.[25] Indeed, there is no greater assurance of redemption than believers knowing that God has chosen them and that it is God who helps them remain faithful unto death (just as was the case with Jesus) despite the disappointments, troubles, temptations, trials, tribulations, and even personal sinfulness, setbacks, and failures that come in life.

Meanwhile, believers may live confidently based on the assurance of victory even in the worst of times. When troubles come, as surely they have and will continue to come upon believers, these difficulties are proof of the "little time" that remains for evil to do its bidding. The Christian journey and its struggle against evil has and will remain in direct proportion to the degree that believers orient their lives to one of the key petitions found in the Lord's Prayer: "Thy kingdom come, thy will be done, on earth as it is in heaven" / ἐλθέτω ἡ βασιλεία σου, γενηθήτω τὸ θέλημά σου, ὡς ἐν οὐρανῷ καὶ ἐπὶ γῆς (Matt 6:10b). Christian anticipation of how earthly life should mirror heavenly life is in every way at the heart of John's vision of a defeated Satan and a victorious church. As idealistic as it may sound that earthly relationships could remotely resemble heavenly ones, local churches and individual believers are indeed God's chosen representatives on earth to that end. The great challenge for believers and churches in the corrupt and fallen world is how to live that anticipated life now while evil tugs, pulls, pushes, and ambushes Christians from every conceivable angle.

Church communities of compassion and forgiveness, patience and kindness, balanced with accountability characterized by genuine love, serve as models of the present yet coming kingdom of God. Case in point was John's sharp rebuke and warning to five of the seven churches (Ephesus, Pergamum, Thyatira, Sardis, and Laodicea) that speaks to the importance of correction similar to that which was given by the Old Testament prophets to the people of God of their day. Discipline, growth, and maturation are always expected of the people of God and as part of the ongoing Christian story for both individuals and churches. Certainly John is not reticent to offer exclusively positive affirmation to two deserving churches (Smyrna and Philadelphia) since their faithful living and service, under the worst of circumstances, warranted nothing but accolades from the Son of Man.

From the Apocalypse's perspective, the foundation for both the censure and the praise of the churches originates in the victory won by the slain Lamb who has taken his place on the heavenly throne (Rev 22:1). Earlier in Revelation, when the Lamb took the book, broke open its seven seals (5:5), and revealed the tragic contents of the human story (6:1-17), God declared that evil has been defeated through God's chosen counterintuitive means. Contemporary recipients of this Revelation who have seen, understood, and embraced this vision of the triumph of the Lamb continue their own journey of living into (and up to) this reality. Nothing short of constant vigilance and a faithful spirit of repentance, birthed in the petition of the Lord's Prayer for the kingdom to come "on earth as it is in heaven," secures believers for their struggle against the fallen yet defeated Dragon.

Living with this kingdom perspective both begins and proceeds from the affirmation that the Lamb of God has won the victory over Satan. This victory includes the overthrow of both human guilt and shame that plague many believers. Jesus asked the woman in the noteworthy scene of John 7:53–8:11, "Where are those who are your *accusers* [emphasis added]?" / Ποῦ εἰσιν ἐκεῖνοι οἱ κατήγοροί σου (John 8:10a); "Has no one condemned you?" / Οὐδείς σε κατέκρινεν (John 8:10b). She honestly replied, "No one, Lord" / Οὐδείς, κύριε (John 8:11a), to which Jesus said, "Neither do I condemn you" / Οὐδὲ ἐγώ σε κρίνω (John 8:11b).

For redeemed believers, the good news is that the accusations brought against them by Satan or his representatives (including even one's own personal shame, guilt-ridden conscience, and self-judgments) have been overcome. Believers are indeed the people that "you ransomed to God by your blood out of every tribe, and tongue, and people, and nation" / ἠγόρασας τῷ θεῷ ἐν τῷ αἵματι σου ἐκ πάσης φυλῆς καὶ γλώσσης καὶ λαοῦ καὶ ἔ"νους (5:9). This truth empowers people to see themselves through and with the "eyes" of heaven—the location from which Satan has been thrown down, where the Lamb sits triumphantly on the mercy seat of judgment, and is the perspective from which Jesus taught his followers to pray: "Thy kingdom come, thy will be done, on earth as it is in heaven" / ἐλθέτω ἡ βασιλεία σου, γενηθήτω τὸ θέλημά σου, ὡς ἐν οὐρανῷ καὶ ἐπὶ ψῆς (Matt 6:10b).

N.T. Wright has suggested similar implications for the meaning of the cross for today:

> "Now is the judgment of this world; now is the ruler of the world cast out; and if I am lifted up from the earth I will draw all people to myself" [John 12:31]. This is what it means that the Messiah died for our sins in accordance with the scriptures. We have some fresh thinking to do, to put it mildly. But thinking, the realm of logos, has become flesh, and must once again become flesh, our flesh, our footwashing flesh, driven by the Spirit to be for the world what Jesus was for Israel, to be the means by which the Spirit holds the world to account as Jesus held Pilate to account. Having loved his own, having revealed the glory, Jesus loved them to the end; and as he resumed his clothes he told them, "This is my command: that you love one another as I have loved you." That is how

the glory will be revealed in tomorrow's world. That is how the world, saved once for all by his victory on the cross, will as he promised be flooded with his glory and knowledge as the waters cover the sea. We are to be, in the power of the Spirit, new Genesis people; people; new Exodus people; new Isaiah people; new gospel people; new Jesus people. That is the meaning of atonement, then and now.[26]

From the vantage point of the kingdom of heaven, God has declared victory over any and everything that separates people from God. Moreover, God extends the gift of spiritual, personal, and emotional peace and hope that overcomes personal shame, guilt, and anxiety. With the personal embrace of the Lamb's redemption comes assurance of salvation and confidence to the forgiven. The key to this life-transforming outcome is the redemptive power of God that the Lamb won for humanity on the cross. The Lamb's redemption is a gift to be received and celebrated with joyful living by his followers in times of personal turmoil, persecution, and tribulation. God has seen it this way "from the foundation of world" / ἀπὸ καταβολῆς κόσμου (Rev 13:8). And John calls believers to see themselves through this unique lens of redemptive atonement as well. When believers accept this reality, they live and model daily not only that they see themselves in the present moment as redeemed people but that they likewise see and relate to others in this world the way that God has seen them from eternity.

Notes

1. Craig R. Koester, *Revelation: A New Translation with Introduction and Commentary*, The Anchor Yale Bible (New Haven: Yale University Press, 2014) 565.

2. See the sharp, two-edged sword of 1:16 and 19:15 as well as the "fire from their mouths" of the two witnesses in 11:5 that speak to the power of the truth. Note especially in the immediate context that it is "by the word of their testimony" (12:11) that the believers conquer.

3. G. K. Beale, *The Book of Revelation: A Commentary on the Greek Text*, The New International Greek Testament Commentary, ed. I. Howard Marshall and Donald A. Hagner (Grand Rapids MI: Eerdmans, 1999) 673.

4. Mitchell G. Reddish, *Revelation*, Smyth & Helwys Commentaries (Macon GA: Smyth & Helwys, 2001) 236.

5. Stanley Hauerwas, "No Enemy, No Christianity: Theology and Preaching between 'Worlds,'" in The *Future of Theology: Essays in Honor of Jürgen Moltmann*, ed. Miroslav Volf, Carmen Krieg, and Thomas Kucharz (Grand Rapids MI: Eerdmans, 1996) 26–34.

THEOLOGICAL CONCLUSIONS   169

6. Richard J. Bauckham, *Theology of the Book of Revelation*, New Testament Theology, ed. James D.G. Dunn (Cambridge: Cambridge University Press, 1993) 91–92.

7. Loren L. Johns, "Atonement and Sacrifice in the Book of Revelation," *The Work of Jesus Christ in Anabaptist Perspective: Essays in Honor of J. Denny Weaver*, ed. Alain Epp Weaver and Gerald J. Mast (Telford PA: Cascadia, 2008) 129.

8. Ibid.

9. M. Eugene Boring, *Revelation*, Interpretation (Louisville KY: John Knox, 1989) 78.

10. Fleming Rutledge, *The Crucifixion: Understanding the Death of Jesus Christ* (Grand Rapids MI: Eerdmans, 2015) 354, partial quotation of J. Christian Beker, *Paul the Apostle: The Triumph of God in Life and Thought* (Philadelphia: Fortress, 1980) 136–37.

11. Ibid., 355.

12. Ibid., 370.

13. Ibid., 329.

14. Ibid., 329.

15. Karl Barth, *Learning Jesus Christ through the Heidelberg Catechism* (Grand Rapids: Eerdmans, 1964), 31.

16. Ibid, 37

17. Karl Barth, *Church Dogmatics: The Doctrine of Reconciliation* 4/1 (London: T & T Clark, 1956) 247, 254.

18. Victor Hugo, *Les Misérables* (New York: Carleton Publishing, 1862) 14.

19. Rutledge, *The Crucifixion*, 329.

20. While this view is attributed to Augustine, *Enchiridion: On Faith, Hope, and Love*, trans. Albert C. Outler (Grand Rapids: Christian Ethereal Library, 1955) 9, it appears in Origen, *De Principiis* ii.9.2 as well.

21. Karl Barth, *Church Dogmatics: The Doctrine of God* 2/2 (London: T & T Clark, 1957) 167.

22. Ibid., 173.

23. Ibid., 174.

24. Ibid. What Barth means by "double predestination" is that (1) God has elected Jesus to be the means of salvation, and (2) God has elected people in Jesus for salvation. Hence, Jesus is God's double predestination. Salvation, therefore, is not based on anything that a person has done or not done, but it is based on what God has done from before the foundation of the world; namely God elected Jesus and God elected salvation of people in Jesus. All of which is to say, God is for humankind, not against humankind.

25. Brian K. Blount, *Revelation: A Commentary* (Louisville: Westminster John Knox, 2009) is a fine example of this emphasis from the perspective of African American persecution and perseverance.

26. N. T. Wright, "Saving the World, Revealing the Glory: Atonement Then and Now," Lecture (St. Mellitus College, London, October 17, 2016).

Bibliography

Abelard, Peter. *Sic et Non: A Critical Edition*. Edited by Blanche B. Boyer and Richard McKeon. Chicago: University of Chicago Press, 1976.

Achtner, Wolfgang, Stefan Kunz, and Thomas Walter. *Dimensions of Time: The Structures of the Time of Humans, of the World, and of God*. Translated by Arthur H. Williams. Grand Rapids: Eerdmans, 1998.

Allen, Garrick V. "Reusing Scripture in the Book of Revelation: Techniques of Reuse and Habits of Reading." *The Book of Revelation: Currents in British Research on the Apocalypse*. Wissenschaftliche Untersuchungen zum Neuen Testament. Tübingen: Mohr Siebeck, 2015.

Allen, Garrick V., Ian Paul, and Simon P. Woodman, eds. *The Book of Revelation: Currents in British Research on the Apocalypse*. Wissenschaftliche Untersuchungen zum Neuen Testament. Tübingen: Mohr Siebeck, 2015.

Anderson, Gary A. "Sacrifice and Sacrificial Offerings (Old Testament)." Pages 870–86 in volume 5 of *Anchor Bible Dictionary*. Edited by David Noel Freedman. 6 volumes. New York: Doubleday, 1992.

Anselm, Saint. *Cur Deus Homo*. Translated by Sidney N. Deane. Fort Worth: Richard D. McCormack, 2005.

Assmann, Jan. *Egyptian Solar Religion in the New Kingdom: Re, Amum and the Crisis of Monotheism*. Translated by A. Alcock. London: Routledge, 1995.

Augustine. *Enchiridion: On Faith, Hope, and Love. In volume 1 of The Nicene and Post-Nicene Fathers*. Series 1. Edited by Philip Schaff. 1886-1889. 14 volumes. Reprint, Peabody MA: Hendrickson, 1994.

Aulén, Gustaf. *Christus Victor: An Historical Study of the Three Main Types of the Idea of the Atonement.* Translated by A.G. Hebert. New York: MacMillan, 1969.

Aune, David E. *Revelation 1–5.* Word Biblical Commentary. Dallas: Word, 1997.

———. *Revelation 6–16.* Word Biblical Commentary. Dallas: Word, 1998.

———. *Revelation 17–22.* Word Biblical Commentary. Dallas: Word, 1998.

Barr, David L. "Tales of the End." *Tales of the End: A Narrative Commentary on the Book of Revelation.* Santa Rosa CA: Polebridge, 1998.

Barrett, C. K. *A Commentary on the Epistle to the Romans.* Harper's New Testament Commentaries. New York: Harper and Row, 1957.

Barth, Karl. *Church Dogmatics: The Doctrine of Reconciliation.* Volume 1. Part 1. London: T & T Clark, 1956.

———. *Church Dogmatics: The Doctrine of God.* Volume 2. Part 2. London: T & T Clark, 1957.

———. *Learning Jesus Christ through the Heidelberg Catechism.* Grand Rapids MI: Eerdmans, 1964.

Bauckham, Richard J. "The Figurae of John of Patmos." *Prophecy and Millenarianism: Essays in Honour of Marjorie Reeves and Ann Williams.* London: Longman, 1980.

———. *The Climax of Prophecy: Studies on the Book of Revelation.* Edinburgh: T&T Clark International, 1993.

———. *Theology of the Book of Revelation.* New Testament Theology. Cambridge: Cambridge University Press, 1993.

———. "Judgment in the Book of Revelation." *The Book of Revelation: Currents in British Research on the Apocalypse.* Wissenschaftliche Untersuchungen zum Neuen Testament. Tübingen: Mohr Siebeck, 2015.

Beale, G. K. *The Book of Revelation: A Commentary on the Greek Text.* The New International Greek Testament Commentary. Grand Rapids MI: Eerdmans, 1999.

Beasley-Murray, G. R. *The Book of Revelation.* New Century Bible Commentary. Grand Rapids MI: Eerdmans, 1974.

Beker, J. Christian. *Paul the Apostle: The Triumph of God in Life and Thought.* Philadelphia: Fortress, 1980.

Ben-Daniel, John and Gloria. *The Apocalypse in the Light of the Temple: A New Approach to the Book of Revelation.* Jerusalem: Beit Yochanan, 2003.

Blount, Brian K. *Revelation: A Commentary.* Louisville: Westminster John Knox, 2009.

Boring, M. Eugene. "What Are We Looking For? Toward a Definition of the Term 'Christian Prophet.'" *Boring Seminar SBL Papers, 1973.* 2 volumes. Society of Biblical Literature Seminar Papers 2. Missoula MT: Scholars Press, 1973.

————. *Revelation.* Interpretation. Louisville: John Knox, 1989.

Boxall, Ian. "The Mighty Angel and the Little Scroll: A Reception-Historical Study of Revelation 10." *The Book of Revelation: Currents in British Research on the Apocalypse.* Wissenschaftliche Untersuchungen zum Neuen Testament. Tübingen: Mohr Siebeck, 2015.

Bredin, Mark R. "Hate Never Dispelled Hate: No Place for the *Pharmakos.*" *Biblical Theology Bulletin 34/3 (2004): 105–13.*

Brock, Rita Nakashima. *Journeys by Heart: A Christology of Erotic Power.* New York: Crossroad, 1988.

Brown, F., S. R. Driver, and C. A. Briggs. *Enhanced Brown-Driver-Briggs Hebrew and English Lexicon.* Oxford: Clarendon, 1977.

Brown, Joan Carlson and Rebecca Parke. "For God so Loved the World." *Christianity, Patriarchy, and Abuse: A Feminist Critique.* Edited by Joan Carlson Brown and Carol R. Bohn. New York: Pilgrim Press, 1989.

Brown, Raymond E. Brown. *The Gospel According to John.* New York: Doubleday, 1966.

Caird, George B. *The Revelation of St. John the Divine.* New York: Harper and Row, 1966.

Calvin, John. *Institutes of the Christian Religion.* Translated by Ford Lewis Battles and Edited by John T. McNeil. Library of Christian Classics. Volume 1. Philadelphia: Westminster, 1960.

Campbell, W. Gordon. "Facing Fire and Fury: One Reading of Revelation's Violence in the Context of Recent Interpretation." *The Book of Revelation: Currents in British Research on the Apocalypse.* Wissenschaftliche Untersuchungen zum Neuen Testament. Tübingen: Mohr Siebeck, 2015.

Carnegie, D. R. "Worthy is the Lamb: The Hymns in Revelation." *Christ the Lord: Studies in Christology Presented to Donald Guthrie.* Edited by Harold H. Rowdon. Downers Grove IL: InterVarsity, 1982.

Carroll, John T. and Joel B. Green. "The Death of Jesus in Hebrews, 1 Peter, and Revelation." *The Death of Jesus in Early Christianity.* Peabody MA: Hendrickson, 1995.

Castelli, Elizabeth A. "Heteroglossia, Hermeneutics, and History: A Review Essay of Recent Feminist Studies of Early Christianity." *Journal of Feminist Studies in Religion* 10/2 (1994): 73–98.

Charles, R. H. *Studies in the Apocalypse.* Edinburgh: T & T Clark, 1913.

Childs, Brevard. *Myth and Reality in the Old Testament,* 2nd ed. Studies in Biblical Theology 27. London: SCM, 1962.

Collins, Adela Yarbro. *The Combat Myth in the Book of Revelation.* Missoula MT: Scholars Press, 1976.

Collins, J. J. "Introduction: Towards the Morphology of Genre," *Semeia* 14 (1979): 1–20.

Cone, James H. *God of the Oppressed.* Revised edition. Maryknoll NY: Orbis, 1997.

Crenshaw, James L. *Defending God: Biblical Response to the Problem of Evil.* New York: Oxford University Press, 2005.

Crossan, John D. *The Greatest Prayer: Rediscovering the Revolutionary Message of the Lord's Prayer.* New York: HarperCollins, 2010.

Cullmann, Oscar. *Christ and Time.* Translated by Floyd V. Filson. Philadelphia: Westminster, 1951.

Davies, G. Henton. "Ark of the Covenant." Pages 222–23 in volume 1 of *The Interpreter's Dictionary of the Bible.* Edited by G. A. Buttrick. 4 volumes. Nashville: Abingdon, 1962.

Day, Peggy L. *An Adversary in Heaven: sātān in the Hebrew Bible.* Atlanta: Scholars Press, 1988.

Defransico, Lesley R, *Washing Away Sin: An Analysis of the Metaphor in the Hebrew Bible and its Influence.* Leuven, Belgium: Peeters Publishers, 2016.

Dixon, Sarah Underwood. "'The Testimony of Jesus' in Light of Internal Self-References in the Books of Daniel and 1 Enoch." *The Book of Revelation: Currents in British Research on the Apocalypse.* Wissenschaftliche Untersuchungen zum Neuen Testament. Tübingen: Mohr Siebeck, 2015.

Dodd, C. H. *Apostolic Preaching and Its Developments.* New York: Harper and Row, 1964.

———. *The Bible and the Greeks.* London: Hodder and Stoughton, 1935.

Downing, Jonathan. "The Women Clothed in the Sun: The Reception of Revelation 12 among Female British Prophets 1780–1814." *The Book of Revelation: Currents in British Research on the Apocalypse.* Wissenschaftliche Untersuchungen zum Neuen Testament. Tübingen: Mohr Siebeck, 2015.

Ellingworth, Paul. "The *Marturia* Debate." *Bible Translator* 41 (1990): 138–39.

Ellul, Jacques. *Apocalypse: The Book of Revelation.* Translated by George W. Schreiner. New York: Seabury, 1977.

Erickson, Millard J. *Christian Theology.* 3rd edition. Grand Rapids MI: Baker, 2013.

Finlan, Stephen. *Sacrifice and Atonement: Psychological Motives and Biblical Patterns.* Minneapolis: Fortress, 2016.

Finlan, Stephen. *The Background and Content of Paul's Cultic Atonement Metaphors.* Atlanta: Society of Biblical Literature, 2004.

Fletcher, Michelle. "Apocalypse Noir: How Revelation Defined and Defied a Genre." *The Book of Revelation: Currents in British Research on the Apocalypse.* Wissenschaftliche Untersuchungen zum Neuen Testament. Tübingen: Mohr Siebeck, 2015.

Foerster, Werner. "διαβάλλω, διάβολος →Σατανᾶς." Pages 72–81 in volume 2 of *Theological Dictionary of the New Testament.* Edited by G. Kittel and G. Friedrich. Translated by G. Bromiley. 10 volumes. Grand Rapids MI: Eerdmans, 1964–1976.

Frilingos, Christopher A. *Spectacles of Empire: Monsters, Martyrs, and the Book of Revelation.* Philadelphia: University of Pennsylvania Press, 2004.

Gadamer, Hans-Georg. *Truth and Method.* New York: Crossroad, 1985.

Gage, Mathilda Joslyn. "Revelation 12." *The Woman's Bible.* Edited by Elizabeth Cady Stanton. New York: European Publishing, 1898.

Ganssle, Gregory E. *God & Time: Four View.* Downers Grove IL: InterVarsity, 2001.

Green, Joel B. *The Gospel of Luke.* New International Commentary on the New Testament Grand Rapids: Eerdmans, 1997.

Gregg, Steve, ed. *Revelation: Four Views. A Parallel Commentary.* Nashville: Nelson, 2002.

Gregory of Nyssa. "An Address on Religious Instruction." *Christology of the Later Fathers.* Edited by Edward Rochie Hardy and Cyril C. Richardson. Library of Christian Classics. Volume 3. Philadelphia: Westminster, 1954.

Guthrie, Donald. "The Lamb in The Structure of the Book of Revelation." *Vox Evangelica* 12 (1981): 64–71.

Hanson, Anthony T. *The Wrath of the Lamb.* London: SPCK, 1957.

Harker, Andrew. "Prophetically Called Sodom and Egypt: The Affective Power of Revelation 11.1–13." *The Book of Revelation: Currents in British Research on the Apocalypse.* Wissenschaftliche Untersuchungen zum Neuen Testament. Tübingen: Mohr Siebeck, 2015.

Hauerwas, Stanley. "No Enemy, No Christianity: Theology and Preaching between 'Worlds.'" *The Future of Theology: Essays in Honor of Jürgen Moltmann.* Edited by Miroslav Volf, Carmen Krieg, and Thomas Kucharz. Grand Rapids MI: Eerdmans, 1996.

Hawking, Stephen W. *A Brief History of Time: From Big Bang to Black Holes.* Toronto: Bantam Books, 1988.

Heidegger, Martin. *Being and Time.* Translated by Joan Stambaugh. Tübingen: Max Niemeyer Verlag, 1953.

Hemer, Colin J. *The Letters to the Seven Churches of Asia in Their Local Contexts.* Grand Rapids MI: Eerdmans, 1986.

Herms, Ronald. "πνευματικῶς and Antagonists in Revelation 11 Reconsidered." *The Book of Revelation: Currents in British Research on the Apocalypse.* Wissenschaftliche Untersuchungen zum Neuen Testament. Tübingen: Mohr Siebeck, 2015.

Hesiod. "To Apollo." *Hesiod, The Homeric Hymns, and Homerica.* Edited by Hugh G. Evelyn-White. Champaign IL: Project Gutenberg, n.d. eBook Collection (EBSCOhost).

Hill, Charles E. "Atonement in the Apocalypse of John: A Lamb Standing as if Slain." *The Glory of the Atonement: Biblical, Historical & Practical Perspectives, Essays in honor of Roger Nicole.* Edited by Charles E. Hill and Frank A. James III. Downers Grove IL: InterVarsity, 2004.

Hill, David. *Greek Words and Hebrew Meanings: Studies in the Semantics of Soteriological Terms.* Cambridge: Cambridge University Press, 1967.

———. *New Testament Prophecy.* London: Marshall, Morgan & Scott, 1979.

Holmes, M. W. *The Greek New Testament: SBL Edition.* Lexham Press, Society of Biblical Literature, 2011–2013.

Hugo, Victor. *Les Misérables.* Translated by Charles E. Wilbour. New York: Carleton Publishing, 1862.

Ice, Thomas D. "Margaret MacDonald" in *Dictionary of Premillennial Theology: A Practical Guide to the People, Viewpoints, and History of Prophetic Studies.* Edited by M. Couch. Grand Rapids MI: Kregel, 1996.

Johns, Loren L. "Atonement and Sacrifice in the Book of Revelation." *The Work of Jesus Christ in Anabaptist Perspective: Essays in Honor of J. Denny Weaver.* Edited by Alain Epp Weaver and Gerald J. Mast. Telford PA: Cascadia, 2008.

———. *The Lamb Christology of the Apocalypse of John: An Investigation into Its Origins and Rhetorical Force.* Tübingen: Mohr Siebeck, 2003.

Käsemann, Ernst. "Die Anfänge christlicher Theologie." ZThK 57 (1960): 162–85.

———. "The Beginnings of Christian Theology." *Journal for Theology and Church* 6. Edited by Robert W. Funk. New York, 1969.

Kelly, Joseph F. *Who is Satan? According to the Scriptures.* Collegeville MN: Liturgical Press, 2013.

Kiddle, Martin. *Revelation of St. John.* The Moffatt New Testament Commentary. New York: Harper & Brothers, 1940.

Kinder, Derek. *Genesis: An Introduction and Commentary.* Tyndale Old Testament Commentaries. Volume 1. Downers Grove IL: InterVarsity, 1967.

Koester, Craig R. *Revelation: A New Translation with Introduction and Commentary.* The Anchor Yale Bible. New Haven: Yale University Press, 2014.

Kovacs, Judith, and Christopher Rowland. *Revelation.* Blackwell Bible Commentaries. Victoria, Australia: Blackwell, 2004.

Ladd, George E. *Jesus and the Kingdom.* New York: Harper and Row, 1964.

———. *A Commentary of the Revelation of John.* Grand Rapids MI: Eerdmans, 1972.

———. "Historic Premillennialism." *The Meaning of the Millennium: Four Views.* Edited by Robert G. Clouse. Downers Grove IL: InterVarsity, 1977.

Lindboe, Inger Marie. "Recent Literature: Development and Perspectives in New Testament Research on Women." *Studia Theologica* 43 (1989): 153–63.

Lindsey, Hal, with C. C. Carlson. *The Late Great Planet Earth.* Grand Rapids MI: Zondervan, 1970.

———. *There Is a New World Coming.* Ventura CA: Vision House, 1973.

Lupieri, Edmondo, F. *A Commentary on the Apocalypse of John.* Translated by Marian Poggi Johnson and Adam Kamesar. Grand Rapids MI: Eerdmans, 1999.

Lyonnet, Stanislas. "The Terminology of Redemption." *Sin, Redemption and Sacrifice: A Biblical and Patristic Study.* Rome: Biblical Institute, 1970.

Lyons, William John, and Jorunn Økland, editors. *The Way the World Ends? The Apocalypse of John in Culture and Ideology.* Sheffield: Sheffield Phoenix, 2009.

Macquarrie, John. "Demonology and the Classic Idea of Atonement." Pts. 1 and 2. *Expository Times* 68/1 (October 1956): 3–6; (November 1956): 60–63.

———. *The Scope of Demythologizing: Bultmann and his Critics*. London: SCM, 1960.

———. *God-Talk: An Examination of the Language and Logic of Theology*. London: SCM, 1967.

———. *Paths in Spirituality*. London: SCM, 1972.

———. *Principles of Christian Theology*. London: SCM, 1977.

———. *Jesus Christ in Modern Thought*. London: SCM, 1990.

Maimonides, Moses. *The Guide for the Perplexed*. Translated from the Original Arabic Text by M. Friedlaender. 4th revised edition. New York: E.P. Dutton, 1904.

Malina, Bruce J. *On the Genre and Message of Revelation: Star Visions and Sky Journeys*. Peabody MA: Hendrickson, 1995.

Mann, Alan. *Atonement for a Sinless Society*. 2nd edition. Eugene OR: Cascade, 2014.

Martin de Viviés, Pierre de. *Apocalypses et cosmologie du salut*. Paris: Cerf, 2002.

Martin, Dale. *Slavery as Salvation: The Metaphor of Slavery in Pauline Christianity*. New Haven CT: Yale University Press, 1990.

Metzger, Bruce M. *A Textual Commentary on the Greek New Testament: A Companion Volume to the United Bible Societies' Greek New Testament*. 3rd edition. London: United Bible Societies, 1975.

Michaels, J. Ramsay. *Interpreting the Book of Revelation*. Grand Rapids MI: Baker, 1992.

Middleton, Paul. "Male Virgins, Male Martyrs, Male Brides: A Reconsideration of the 144,000 'who have not dirtied themselves with women' (Revelation 14.4)." *The Book of Revelation: Currents in British Research on the Apocalypse*. Wissenschaftliche Untersuchungen zum Neuen Testament. Tübingen: Mohr Siebeck, 2015.

Milne, Pamela J. "Toward Feminist Companionship: The Future of Feminist Biblical Studies and Feminism." *A Feminist Companion to Reading the Bible: Approaches, Methods and Strategies*. Edited by Athalya Brenner and Carole Fontaine. Sheffield: Sheffield Academic, 1997.

Moltmann, Jürgen. *Theology of Hope: On the Ground and the Implications of a Christian Eschatology*. London: SCM, 1967.

————. *The Crucified God: The Cross of Christ as the Foundation and Criticism of Christian Theology.* New York: Harper and Row, 1974.

Morris, Charles W. *Foundations of the Theory of Signs.* Chicago: University of Chicago Press, 1938.

Morris, Leon. *The Apostolic Preaching of the Cross.* Grand Rapids MI: Eerdmans, 1955.

Moulton, J. H., W. F. Howard, and M. Turner. *A Grammar of New Testament Greek III* Edinburgh: T & T Clark, 1906–76.

Mounce, Robert. *The Book of Revelation.* New International Commentary on the New Testament. Grand Rapids MI: Eerdmans, 1977.

Moyise, Steve. "A Response to Currents in British Research on the Apocalypse." *The Book of Revelation: Currents in British Research on the Apocalypse.* Wissenschaftliche Untersuchungen zum Neuen Testament. Tübingen: Mohr Siebeck, 2015.

Murphy, Frederick J. "Introduction to Apocalyptic Literature." *The New Interpreter's Bible.* Volume 7. Nashville: Abingdon, 1996.

Newson, Carol A. "The Book of Job: Introduction, Commentary, and Reflections." *The New Interpreter's Bible.* Volume 4. Nashville: Abingdon, 1996.

Northcott, Michael S. "Earth Left Behind? Ecological Readings of the Apocalypse of John in Contemporary America." *The Way the World Ends? The Apocalypse of John in Culture and Ideology.* Edited by William John Lyons and Jorunn Økland. Sheffield: Sheffield Phoenix, 2009.

Økland, Jorunn. "Setting the Scene: The End of the Bible, the End of the World." *The Way the World Ends? The Apocalypse of John in Culture and Ideology.* Sheffield: Sheffield Phoenix, 2009.

Origen. *De Principiis.* In volume 4 of *The Ante-Nicene Fathers.* Edited by Alexander Roberts and James Donaldson. 1885–1887. 10 volumes. Reprint, Peabody MA: Hendrickson, 1994.

Packer, J. I. *Knowing God.* Downers Grove IL: InterVarsity, 1973.

Pagels, Elaine. *The Origin of Satan.* New York: Random House, 1995.

Panagopoulos, J. "Prophecy in the Early Church: Its Character and Function." *Prophetic Vocation.* Brill: Leiden, 1977.

Pataki, András Dávid. "A Non-Combat Myth in Revelation 12." *New Testament Studies* 57/2 (April 2011): 258–72.

Pattison, Stephen. *Shame: Theory, Therapy, Theology.* Cambridge: Cambridge University Press, 2000.

Paul, Ian. "Source, Structure, and Composition in the Book of Revelation." *The Book of Revelation: Currents in British Research on the Apocalypse.* Wissenschaftliche Untersuchungen zum Neuen Testament. Tübingen: Mohr Siebeck, 2015.

Pinch, Geraldine. *Egyptian Mythology: A Guide to the Gods, Goddesses, and Traditions of Ancient Egypt.* Oxford: Oxford University Press, 2002.

Pippin, Tina. "Eros and the End: Reading for Gender in the Apocalypse of John." *Semeia* 59 (1992): 193–217.

———. "The Heroine and the Whore: Fantasy and the Female in the Apocalypse of John." *Semeia* 60 (1992): 67–82.

———. *Death and Desire: The Rhetoric of Gender in the Apocalypse of John.* Louisville: Westminster/John Knox, 1992.

———. "Jezebel Re-Vamped." *Semeia* 69/70: Intertextuality and the Bible (1995): 221–34.

Räisänen, Heikki. "Revelation, Violence, and War: Glimpses of a Dark Side." *The Way the World Ends? The Apocalypse of John in Culture and Ideology.* Edited by William John Lyons and Jorunn Økland. Sheffield: Sheffield Phoenix, 2009.

Reddish, Mitchell G. "Martyr Christology in the Apocalypse." *Journal for the Study of the New Testament* 33 (1988).

———. *Revelation.* Smyth & Helwys Commentaries. Macon GA: Smyth & Helwys, 2001.

Ricoeur, Paul. *The Symbolism of Evil.* New York: Harper and Row, 1967.

Rist, Martin. "The Revelation of St. John the Divine." *The Interpreter's Bible.* Volume 12. Nashville: Abingdon, 1957.

Roberts, Jonathon. "Decoding, Reception History, Poetry: Three Hermeneutical Approaches to the Apocalypse." *The Way the World Ends? The Apocalypse of John in Culture and Ideology.* Sheffield: Sheffield Phoenix, 2009.

Rowland, Christopher C. "The Book of Revelation: Introduction, Commentary and Reflections." *The New Interpreter's Bible*. Volume 12. Nashville: Abingdon, 1998.

———. "British Interpretation of the Apocalypse: A Historical Perspective." *The Book of Revelation: Currents in British Research on the Apocalypse*. Wissenschaftliche Untersuchungen zum Neuen Testament. Tübingen: Mohr Siebeck, 2015.

Russell, Jeffrey Burton. *The Devil: Perceptions of Evil from Antiquity to the Middle Ages*. Ithaca NY: Cornell University Press, 1977.

———. *Satan: The Early Christian Tradition*. Ithaca NY: Cornell University Press, 1981.

———. *Lucifer: The Devil in Middle Ages*. Ithaca NY: Cornell University Press, 1984.

———. *Mephistopheles: The Devil in the Modern World*. Ithaca NY: Cornell University Press, 1986

———. *The Prince of Darkness: Radical Evil and the Power of Good in History*. Ithaca NY: Cornell University Press, 1988.

Rutledge, Fleming. *The Crucifixion: Understanding the Death of Jesus Christ*. Grand Rapids MI: Eerdmans, 2015.

Ryan, Sean Michael. "'The Testimony of Jesus' and 'The Testimony of Enoch': An *emic* Approach to the Genre of the Apocalypse." *The Book of Revelation: Currents in British Research on the Apocalypse*. Wissenschaftliche Untersuchungen zum Neuen Testament. Tübingen: Mohr Siebeck, 2015.

Sandeen, Ernest R. *The Roots of Fundamentalism: British and American Millenarianism 1800–1930*. Grand Rapids MI: Baker, 1970.

Schmidt, H. W. *Zeit und Ewigkeit Die letzen Voraussetzungen der dialektishcen Theologie*. Gütersloh, 1927.

Schüssler Fiorenza, Elisabeth. *The Book of Revelation: Justice and Judgment*. Philadelphia: Fortress, 1985.

Seal, D. "Satan," *The Lexham Bible Dictionary*. Edited by J. D. Barry, D. Bomar, D. R. Brown, R. Klippenstein, D. Mangum, C. Sinclair Wolcott, W. Widder. Bellingham WA: Lexham, 2012, 2013, 2014, 2015.

Smalley, Stephen S. *The Revelation of John: A Commentary on the Greek Text of the Apocalypse.* Downers Grove IL: InterVarsity, 2005.

Smith, Martyn John. *Divine Violence and the Christus Victor Atonement Model: God's Reluctant Use of Violence for Soteriological Ends.* Kindle Edition. Eugene OR: Pickwick, 2016.

Stenström, Hanna. "Feminists in Search for a Usable Future: Feminist Reception of the Book of Revelation." *The Way the World Ends? The Apocalypse of John in Culture and Ideology.* Edited by William John Lyons and Jorunn Økland. Sheffield: Sheffield Phoenix, 2009.

Stern, Josef. *Problems and Parables of Law: Maimonides and Nahmanides on Reasons for the Commandments (Ta'Amei Ha-Mitzvot).* Albany: State University of New York Press, 1989.

Steven, Gerald L. *Revelation: The Past and Future of John's Apocalypse.* Eugene OR: Pickwick, 2014.

Tate, Marvin E. "Satan in the Old Testament." *Review & Expositor* 89/4 (1992): 461–74.

Thomas, John Christopher and Frank D. Macchia. *Revelation.* New Horizons New Testament Commentary. Grand Rapids: Eerdmans, 2016.

Tucker, Gene M. "The Book of Isaiah: Introduction, Commentary and Reflections." *The New Interpreter's Bible.* Volume 6. Nashville: Abingdon, 2001.

Weaver, J. Denny. *The Nonviolent Atonement.* Grand Rapids MI: Eerdmans, 2001.

Westermann, Claus. *Creation.* Philadelphia: Fortress, 1974.

Wilckens, Ulrich. "οτολή." Pages 687–91 in volume 7 of *Theological Dictionary of the New Testament.* Edited by G. Kittel and G. Friedrich. Translated by G. Bromiley. 10 vols. Grand Rapids: Eerdmans. 1964-1976.

Williams, Delores. *Sisters in the Wilderness: The Challenge of Womanist God-Talk.* Maryknoll NY: Orbis, 1993.

Williams, James G., editor. *The Girard Reader.* New York: Crossroad, 1996.

Wood, Shane J. "God's Triumphal Procession: Re-examining the Release of Satan in the Light of Roman Imperial Imagery." *The Book of Revelation: Currents in British Research on the Apocalypse.* Wissenschaftliche Untersuchungen zum Neuen Testament. Tübingen: Mohr Siebeck, 2015.

Woodman, Simon P. "Fire from Heaven: Divine Judgment in the Book of Revelation." *The Book of Revelation: Currents in British Research on the Apocalypse.* Wissenschaftliche Untersuchungen zum Neuen Testament. Tübingen: Mohr Siebeck, 2015.

Wray, T. J. and Gregory Mobley. *The Birth of Satan: Tracing the Devil's Biblical Roots.* New York: Palgrave MacMillan, 2005.

Wright, N. T. *The Day the Revolution Began: Reconsidering the Meaning of Jesus's Crucifixion.* New York: HarperOne, 2016.

———. "Saving the World, Revealing the Glory: Atonement Then and Now." Lecture. St. Mellitus College, London. October 17, 2016.

Other available titles from

#Connect
Reaching Youth Across the Digital Divide
Brian Foreman

Reaching our youth across the digital divide is a struggle for parents, ministers, and other adults who work with Generation Z—today's teenagers. *#Connect* leads readers into the technological landscape, encourages conversations with teenagers, and reminds us all to be the presence of Christ in every facet of our lives. *978-1-57312-693-9 120 pages/pb* **$13.00**

Atonement in the Apocalypse
An Exposé of the Defeat of Evil
Robert W. Canoy

Revelation calls believers to see themselves through the unique lens of redemptive atonement and to live and model daily that they see themselves in the present moment as redeemed people. Having thus seen themselves, believers likewise are directed to see and to relate to others in this world the very way that God has seen them from eternity.

978-1-57312-946-6 218 pages/pb **$22.00**

Beginnings
A Reverend and a Rabbi Talk About the Stories of Genesis
Michael Smith and Rami Shapiro

Editor Aaron Herschel Shapiro declares that stories "must be retold—not just repeated, but reinvented, reimagined, and reexperienced" to remain vital in the world. Mike and Rami continue their conversations from the *Mount and Mountain* books, exploring the places where their traditions intersect and diverge, listening to each other as they respond to the stories of Genesis. *978-1-57312-772-1 202 pages/pb* **$18.00**

Bugles in the Afternoon
Dealing with Discouragement and Disillusionment in Ministry
Judson Edwards

In *Bugles in the Afternoon*, Edwards writes, "My long experience in the church has convinced me that most ministers—both profession-al and lay—spend time under the juniper tree. Those ministers who have served more than ten years and not been depressed, discouraged, or disillu-sioned can hold their annual convention in a phone booth."

978-1-57312-865-0 148 pages/pb **$16.00**

A Christian's Guide to Islam
Michael D. McCullar

A *Christian's Guide to Islam* provides a brief but accurate guide to Muslim formation, history, structure, beliefs, practices, and goals. It explores to what degree the tenets of Islam have been misinterpreted, corrupted, or abused over the centuries.

978-1-57312-512-3 *128 pages/pb* **$16.00**

Choosing Gratitude
Learning to Love the Life You Have

James A. Autry

Autry reminds us that gratitude is a choice, a spiritual—not social— process. He suggests that if we cultivate gratitude as a way of being, we may not change the world and its ills, but we can change our response to the world. If we fill our lives with moments of gratitude, we will indeed love the life we have.

978-1-57312-614-4 *144 pages/pb* **$15.00**

Choosing Gratitude 365 Days a Year
Your Daily Guide to Grateful Living

James A. Autry and Sally J. Pederson

Filled with quotes, poems, and the inspired voices of both Pederson and Autry, in a society consumed by fears of not having "enough"— money, possessions, security, and so on—this book suggests that if we cultivate gratitude as a way of being, we may not change the world and its ills, but we can change our response to the world.

978-1-57312-689-2 *210 pages/pb* **$18.00**

Countercultural Worship
A Plea to Evangelicals in a Secular Age

Mark G. McKim

Evangelical worship, McKim argues, has drifted far from both its biblical roots and historic origins, leaving evangelicals in danger of becoming mere chaplains to the wider culture, oblivious to the contradictions between what the secular culture says is real and important and what Scripture says is real and important.

978-1-57312-873-5 *174 pages/pb* **$19.00**

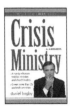

Crisis Ministry: A Handbook
Daniel G. Bagby

Covering more than 25 crisis pastoral care situations, this book provides a brief, practical guide for church leaders and other caregivers responding to stressful situations in the lives of parishioners. It tells how to resource caregiving professionals in the community who can help people in distress.

978-1-57312-370-9 *154 pages/pb* **$15.00**

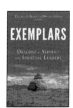

Exemplars
Deacons as Servant and Spiritual Leaders
Elizabeth Allen and Daniel Vestal, eds.

Who Do Deacons Need to Be? What Do Deacons Need to Know? What Do Deacons Need to Do? These three questions form the basis for *Exemplars: Deacons as Servant and Spiritual Leaders*. They are designed to encourage robust conversation within diaconates as well as between deacons, clergy, and other laity.   *978-1-57312-876-6 128 pages/pb* **$15.00**

The Exile and Beyond (All the Bible series)
Wayne Ballard

The Exile and Beyond brings to life the sacred literature of Israel and Judah that comprises the exilic and postexilic communities of faith. It covers Ezekiel, Isaiah, Haggai, Zechariah, Malachi, 1 & 2 Chronicles, Ezra, Nehemiah, Joel, Jonah, Song of Songs, Esther, and Daniel.   *978-1-57312-759-2 196 pages/pb* **$16.00**

Fierce Love
Desperate Measures for Desperate Times
Jeanie Miley

Fierce Love is about learning to see yourself and know yourself as a conduit of love, operating from a full heart instead of trying to find someone to whom you can hook up your emotional hose and fill up your empty heart.   *978-1-57312-810-0 276 pages/pb* **$18.00**

Five Hundred Miles
Reflections on Calling and Pilgrimage
Lauren Brewer Bass

Spain's Camino de Santiago, the Way of St. James, has been a cherished pilgrimage path for centuries, visited by countless people searching for healing, solace, purpose, and hope. These stories from her five-hundred-mile-walk is Lauren Brewer Bass's honest look at the often winding, always surprising journey of a calling.   *978-1-57312-812-4 142 pages/pb* **$16.00**

A Five-Mile Walk
Exploring Themes in the Experience of Christian Faith and Discipleship
Michael B. Brown

Sometimes the Christian journey is a stroll along quiet shores. Other times it is an uphill climb on narrow, snow-covered mountain paths. Usually, it is simply walking in the direction of wholeness, one step after another, sometimes even two steps forward and one step back.

978-1-57312-852-0 196 pages/pb **$18.00**

Glimpses from State Street
Wayne Ballard

As a collection of devotionals, *Glimpses from State Street* provides a wealth of insights and new ways to consider and develop our fellowship with Christ. It also serves as a window into the relationship between a small town pastor and a welcoming congregation.

978-1-57312-841-4 158 pages/pb **$15.00**

God's Servants, the Prophets
Bryan Bibb

God's Servants, the Prophets covers the Israelite and Judean prophetic literature from the preexilic period. It includes Amos, Hosea, Isaiah, Micah, Zephaniah, Nahum, Habakkuk, Jeremiah, and Obadiah.

978-1-57312-758-5 208 pages/pb **$16.00**

Hermeneutics of Hymnody
A Comprehensive and Integrated Approach to Understanding Hymns
Scotty Gray

Scotty Gray's *Hermeneutics of Hymnody* is a comprehensive and integrated approach to understanding hymns. It is unique in its holistic and interrelated exploration of seven of the broad facets of this most basic forms of Christian literature. A chapter is devoted to each and relates that facet to all of the others.

978-157312-767-7 432 pages/pb **$28.00**

Holy Hilarity
A Funny Study of Genesis
Mark Roncace

In this fun, meaningful, and practical study of Genesis, Mark Roncace brings readers fifty-three short chapters of wit and amusing observations about the biblical stories, followed by five thought-provoking questions for individual reflection or group discussion. Humorous, yet reverent, this refreshing approach to Bible study invites us, whatever our background, to wrestle with the issues in the text and discover the ways those issues intersect our own messy lives. It's seriously entertaining.

978-157312-892-6 230 pages/pb **$17.00**

If Jesus Isn't the Answer . . . He Sure Asks the Right Questions!
J. Daniel Day

Taking eleven of Jesus' questions as its core, Day invites readers into their own conversation with Jesus. Equal parts testimony, theological instruction, pastoral counseling, and autobiography, the book is ultimately an invitation to honest Christian discipleship.

978-1-57312-797-4 148 pages/pb **$16.00**

Jonah (Annual Bible Study series)
Reluctant Prophet, Merciful God
Taylor Sandlin

The book of Jonah invites readers to ask important questions about who God is and who God calls us to be in response. Along with the prophet, we ask questions such as What kind of God is the God of Israel? and Who falls within the sphere of God's care? Most importantly, perhaps, we find ourselves asking How will I respond when I discover that God loves the people I love to hate? These sessions invite readers to wrestle with these questions and others like them as we discover God's mercy for both the worst of sinners and the most reluctant of prophets.   *Teaching Guide 978-1-57312-910-7 164 pages/pb* **$14.00**

Study Guide 978-1-57312-911-4 96 pages/pb **$6.00**

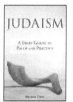

Judaism
A Brief Guide to Faith and Practice
Sharon Pace

Sharon Pace's newest book is a sensitive and comprehensive introduction to Judaism. How does belief in the One God and a universal morality shape the way in which Jews see the world? How does one find meaning in life and the courage to endure suffering? How does one mark joy and forge community ties?   *978-1-57312-644-1 144 pages/pb* **$16.00**

Live the Stories
50 Interactive Children's Sermons
Andrew Noe

Live the Stories provides church leaders a practical guide to teaching children during the worship service through play—and invites the rest of the congregation to join the fun. Noe's lessons allow children to play, laugh, and act out the stories of our faith and turn the sanctuary into a living testimony to what God has done in the past, is doing in the present, and will do in the future. As they learn the stories and grow, our children will develop in their faith.   *978-1-57312-943-5 128 pages/pb* **$14.00**

Loyal Dissenters
Reading Scripture and Talking Freedom with 17th-century English Baptists
Lee Canipe

When Baptists in 17th-century England wanted to talk about freedom, they unfailingly began by reading the Bible—and what they found in Scripture inspired their compelling (and, ultimately, successful) arguments for religious liberty. In an age of widespread anxiety, suspicion, and hostility, these early Baptists refused to worship God in keeping with the king's command.   *978-1-57312-872-8 178 pages/pb* **$19.00**

To order call **1-800-747-3016** or visit **www.helwys.com**

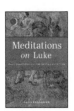

Meditations on Luke
Daily Devotions from the Gentile Physician
Chris Cadenhead

Readers searching for a fresh encounter with Scripture can delve into *Meditations on Luke*, a collection of daily devotions intended to guide the reader through the book of Luke, which gives us some of the most memorable stories in all of Scripture. The Scripture, response, and prayer will guide readers' own meditations as they listen and respond to God's voice, coming to us through Luke's Gospel. 978-1-57312-947-3 328 pages/pb **$22.00**

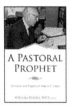

A Pastoral Prophet
Sermons and Prayers of Wayne E. Oates
William Powell Tuck, ed.

Read these sermons and prayers and look directly into the heart of Wayne Oates. He was a consummate counselor, theologian, and writer, but first of all he was a pastor. . . . He gave voice to our deepest hurts, then followed with words we long to hear: you are not alone.

—Kay Shurden
Associate Professor Emeritus, Clinical Education,
Mercer University School of Medicine, Macon, Georgia
978-157312-955-8 160 pages/pb **$18.00**

Place Value
The Journey to Where You Are
Katie Sciba

Does a place have value? Can a place change us? Is it possible for God to use the place you are in to form you? From Victoria, Texas to Indonesia, Belize, Australia, and beyond, Katie Sciba's wanderlust serves as a framework to understand your own places of deep emotion and how God may have been weaving redemption around you all along.

978-157312-829-2 138 pages/pb **$15.00**

Portraits of Jesus
for an Age of Biblical Illiteracy
Gerald L. Borchert

Despite our era of communication and information overload, biblical illiteracy is widespread. In *Portraits of Jesus*, Gerald L. Borchert assists both ministers and laypeople with a return to what the New Testament writers say about this stunning Jesus who shocked the world and called a small company of believers into an electrifying transformation.

978-157312-940-4 212 pages/pb **$20.00**

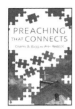

Preaching that Connects
Charles B. Bugg and Alan Redditt

How does the minister stay focused on the holy when the daily demands of the church seem relentless? How do we come to a preaching event with a sense that God is working in us and through us? In *Preaching that Connects*, Charles Bugg and Alan Redditt explore the balancing act of a minister's authority as preacher, sharing what the congregation needs to hear, and the communal role as pastor, listening to God alongside congregants.   *978-157312-887-2 128 pages/pb* **$15.00**

Reading Isaiah
(Reading the Old Testament series)
A Literary and Theological Commentary
Hyun Chul Paul Kim

While closely exegeting key issues of each chapter, this commentary also explores interpretive relevance and significance between ancient texts and the modern world. Engaging with theological messages of the book of Isaiah as a unified whole, the commentary will both illuminate and inspire readers to wrestle with its theological implications for today's church and society.
978-1-57312-925-1 352 pages/pb **$33.00**

Reading Jeremiah
(Reading the Old Testament series)
A Literary and Theological Commentary
Corrine Carvalho

Reflecting the ways that communal tragedy permeates communal identity, the book of Jeremiah as literary text embodies the confusion, disorientation, and search for meaning that all such tragedy elicits. Just as the fall of Jerusalem fractured the Judean community and undercut every foundation on which it built its identity, so too the book itself (or more properly, the scroll) jumbles images, genres, and perspectives.   *978-1-57312-924-4 186 pages/pb* **$32.00**

Ruth & Esther (Smyth & Helwys Bible Commentary)
Kandy Queen-Sutherland

Ruth and Esther are the only two women for whom books of the Hebrew Bible are named. This distinction in itself sets the books apart from other biblical texts that bear male names, address the community through its male members, recall the workings of God and human history through a predominately male perspective, and look to the future through male heirs. These books are particularly stories of survival. The story of Ruth focuses on the survival of a family; Esther focuses on the survival of a people.   *978-1-57312-891-9 544 pages/hc* **$60.00**

To order call **1-800-747-3016** or visit **www.helwys.com**

Sessions with Psalms (Sessions Bible Studies series)
Prayers for All Seasons
Eric and Alicia D. Porterfield

Useful to seminar leaders during preparation and group discussion, as well as in individual Bible study, *Sessions with Psalms* is a ten-session study designed to explore what it looks like for the words of the psalms to become the words of our prayers. Each session is followed by a thought-provoking page of questions.   *978-1-57312-768-4 136 pages/pb* **$14.00**

Sessions with Isaiah (Sessions Bible Studies series)
What to Do When the World Caves In
James M. King

The book of Isaiah begins in the years of national stress when, under various kings, Israel was surrounded by more powerful neighbors and foolishly sought foreign alliances rather than dependence on Yahweh. It continues with the natural result of that unfaithfulness: conquest by the great power in the region, Babylon, and the captivity of many of Israel's best and brightest in that foreign land. The book concludes anticipating their return to the land of promise and strong admonitions about the people's conduct—but we also hear God's reassuring messages of comfort and restoration, offered to all who repent.

978-1-57312-942-8 130 pages/pb **$14.00**

Stained-Glass Millennials
Rob Lee

We've heard the narrative that millennials are done with the institutional church; they've packed up and left. This book is an alternative to that story and chronicles the journey of millennials who are investing their lives in the institution because they believe in the church's resurrecting power. Through anecdotes and interviews, Rob Lee takes readers on a journey toward God's unfolding future for the church, a beloved institution in desperate need of change.   *978-1-57312-926-8 156 pages/pb* **$16.00**

Star Thrower
A Pastor's Handbook
William Powell Tuck

In *Star Thrower: A Pastor's Handbook*, William Powell Tuck draws on over fifty years of experience to share his perspective on being an effective pastor. He describes techniques for sermon preparation, pastoral care, and church administration, as well as for conducting Communion, funeral, wedding, and baptismal services. He also includes advice for working with laity and church staff, coping with church conflict, and nurturing one's own spiritual and family life.   *978-1-57312-889-6 244 pages/pb* **$15.00**

Tell the Truth, Shame the Devil
Stories about the Challenges of Young Pastors

James Elllis III, ed.

A pastor's life is uniquely difficult. *Tell the Truth, Shame the Devil*, then, is an attempt to expose some of the challenges that young clergy often face. While not exhaustive, this collection of essays is a superbly compelling and diverse introduction to how tough being a pastor under the age of thirty-five can be.   *978-1-57312-839-1 198 pages/pb* **$18.00**

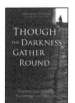

Though the Darkness Gather Round
Devotions about Infertility, Miscarriage, and Infant Loss

Mary Elizabeth Hill Hanchey and Erin McClain, eds.

Much courage is required to weather the long grief of infertility and the sudden grief of miscarriage and infant loss. This collection of devotions by men and women, ministers, chaplains, and lay leaders who can speak of such sorrow, is a much-needed resource and precious gift for families on this journey and the faith communities that walk beside them.

978-1-57312-811-7 180 pages/pb **$19.00**

Time for Supper
Invitations to Christ's Table

Brett Younger

Some scholars suggest that every meal in literature is a communion scene. Could every meal in the Bible be a communion text? Could every passage be an invitation to God's grace? These meditations on the Lord's Supper help us listen to the myriad of ways God invites us to gratefully, reverently, and joyfully share the cup of Christ.   *978-1-57312-720-2 246 pages/pb* **$18.00**

A True Hope
Jedi Perils and the Way of Jesus

Joshua Hays

Star Wars offers an accessible starting point for considering substantive issues of faith, philosophy, and ethics. In A *True Hope*, Joshua Hays explores some of these challenging ideas through the sayings of the Jedi Masters, examining the ways the worldview of the Jedi is at odds with that of the Bible.   *978-1-57312-770-7 186 pages/pb* **$18.00**